# Learning Apache Cassandra

*Second Edition*

Managing fault-tolerant and scalable data

**Sandeep Yarabarla**

BIRMINGHAM - MUMBAI

# Learning Apache Cassandra

## *Second Edition*

First published: February 2015
Second Edition: April 2017

Production reference: 1200417

Published by Packt Publishing Ltd.
Livery Place
35 Livery Street
Birmingham
B3 2PB, UK.

ISBN 978-1-78712-729-6

www.packtpub.com

# Credits

**Author**

Sandeep Yarabarla

**Reviewers**

Graham Doman
Michael Klishin

**Commissioning Editor**

Amey Varangaonkar

**Acquisition Editor**

Ajith Menon

**Content Development Editor**

Tejas Limkar

**Technical Editor**

Dinesh Chaudhary

**Copy Editor**

Manisha Sinha

**Project Coordinator**

Nidhi Joshi

**Proofreader**

Safis Editing

**Indexer**

Francy Puthiry

**Graphics**

Tania Dutta

**Production Coordinator**

Deepika Naik

# About the Author

**Sandeep Yarabarla** is a professional software engineer working for Verizon Labs, based out of Palo Alto, CA. After graduating from Carnegie Mellon University, he has worked on several big data technologies for a spectrum of companies. He has developed applications primarily in Java and Go.

His experience includes handling large amounts of unstructured and structured data in Hadoop, and developing data processing applications using Spark and MapReduce. Right now, he is working with some cutting-edge technologies such as Cassandra, Kafka, Mesos, and Docker to build fault-tolerant and highly scalable applications.

*I would like to thank my mom and dad for their love and support throughout my career. I would also like to thank my relatives and friends for their help during various stages of my life. Lastly, I would like to thank Packt for giving me this opportunity to write this book and all the staff involved who helped me with the book's completion.*

# About the Reviewer

**Graham Doman** is a passionate software architect who has worked in a wide variety of business domains over his 20-year career. He started off as a junior working with C++, before moving onto C# and JavaScript, which have been his main languages for many years. He's worked on a variety of projects and products, ranging from recruitment agency systems, medical devices, back of bridge route planning software, air powered printer drivers, and many more.

He had the opportunity to study for an MSc in Data Science, and having worked in data-focused projects throughout his career, he jumped at the chance, graduating in 2015. He has been passionate about NoSQL, big data, and their application in IoTT projects ever since. As a result of this newfound passion, he's delved into Hadoop, Cassandra, Spark, MQTT, Python, R, Scala, and Java. Though he's not particularly mathematical minded, he's even delved into the curious world of statistics.

He has his own IT consultancy company, Buteo Consultancy Ltd (`http://www.bizdb.co.uk/`), which specialises in data and software engineering, data science, and IoT. He is actively working on a number of different contracts and forging new connections.

*I would like to thank my family, Sally, Ewan, Erin, William and Felix, who have supported me in all my endeavours these past few years. I couldn't do it without you guys.*

# www.PacktPub.com

For support files and downloads related to your book, please visit www.PacktPub.com.

Did you know that Packt offers eBook versions of every book published, with PDF and ePub files available? You can upgrade to the eBook version at www.PacktPub.com and as a print book customer, you are entitled to a discount on the eBook copy. Get in touch with us at service@packtpub.com for more details.

At www.PacktPub.com, you can also read a collection of free technical articles, sign up for a range of free newsletters and receive exclusive discounts and offers on Packt books and eBooks.

https://www.packtpub.com/mapt

Get the most in-demand software skills with Mapt. Mapt gives you full access to all Packt books and video courses, as well as industry-leading tools to help you plan your personal development and advance your career.

## Why subscribe?

- Fully searchable across every book published by Packt
- Copy and paste, print, and bookmark content
- On demand and accessible via a web browser

# Customer Feedback

Thanks for purchasing this Packt book. At Packt, quality is at the heart of our editorial process. To help us improve, please leave us an honest review on this book's Amazon page at `https://www.amazon.com/dp/178712729X`.

If you'd like to join our team of regular reviewers, you can e-mail us at `customerreviews@packtpub.com`. We award our regular reviewers with free eBooks and videos in exchange for their valuable feedback. Help us be relentless in improving our products!

# Table of Contents

# Preface

The crop of distributed databases that have come to the market in recent years appeals to application developers for several reasons. Their storage capacity is nearly limitless, bounded only by the number of machines you can afford to spin up. Masterless replication makes them resilient to adverse events, handling even a complete machine failure without any noticeable effect on the applications that rely on them. Log-structured storage engines allow these databases to handle high volume write loads without blinking an eye.

But compared to traditional relational databases, not to mention newer document stores, distributed databases are typically feature-poor and inconvenient to work with. Read and write functionality is frequently confined to simple key-value operations, with more complex operations demanding arcane map-reduce implementations. Happily, Cassandra provides all of the benefits of a fully distributed data store while also exposing a familiar, user-friendly data model and query interface.

By the time I began writing this book, Cassandra had seen plenty of improvements with regards to performance and feature set since its inception. The earliest versions of Cassandra were optimized for fast and large volumes of writes. The read performance was good, but not at par with the write performance. Several improvements were made to make reads considerably faster, such as the addition of bloom filters, caching mechanisms, better indexing, and partitioning.

Over the past couple of years, we have had several successful deployments of Cassandra, both on premise and in the cloud. I have helped several teams migrate from traditional databases to Cassandra without a hitch. Since it is a fully distributed database with masterless architecture, it works well with a scheduling framework such as Mesos. The toughest challenge one would face when transitioning from a relational database to Cassandra would be to come up with an optimal data model. While Cassandra allows you to have flexible models, it is still vital to ensure you get the maximum performance out of it.

The goal of this book is to teach: how to use Cassandra effectively, powerfully, and efficiently. We'll explore Cassandra's ins and outs by designing the persistence layer for a messaging service that allows users to post status updates that are visible to their friends. By the end of the book, you'll be fully prepared to build your own highly scalable and highly available applications.

# What this book covers

Chapter 1, *Getting Up and Running with Cassandra*, introduces the major reasons to choose Cassandra over a traditional relational or document database. It then provides step-by-step instructions on installing Cassandra on various operating systems, creating a keyspace, and interacting with the database using the CQL language and cqlsh tool.

Chapter 2, *The First Table*, is a walkthrough of creating a table, inserting data, and retrieving rows by primary key. Along the way, it discusses how Cassandra tables are structured, and provides a tour of the Cassandra type system.

Chapter 3, *Organizing Related Data*, introduces more complex table structures that group related data together using compound primary keys and composite partition keys.

Chapter 4, *Beyond Key-Value Lookup*, puts the more robust schema developed in the previous chapter to use, explaining how to query for sorted ranges of rows. It also touches upon the JSON support that was introduced in Cassandra 2.2.

Chapter 5, *Establishing Relationships*, develops table structures for modeling relationships between rows. The chapter introduces static columns and row deletion. This chapter also touches upon secondary indexes and materialized views, which can be used to avoid denormalization of data.

Chapter 6, *Denormalizing Data for Maximum Performance*, explains when and why storing multiple copies of the same data can make your application more efficient. The chapter introduces batching mechanisms in Cassandra and when to use them.

Chapter 7, *Expanding Your Data Model*, demonstrates the use of lightweight transactions to ensure data integrity. It also introduces schema alteration, row updates, and single-column deletion.

Chapter 8, *Collections, Tuples, and User-Defined Types*, introduces collection columns and explores Cassandra's support for advanced, atomic collection manipulation. It also introduces tuples, nested collections, and user-defined types.

Chapter 9, *Aggregating Time-Series Data*, covers the common use case of collecting high-volume time-series data and introduces counter columns. It also introduces user-defined functions and user-defined aggregates.

Chapter 10, *How Cassandra Distributes Data*, explores what happens when you save a row to Cassandra. It considers eventual consistency and teaches you how to use tunable consistency to get the right balance between consistency and fault-tolerance.

Chapter 11, *Cassandra Multi-Node Cluster,* explains how the dynamics of consistency levels and replication factor, change with a multi-node cluster. This chapter also touches upon some of the architectural aspects of Cassandra, including the read/write paths and data repair mechanisms.

Chapter 12, *Application Development Using the Java Driver,* introduces the DataStax Java driver which can be used to develop applications in Java with appropriate load balancing, reconnection, and retry policies to work with Cassandra.

Appendix A, *Peeking under the Hood,* peels away the abstractions provided by CQL to reveal how Cassandra represents data at the lower column family level.

Appendix B, *Authentication and Authorization,* introduces ways to control access to your Cassandra cluster and specific data structures within it.

# What you need for this book

You will need the following software to work with the examples in this book:

- Java Runtime Environment 8.0 (http://www.oracle.com/technetwork/java/ja vase/downloads/jdk8-downloads-2133151.html)
- Apache Cassandra 3.X (http://cassandra.apache.org/download/)
- Java IDE (IntelliJ or Eclipse) to edit, compile, and run Java code

Further instructions on installing these are presented in the upcoming chapters of the book.

# Who this book is for

This book is for first-time users of Cassandra, as well as anyone who wants a better understanding of Cassandra in order to evaluate it as a solution for their application. Since Cassandra is a standalone database, we don't assume any particular coding language or framework; anyone who builds applications for a living, and who wants those applications to scale, will benefit from reading the book. Later on, some examples have been presented in Java, but anyone with a minimalistic understanding of object-oriented programming should be able to grasp them.

# Conventions

In this book, you will find a number of text styles that distinguish between different kinds of information. Here are some examples of these styles and an explanation of their meaning.

Code words in text, database table names, folder names, filenames, file extensions, pathnames, dummy URLs, user input, and Twitter handles are shown as follows: "The next lines of code read the link and assign it to the to the `BeautifulSoup` function."

A block of code is set as follows:

```
import com.datastax.driver.core.Cluster;
import com.datastax.driver.core.ResultSet;
import com.datastax.driver.core.Row;
import com.datastax.driver.core.Session;
```

Any command-line input or output is written as follows:

```
C:> cd %CASSANDRA_HOME%
C:> bin\nodetool status
```

**New terms** and **important words** are shown in bold. Words that you see on the screen, for example, in menus or dialog boxes, appear in the text like this: "In order to download new modules, we will go to **Files** | **Settings** | **Project Name** | **Project Interpreter**."

Warnings or important notes appear in a box like this.

Tips and tricks appear like this.

# Reader feedback

Feedback from our readers is always welcome. Let us know what you think about this book-what you liked or disliked. Reader feedback is important for us as it helps us develop titles that you will really get the most out of.

To send us general feedback, simply e-mail feedback@packtpub.com, and mention the book's title in the subject of your message.

If there is a topic that you have expertise in and you are interested in either writing or contributing to a book, see our author guide at `www.packtpub.com/authors`.

# Customer support

Now that you are the proud owner of a Packt book, we have a number of things to help you to get the most from your purchase.

# Downloading the example code

You can download the example code files for this book from your account at `http://www.packtpub.com`. If you purchased this book elsewhere, you can visit `http://www.packtpub.com/support` and register to have the files e-mailed directly to you.

You can download the code files by following these steps:

1. Log in or register to our website using your e-mail address and password.
2. Hover the mouse pointer on the **SUPPORT** tab at the top.
3. Click on **Code Downloads & Errata**.
4. Enter the name of the book in the **Search** box.
5. Select the book for which you're looking to download the code files.
6. Choose from the drop-down menu where you purchased this book from.
7. Click on **Code Download**.

Once the file is downloaded, please make sure that you unzip or extract the folder using the latest version of:

- WinRAR / 7-Zip for Windows
- Zipeg / iZip / UnRarX for Mac
- 7-Zip / PeaZip for Linux

The code bundle for the book is also hosted on GitHub at `https://github.com/PacktPublishing/Learning-Apache-Cassandra-Second-Edition`. We also have other code bundles from our rich catalog of books and videos available at `https://github.com/PacktPublishing/`. Check them out!

# Downloading the color images of this book

We also provide you with a PDF file that has color images of the screenshots/diagrams used in this book. The color images will help you better understand the changes in the output.

You can download this file from `https://www.packtpub.com/sites/default/files/down loads/LearningApacheCassandraSecondEdition_ColorImages.pdf`.

# Errata

Although we have taken every care to ensure the accuracy of our content, mistakes do happen. If you find a mistake in one of our books-maybe a mistake in the text or the code-we would be grateful if you could report this to us. By doing so, you can save other readers from frustration and help us improve subsequent versions of this book. If you find any errata, please report them by visiting `http://www.packtpub.com/submit-errata`, selecting your book, clicking on the **Errata Submission Form** link, and entering the details of your errata. Once your errata are verified, your submission will be accepted and the errata will be uploaded to our website or added to any list of existing errata under the Errata section of that title.

To view the previously submitted errata, go to `https://www.packtpub.com/books/conten t/support` and enter the name of the book in the search field. The required information will appear under the **Errata** section.

# Piracy

Piracy of copyrighted material on the Internet is an ongoing problem across all media. At Packt, we take the protection of our copyright and licenses very seriously. If you come across any illegal copies of our works in any form on the Internet, please provide us with the location address or website name immediately so that we can pursue a remedy.

Please contact us at `copyright@packtpub.com` with a link to the suspected pirated material.

We appreciate your help in protecting our authors and our ability to bring you valuable content.

# Questions

If you have a problem with any aspect of this book, you can contact us at `questions@packtpub.com`, and we will do our best to address the problem.

# 1
# Getting Up and Running with Cassandra

As an application developer, you have almost certainly worked with databases extensively. You must have built products using relational databases such as **MySQL** and **PostgreSQL**, and perhaps experimented with **NoSQL** databases including a document store such as **MongoDB** or a key value store such as **Redis**. While each of these tools has its strengths, you will now consider whether a distributed database such as **Cassandra** might be the best choice for the task at hand.

In this chapter, we'll begin with the need for NoSQL databases to satisfy the conundrum of ever-growing data. We will see why NoSQL databases are becoming the de facto choice for big data and real-time web applications. We will also talk about the major reasons to choose Cassandra from among the many database options available to you. Having established that Cassandra is a great choice, we'll go through the nuts and bolts of getting a local Cassandra installation up and running. By the end of this chapter, you'll know the following:

- What big data is and why relational databases are not a good choice
- When and why Cassandra is a good choice for your application
- How to install Cassandra on your development machine
- How to interact with Cassandra using `cqlsh`
- How to create a `keyspace`, table, and write a simple query

# What is big data?

Big data is a relatively new term which has been gathering steam over the past few years. Big data is a term used for datasets that are relatively large to be stored in a traditional database system or processed by traditional data-processing pipelines. This data could be structured, semi-structured, or unstructured data. The datasets that belong to this category usually scale to terabytes or petabytes of data. Big data usually involves one or more of the following:

- **Velocity**: Data moves at an unprecedented speed and must be dealt with it in a timely manner.

  For example, online systems, sensors, social media, web clickstream, and so on.

- **Volume**: Organizations collect data from a variety of sources, including business transactions, social media, and information from sensor or machine-to-machine data. This could involve terabytes to petabytes of data. In the past, storing it would've been a problem, but new technologies have eased the burden.
- **Variety**: Data comes in all sorts of formats ranging from structured data to be stored in traditional databases to unstructured data (blobs) such as images, audio files, and text files.

These are known as the 3Vs of big data.

In addition to these, we tend to associate another term with big data:

- **Complexity**: Today's data comes from multiple sources, which makes it difficult to link, match, cleanse, and transform data across systems. However, it's necessary to connect and correlate relationships, hierarchies, and multiple data linkages, or your data can quickly spiral out of control. It must be able to traverse multiple data centers, cloud, and geographical zones.

# Challenges of modern applications

Before we delve into the shortcomings of relational systems to handle big data, let's take a look at some of the challenges faced by modern web-facing and big data applications.

Later, this will give an insight into how NoSQL data stores or Cassandra, in particular, help solve these issues:

- One of the most important challenges faced by a web-facing application is the ability to handle a large number of concurrent users. Think of a search engine such as Google, which handles millions of concurrent users at any given point of time, or a large online retailer. The response from these applications should be swift even as the number of users keeps on growing.
- Modern applications need to be able to handle large amounts of data, which can scale to several petabytes of data and beyond. Consider a large social network with a few hundred million users:
    - Think of the amount of data generated in tracking and managing those users
    - Think of how this data can be used for analytics
- Business-critical applications should continue running without much impact even when there is a system failure or multiple system failures (server failure, network failure, and so on). The applications should be able to handle failures gracefully without any data loss or interruptions.
- These applications should be able to scale across multiple data centers and geographical regions to support customers from different regions around the world with minimum delay. Modern applications should be implementing fully distributed architectures and should be capable of scaling out horizontally to support any data size or any number of concurrent users.

# Why not relational databases?

**Relational database systems** (**RDBMS**) have been the primary data store for enterprise applications for 20 years. Lately, NoSQL databases have been picking up a lot of steam, and businesses are slowly seeing a shift towards non-relational databases. There are a few reasons why relational databases don't seem like a good fit for modern big data web applications:

- Relational databases are not designed for clustered solutions. There are some solutions that shard data across servers, but these are fragile, complex, and generally don't work well.

Sharding solutions implemented by RDBMS are as follows:

- MySQL's product MySQL cluster provides clustering support which adds many capabilities of non-relational systems. It is actually an NoSQL solution that integrates with the MySQL relational database. It partitions the data onto multiple nodes, and the data can be accessed via different APIs.
- Oracle provides a clustering solution, Oracle RAC, which involves multiple nodes running an Oracle process accessing the same database files. This creates a single point of failure as well as resource limitations in accessing the database itself.

- They are not a good fit for current hardware and architectures. Relational databases are usually scaled up using larger machines with more powerful hardware and maybe clustering and replication among a small number of nodes. Their core architecture is not a good fit for commodity hardware and thus doesn't work with scale-out architectures.

Scale-out versus scale-up architecture:

- Scaling out means adding more nodes to a system, such as adding more servers to a distributed database or filesystem. This is also known as horizontal scaling.
- Scaling up means adding more resources to a single node within the system, such as adding more CPU, memory, or disks to a server. This is also known as vertical scaling.

# How to handle big data

Now that we are convinced the relational model is not a good fit for big data, let's try to figure out ways to handle big data. These are the solutions that paved the way for various NoSQL databases:

- **Clustering**: The data should be spread across different nodes in a cluster. The data should be replicated across multiple nodes in order to sustain node failures. This helps spread the data across the cluster, and different nodes contain different subsets of data. This improves performance and provides fault tolerance.

A node is an instance of database software running on a server. Multiple instances of the same database could be running on the same server.

- **Flexible schema**: Schemas should be flexible unlike the relational model and should evolve with the data.
- **Relax consistency**: We should embrace the concept of eventual consistency, which means data will eventually be propagated to all the nodes in the cluster (in case of replication). Eventual consistency allows data replication across nodes with minimum overhead. This allows for fast writes with the need for distributed locking.
- **Denormalization of data**: Denormalize data to optimize queries. This has to be done at the cost of writing and maintaining multiple copies of the same data.

# What is Cassandra and why Cassandra?

Cassandra is a fully distributed, masterless database, offering superior scalability, and fault tolerance to traditional single-master databases. Compared with other popular distributed databases such as **Riak**, **HBase**, and **Voldemort**, Cassandra offers a uniquely robust and expressive interface for modeling and querying data. What follows is an overview of several desirable database capabilities, with accompanying discussions of what Cassandra has to offer in each category. Apart from the following features, Apache Cassandra has a large user base including some top technology firms such as Apple, Netflix, and Instagram, who also open-source new features. It is being actively developed and has one of largest open source communities with close to 200 contributors and over 20,000 commits.

# Horizontal scalability

**Horizontal scalability** refers to the ability to expand the storage and processing capacity of a database by adding more servers to a database cluster. A traditional single-master database's storage capacity is limited by the capacity of the server that hosts the master instance. If the data set outgrows this capacity and a more powerful server isn't available, the data set must be shared among multiple independent database instances that know nothing of each other. Your application bears responsibility for knowing to which instance a given piece of data belongs.

Cassandra, on the other hand, is deployed as a **cluster** of instances that are all aware of each other. From the client application's standpoint, the cluster is a single entity; the application need not know, nor care, which machine a piece of data belongs to. Instead, data can be read or written to any instance in the cluster, referred to as a **node**; this node will forward the request to the instance where the data actually belongs. The result is that Cassandra deployments have an almost limitless capacity to store and process data. When additional capacity is required, more machines can simply be added to the cluster. When new machines join the cluster, Cassandra takes care of rebalancing the existing data so that each node in the expanded cluster has a roughly equal share. Also, the performance of a Cassandra cluster is directly proportional to the number of nodes within the cluster. As you keep on adding instances, the read and write throughput will keep increasing linearly.

 Cassandra is one of the several popular distributed databases inspired by the Dynamo architecture, originally published in a paper by Amazon. Other widely used implementations of Dynamo include Riak and Voldemort. You can read the original paper at http://s3.amazonaws.com /AllThingsDistributed/sosp/amazon-dynamo-sosp2007.pdf.

# High availability

The simplest database deployments are run as a single instance on a single server. This sort of configuration is highly vulnerable to interruption: if the server is affected by a hardware failure or network connection outage, the application's ability to read and write data is completely lost until the server is restored. If the failure is catastrophic, the data on that server might be lost completely.

Master-slave architectures improve this picture a bit. The master instance receives all write operations, and then these operations are replicated to follower instances. The application can read data from the master or any of the follower instances, so a single host becoming unavailable will not prevent the application from continuing to read the data. A failure of the master, however, will still prevent the application from performing any write operations, so while this configuration provides high read availability, it doesn't completely provide high availability.

Cassandra, on the other hand, has no single point of failure for reading or writing data. Each piece of data is replicated to multiple nodes, but none of these nodes holds the authoritative master copy. All the nodes in a Cassandra cluster are peers without a master node. If a machine becomes unavailable, Cassandra will continue writing data to the other nodes that share data with that machine and will queue the operations and update the failed node when it rejoins the cluster. This means that in a typical configuration, multiple nodes must fail simultaneously for there to be any application - visible interruption in Cassandra's availability.

**How many copies?**

When you create a keyspace, Cassandra's version of a database, you specify how many copies of each piece of data should be stored; this is called the replication factor. A replication factor of 3 is a common choice for most use cases.

The image below perfectly illustrates high availability in Cassandra. Clients reconnect to different node in case a node is down:

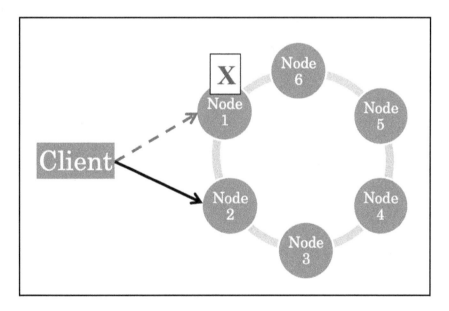

# Write optimization

Traditional relational and document databases are optimized for read performance. Writing data to a relational database will typically involve making in - place updates to complicated data structures on disk, in order to maintain a data structure that can be read efficiently and flexibly. Updating these data structures is a very expensive operation from a standpoint of disk I/O, which is often the limiting factor for database performance. Since writes are more expensive than reads, you'll typically avoid any unnecessary updates to a relational database, even at the expense of extra read operations.

Cassandra, on the other hand, is highly optimized for write throughput and, in fact, never modifies data on disk; it only appends to existing files or creates new ones. This is much easier on disk I/O and means that Cassandra can provide astonishingly high write throughput. Since both writing data to Cassandra and storing data in Cassandra are inexpensive, denormalization carries little cost and is a good way to ensure that data can be efficiently read in various access scenarios.

 Because Cassandra is optimized for write volume, you shouldn't shy away from writing data to the database. In fact, it's most efficient to write without reading whenever possible, even if doing so might result in redundant updates.

Just because Cassandra is optimized for writes doesn't make it bad at reads; in fact, a well-designed Cassandra database can handle very heavy read loads with no problem. We'll cover the topic of efficient data modeling in great depth in the next few chapters.

# Structured records

The first three database features we looked at are commonly found in distributed data stores. However, databases such as Riak and Voldemort are purely key value stores; these databases have no knowledge of the internal structure of a record that's stored in a particular key. This means useful functions such as updating only part of a record, reading only certain fields from a record, or retrieving records that contain a particular value in a given field are not possible.

Relational databases such as PostgreSQL, document stores such as MongoDB, and, to a limited extent, newer key-value stores such as Redis, do have a concept of the internal structure of their records, and most application developers are accustomed to taking advantage of the possibilities this allows. None of these databases, however, offer the advantages of a masterless distributed architecture.

In Cassandra, records are structured much in the same way as they are in a relational database—using tables, rows, and columns. Thus, applications using Cassandra can enjoy all the benefits of masterless distributed storage while also getting all the advanced data modeling and access features associated with structured records.

# Secondary indexes

A secondary index, commonly referred to as an index in the context of a relational database, is a structure allowing efficient lookup of records by some attribute other than their primary key. This is a widely useful capability; for instance, when developing a blog application, you would want to be able to easily retrieve all of the posts written by a particular author. Cassandra supports secondary indexes; while Cassandra's version is not as versatile as indexes in a typical relational database, it's a powerful feature in the right circumstances. A query on a secondary index can perform poorly in certain cases; hence, it should be used sparingly and only in certain cases, which we will touch upon later in `Chapter 5,` *Establishing Relationships*.

# Materialized views

Data modeling principles in Cassandra compel us to denormalize data as much as possible. Prior to Cassandra 3.0, the only way to query on a non-primary key column was to create a secondary index and query on it. However, secondary indexes have a performance trade-off if they contain high cardinality data. Often, high cardinality secondary indexes have to scan data on all the nodes and aggregate them to return the query results. This defeats the purpose of having a distributed system.

To avoid secondary indexes and client-side denormalization, Cassandra introduced the feature of materialized views, which does server side denormalization. You can create views for a base table and Cassandra ensures eventual consistency between the base and view. This lets us do very fast lookups on each view following the normal Cassandra read path. Materialized views maintain a correspondence of one CQL row each in the base and the view, so we need to ensure that each CQL row that is required for the views will be reflected in the base table's primary keys. Although a materialized view allows for fast lookups on non-primary key indexes, this comes at a performance hit to writes. Also, using secondary indexes and materialized views increases the disk usage by a considerable margin. Thus, it is important to take this into consideration when sizing your cluster.

# Efficient result ordering

It's quite common to want to retrieve a record set ordered by a particular field; for instance, a photo-sharing service will want to retrieve the most recent photographs in descending order of creation. Since sorting data on the fly is a fundamentally expensive operation, databases must keep information about record ordering persisted on disk in order to efficiently return results in order. In a relational database, this is one of the jobs of a secondary index.

In Cassandra, secondary indexes can't be used for result ordering, but tables can be structured such that rows are always kept sorted by a given column or columns, called **clustering columns**. Sorting by arbitrary columns at read time is not possible, but the capacity to efficiently order records in any way and to retrieve ranges of records based on this ordering is an unusually powerful capability for a distributed database.

# Immediate consistency

When we write a piece of data to a database, it is our hope that that data is immediately available to any other process that may wish to read it. From another point of view, when we read some data from a database, we would like to be guaranteed that the data we retrieve is the most recently updated version. This guarantee is called **immediate consistency**, and it's a property of most common single-master databases such as MySQL and PostgreSQL.

Distributed systems such as Cassandra typically do not provide an immediate consistency guarantee. Instead, developers must be willing to accept **eventual consistency**, which means when data is updated, the system will reflect that update at some point in the future. Developers are willing to give up immediate consistency precisely because it is a direct trade-off with high availability.

In the case of Cassandra, that trade-off is made explicit through **tunable consistency**. Each time you design a write or read path for data, you have the option of immediate consistency with less resilient availability, or eventual consistency with extremely resilient availability. We'll cover consistency tuning in great detail in `Chapter 10`, *How Cassandra Distributes Data*.

# Discretely writable collections

While it's useful for records to be internally structured into discrete fields, a given property of a record isn't always a single value such as a string or an integer. One simple way to handle fields that contain collections of values is to serialize them using a format such as JSON and then save the serialized collection into a `text` field. However, in order to update collections stored in this way, the serialized data must be read from the database, decoded, modified, and then written back to the database in its entirety. If two clients try to perform this kind of modification to the same record concurrently, one of the updates will be overwritten by the other. For this reason, many databases offer built-in collection structures that can be discretely updated: values can be added to and removed from collections without reading and rewriting the entire collection. Cassandra is no exception, offering list, set, and map collections, and supporting operations such as *append the number 3 to the end of this list*. Neither the client nor Cassandra itself needs to read the current state of the collection in order to update it, meaning collection updates are also blazingly efficient.

# Relational joins

In real-world applications, different pieces of data relate to each other in a variety of ways. Relational databases allow us to perform queries that make these relationships explicit; for instance, to retrieve a set of events whose location is in the state of New York (this is assuming events and locations are different record types). Cassandra, however, is not a relational database and does not support anything such as joins. Instead, applications using Cassandra typically denormalize data and make clever use of clustering in order to perform the sorts of data access that would use a join in a relational database.

For data sets that aren't already denormalized, applications can also perform client-side joins, which mimic the behavior of a relational database by performing multiple queries and joining the results at the application level. Client-side joins are less efficient than reading data that has been denormalized in advance, but they offer more flexibility. We'll cover both of these approaches in `Chapter 6`, *Denormalizing Data for Maximum Performance*.

# MapReduce and Spark

**MapReduce** is a technique for performing aggregate processing on large amounts of data in parallel; it's a particularly common technique in data analytics applications. Cassandra does not offer built-in MapReduce capabilities, but it can be integrated with Hadoop in order to perform MapReduce operations across Cassandra data sets, or Spark for real-time data analysis. The DataStax enterprise product provides integration with both of these tools out of the box.

**Spark** is a fast, distributed, and expressive computational engine used for large-scale data processing similar to MapReduce. It is much more efficient than MapReduce and runs with resource managers such as Mesos and Yarn. It can read data from various sources such as Hadoop or Cassandra or even streams such as Kafka. DataStax provides a Spark-Cassandra connector to load data from Cassandra into Spark and run batch computations on the data.

# Rich and flexible data model

Cassandra provides an SQL-like syntax to interact with the database. **Cassandra Query Language (CQL)** presents a familiar row column representation of data. CQL provides a familiar SQL-like table definition with columns and defined data types. Schema is flexible, and new columns can be added while using the existing data. The data model doesn't support features problematic in distributed systems such as joins. On top of this, Cassandra provides other features such as collections to store multiple items in a single column. It also lets you easily define secondary indexes and materialized views for fast lookups on non-primary key columns.

> The previous thrift-based interface was closely tied to the internal storage view. This was fairly complex and had a relatively high learning curve to adopt. The CQL interface is much easier to understand because of its similarity to SQL.

# Lightweight transactions

As discussed before, Cassandra provides eventual consistency rather than immediate consistency, which means data written will eventually be consistent across multiple replicas of the data. This has implications on the data returned by read queries. There is a possibility that reads could return stale data depending on how writes and reads are configured (the consistency levels at which both queries are performed). Strong consistency, which means reading the most recently written value, can be achieved using quorum reads and writes. But what if strong consistency is not enough? What if we have some operations to perform in sequence that must not be interrupted by others, that is, we must perform them one at a time, or make sure that any that we do run concurrently get the same results as if they really were processed independently. Cassandra provides lightweight transactions with linearizable consistency to ensure a transaction isolation level similar to the serializable level offered by RDBMSs. They are also known as compare and set transactions. You can use lightweight transactions instead of durable transactions with eventual/tunable consistency for situations that require the nodes in the distribution system to agree on changes to the data.

# Multidata center replication

Another interesting feature provided by Cassandra is the ability to replicate data across multiple data centers or geographical zones in near real-time. This is natively supported by Cassandra and doesn't need to be managed at the application level. Cassandra also provides local consistency levels to ensure cross-region latency doesn't impact client queries. A multiregion cluster can sustain disasters or entire data centers going down. Ideally, there is no need for backups or disaster recovery when running multidata center clusters except for cases of data corruption.

 On April 21, 2011, Amazon experienced a large outage in AWS US-East. Some websites were impacted, while others were not. For Netflix, their systems are designed explicitly for these sorts of failures. The SimpleDB, S3, and Cassandra services that Netflix depends upon were not affected by the outage because of the cross-region replication that these services provide.

# Comparing Cassandra to the alternatives

Now that you've got an in-depth understanding of the feature set that Cassandra offers, it's time to figure out which features are most important to you and which database is the best fit. The following table lists a handful of commonly used databases and key features that they do or don't have:

| Feature | Cassandra | PostgreSQL | MongoDB | Redis | Riak |
|---|---|---|---|---|---|
| Structured records | Yes | Yes | Yes | Limited | No |
| Secondary indexes | Yes | Yes | Yes | No | Yes |
| Discretely writable collections | Yes | Yes | Yes | Yes | No |
| Relational joins | No | Yes | No | No | No |
| Built-in MapReduce | No | No | Yes | No | Yes |
| Fast result ordering | Yes | Yes | Yes | Yes | No |
| Immediate consistency | Configurable at query level | Yes | Yes | Yes | Configurable at cluster level |
| Transparent sharding | Yes | No | Yes | No | Yes |
| No single point of failure | Yes | No | No | No | Yes |
| High throughput writes | Yes | No | No | Yes | Yes |

As you can see, Cassandra offers a unique combination of scalability, availability, and a rich set of features for modeling and accessing data.

# Installing Cassandra

Now that you're acquainted with Cassandra's substantial powers, you're no doubt chomping at the bit to try it out. Happily, Cassandra is free, open source, and very easy to get running:

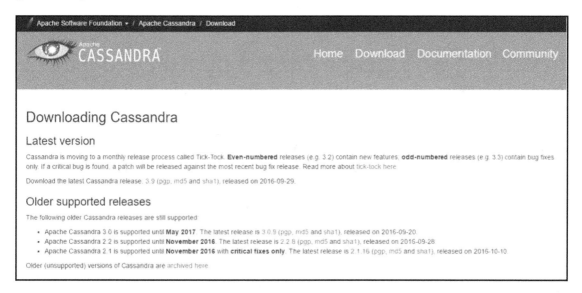

Since some of the features are specific to Cassandra 3.0, we will be installing the latest version of Cassandra 3.0.x available for each OS. Also since it is easier to add apt and yum repositories from DataStax, we will be using the DataStax Community version of Cassandra wherever possible. DataStax Community is open source Apache Cassandra with a few added features.

# Installing the JDK

First, we need to make sure that we have an up-to-date installation of the **Java Runtime Environment** (JRE). The recommended Java version for Cassandra 3.0 is Oracle Java 1.8. Make sure you have the correct **Java Development Kit** (JDK) version installed. Go to `http ://www.oracle.com/technetwork/java/javase/downloads/index.html`, and download and install the appropriate JDK. Open the Terminal application, and type the following into the command prompt:

```
$ java -version
```

You will see an output that looks similar to the following:

```
java version "1.8.0_65"
Java(TM) SE Runtime Environment (build 1.8.0_65-b17)
Java HotSpot(TM) 64-Bit Server VM (build 25.65-b01, mixed mode)
```

Once you've got the right version of Java, you're ready to install Cassandra.

# Installing on Debian-based systems (Ubuntu)

To install Cassendra on Debian-based systems (Ubuntu), perform the following steps:

1. Add the repository to the
   `/etc/apt/sources.list.d/cassandra.sources.list`:

   ```
   $ echo "deb http://debian.datastax.com/community stable main" |
     sudo tee -a /etc/apt/sources.list.d/cassandra.sources.list
   ```

2. Add the DataStax repository key to your aptitude trusted keys:

   ```
   $ curl -L https://debian.datastax.com/debian/repo_key | sudo
     apt-key add -
   ```

3. Install the latest package:

   ```
   $ sudo apt-get update
   $ sudo apt-get install dsc30
   ```

4. Start Cassandra:

   ```
   $ sudo service cassandra start
   ```

5. Verify the Cassandra installation:

   ```
   $ nodetool status
   ```

```
Datacenter: datacenter1
========================
Status=Up/Down
|/ State=Normal/Leaving/Joining/Moving
--  Address    Load       Tokens    Owns (effective)  Host ID                                Rack
UN  127.0.0.1  234.32 KB  256       100.0%            9e35777b-f2fa-460f-bb87-26fe0507fecd   rack1
```

Your result should look something like the preceding except for a different Host ID.

6. Stop Cassandra:

```
$ sudo service cassandra stop
```

# Installing on RHEL-based systems

To install Cassendra on RHEL-based systems, perform the following steps:

1. Add the Apache Cassandra 3.0 repository to
   /etc/yum.repos.d/datastax.repo:

```
[datastax]
name = DataStax Repo for Apache Cassandra
baseurl = http://rpm.datastax.com/community
enabled = 1
gpgcheck = 0
```

2. Install the latest packages:

```
$ sudo yum install dsc30
```

3. Start Cassandra:

```
$ sudo service cassandra start
```

On some Linux distributions, you many need to use the following:

```
$ sudo /etc/init.d/cassandra start
```

# Installing on Windows

The easiest way to install Cassandra on Windows is to use the DataStax Community Edition. DataStax is a company that provides enterprise-level support for Cassandra; they also release Cassandra packages at both free and paid tiers. The DataStax Community Edition is free and does not differ from the Apache package in any meaningful way.

DataStax offers a graphical installer for Cassandra on Windows, which is available for download at http://planetcassandra.org/cassandra.

On this page, locate **MSI Installer** (32 bit or 64 bit depending on your operating system) under Download **DataStax Community Edition v3.0.9**. Install the downloaded binary:

 From Windows PowerShell, set the execution policy to unrestricted from an elevated command-prompt:
```
C:> powershell Set-ExecutionPolicy Unrestricted
```

1. Follow the setup wizard to install.
2. The installation wizard lets you set up the DataStax services to start automatically when the installation completes and whenever the computer reboots. If you select this option, the services start automatically—you can skip the next step.

3. If you did not elect to have Datastax services start automatically, start Cassandra by entering the following in Command Prompt:

```
C:> net start DataStax_Cassandra_Community_Server
C:> net start DataStax_DDC_Server
```

- To verify that Apache Cassandra 3.0 for Windows is running, use the nodetool status command,

  For example:

```
C:> cd %CASSANDRA_HOME%
C:> bin\nodetool status
```

The following is the output:

```
C:\Program Files\DataStax Community\apache-cassandra>bin\nodetool status
Datacenter: datacenter1
=========================
Status=Up/Down
|/ State=Normal/Leaving/Joining/Moving
--  Address    Load       Tokens     Owns (effective)  Host ID                               Rack
UN  127.0.0.1  155.59 KB  256        100.0%            86aa8bfc-8d69-4b28-8226-87f2d1b05c8e  rack1


C:\Program Files\DataStax Community\apache-cassandra>
```

- Stop Cassandra:

```
C:> net stop DataStax_Cassandra_Community_Server
```

# Installing on Mac OS X

You'll need to set up your environment so that Cassandra knows where to find the latest version of Java. To do this, set up your JAVA_HOME environment variable to the install location, and your PATH to include the executable in your new Java installation, as follows:

```
$ export JAVA_HOME="
/Library/Java/JavaVirtualMachines/jdk1.8.0_65.jdk/Contents/Home"
$ export PATH="$JAVA_HOME/bin":$PATH
```

You should put these two lines at the bottom of your .bashrc or .bash_profile file to ensure that things still work when you open a new terminal.

The installation instructions given earlier assume that you're using the latest version of Mac OS X (at the time of writing this, 10.11.6 El Capitan). If you're running a different version of OS X, installing Java might require different steps. Check out `https://www.java.com/en/download/faq/jav a_mac.xml` for detailed installation information.

Once you've got the right version of Java, you're ready to install Cassandra. It's very easy to install Cassandra using **Homebrew**; simply type the following:

```
$ brew install cassandra
$ pip install cassandra-driver cql
$ cassandra
```

Here's what we just did:

- Installed Cassandra using the Homebrew package manager
- Installed the CQL shell and its dependency, the Python Cassandra driver
- Started the Cassandra server

# Installing the binary tarball

You can use the binary tarball to install Cassandra on any Linux-based platform including Mac OS X and platforms without package support or if you do not want a root installation:

1. Download the Apache `Cassandra` 3.0.9 binary tarball from the following:

    `http://www.apache.org/dyn/closer.lua/cassandra/3.0.9/apache-cassandra-3.0.9-bin.tar.gz.`

2. Use the following command to untar:

    ```
    $ tar -xvzf apache-cassandra-3.0.9-bin.tar.gz
    ```

3. To configure `Cassandra`, go to the `$INSTALL_LOCATION/conf` directory and make the relevant changes. You can do this once you get an idea of Cassandra internals later in the book. `INSTALL_LOCATION` in this case will be `$CURRENT_DIRECTORY/apache-cassandra-3.0.9/`.

4. Start `Cassandra`:

    ```
    $ cd apache-cassandra-3.0.9/
    $ bin/cassandra # Use -f to start Cassandra in the foreground
    ```

5.  Verify that Cassandra is running:

```
$ bin/nodetool status
```

You might want to add `CASSANDRA_HOME=$INSTALL_LOCATION` and `PATH=$PATH:$INSTALL_LOCATION/bin` in the `.bashrc` or `.bash_profile` files so every time you open a new terminal, you can simply launch `cassandra`, `nodetool`, or `cqlsh` by entering the command on terminal without changing directory every time.

# Bootstrapping the project

Throughout the remainder of this book, we will build an application called **MyStatus**, which allows users to post status updates for their friends to read. In each chapter, we'll add new functionality to the MyStatus application; each new feature will also introduce a new aspect of Cassandra.

# CQL—the Cassandra Query Language

Since this is a book about Cassandra and not targeted to users of any particular programming language or application framework, we will focus entirely on the database interactions that MyStatus will require. Code examples will be in **Cassandra Query Language** (CQL). Specifically, we'll use version 3.4.0 of CQL, which is available in Cassandra 3.0 and later versions.

As the name implies, CQL is heavily inspired by SQL; in fact, many CQL statements are equally valid SQL statements. However, CQL and SQL are not interchangeable. CQL lacks grammar for relational features such as JOIN statements, which are not possible in Cassandra. Conversely, CQL is not a subset of SQL; constructs for retrieving the update time of a given column, or performing an update in a lightweight transaction, which are available in CQL, do not have an SQL equivalent.

Throughout this book, you'll learn the important constructs of CQL. Once you've completed reading this book, I recommend you to turn to the DataStax CQL documentation for additional reference. This documentation is available at `http://www.datastax.com/documentation/cql/3.3`.

# Interacting with Cassandra

Most common programming languages have drivers for interacting with Cassandra. When selecting a driver, you should look for libraries that support the CQL binary protocol, which is the latest and most efficient way to communicate with Cassandra.

 The CQL binary protocol is a relatively new introduction; older versions of Cassandra used the Thrift protocol as a transport layer. Although Cassandra continues to support Thrift, avoid Thrift-based drivers as they are less performant than the binary protocol.

Here are the CQL binary drivers available for some popular programming languages:

| Language | Driver | Available at |
|----------|--------|--------------|
| Java | DataStax Java Driver | `https://github.com/datastax/java-driver` |
| Python | DataStax Python Driver | `https://github.com/datastax/python-driver` |
| Ruby | DataStax Ruby Driver | `https://github.com/datastax/ruby-driver` |
| C++ | DataStax C++ Driver | `https://github.com/datastax/cpp-driver` |
| C# | DataStax C# Driver | `https://github.com/datastax/csharp-driver` |
| JavaScript (Node.js) | node-cassandra-cql | `https://github.com/jorgebay/node-cassandra-cql` |
| PHP | phpbinarycql | `https://github.com/rmcfrazier/phpbinarycql` |

While you are likely to use one of these drivers in your applications, to try out the code examples in this book, you can simply use the cqlsh tool, which is a command-line interface for executing CQL queries and viewing the results. To start cqlsh on OS X or Linux, simply type `cqlsh` into your command line; you should see something like this:

```
$ cqlsh
Connected to Test Cluster at 127.0.01:9042.
[cqlsh 5.0.1 | Cassandra 3.0.9 | CQL spec 3.4.0 | Native protocol v4]
```

```
Use HELP for help.
cqlsh>
```

On Windows, you can start `cqlsh` just the way you ran nodetool:

```
C:> cd %CASSANDRA_HOME%
C:> bin\cqlsh
```

Once you open it, you should see the same output we just saw.

# Getting started with CQL

To get started with CQL, we will create a simple keyspace and table. We will insert a record into the table and read it back. Let's create a simple table which stores some personal information of a social network user.

# Creating a keyspace

A **keyspace** is a collection of related tables equivalent to a database in a relational system. To create `keyspace`, issue the following statement in the CQL shell:

```
cqlsh> CREATE KEYSPACE "users"
WITH REPLICATION = {
  'class': 'SimpleStrategy', 'replication_factor': 1
};
```

Here, we created a keyspace called `users`. When we create a keyspace, we have to specify replication options. Cassandra provides several strategies for managing replication of data; `SimpleStrategy` is the best strategy as long as your Cassandra deployment does not span across multiple data centers. The `replication_factor` value tells Cassandra how many copies of each piece of data are to be kept in the cluster; since we are only running a single instance of Cassandra, there is no point in keeping more than one copy of the data. In a production deployment, you would certainly want a higher replication factor; three is a good place to start.

A few things at this point are worth noting about CQL's syntax:

- It's syntactically very similar to SQL; as we further explore CQL, the impression of similarity will not diminish.
- Double quotes are used for identifiers such as keyspace, table, and column names. As in SQL, quoting identifier names is usually optional, unless the identifier is a keyword or contains a space or another character that will trip up the parser.
- Single quotes are used for string literals; the key value structure we use for replication is a map literal, which is syntactically similar to an object literal in JSON.

# Selecting a keyspace

Once you've created a keyspace, you would want to use it. In order to do this, employ the USE command:

```
cqlsh> USE "users";
```

This tells Cassandra that all future commands will implicitly refer to tables inside the users keyspace. If you close the CQL shell and reopen it, you'll need to reissue this command.

# Creating a table

Let's create a table within our users keyspace to store personal information. You can create a table by issuing the following command:

```
CREATE TABLE "personal_info" (id int PRIMARY KEY, name text, dob text);
```

I will be omitting cqlsh> in the text from now on. You should always run the commands after entering cqlsh.

So we created the table `personal_info` with three columns: `id` , which is a unique integer identifier for a user which also happens to be the primary key for this table, `name`, and `dob` (date of birth) columns which are text values (strings).

## Inserting and reading data

To insert data into the table, run the following command:

```
INSERT INTO personal_info (id, name, dob) VALUES ( 1 , 'Alice' ,
'02-25-1954' );
```

This will insert a record for a user named `Alice` whose date of birth is `02-25-1954` and has been assigned the `id 1`. To read the data from the table, run the following query:

```
SELECT * FROM personal_info WHERE id = 1;
```

You should get an output that looks like this:

```
id | dob        | name
---+------------+-------
 1 | 02-25-1954 | Alice
```

Voila! You have created your first keyspace and table, inserted a record, and queried the record back.

# New features in Cassandra 2.2, 3.0, and 3.X

Since the first edition of this mostly covered Cassandra versions 2.1 and below, here is a list of features and improvements that have been made to Cassandra starting version 2.2 and beyond. This will give you a gist of how Cassandra has matured over the last year:

- **JSON in CQL3**: Cassandra 2.2 has support for inserting and selecting JSON data
- **User-defined functions**: These can be defined to apply a function to data stored in Cassandra
- **User-defined aggregates**: Using user-defined functions, custom aggregation functions can be stored in Cassandra
- **Role-based access control**: In addition to per-user access control, now roles can be defined for role-based access control

- Support for Windows 7, Windows 8, Windows 10, Windows Server 2008, and Windows Server 2012
- The storage engine has been refactored
- **Materialized views**: Materialized views have been added to handle server side denormalization, with consistency between base and view
- **G1 garbage collector**: The default garbage collector has been changed to G1 from CMS (concurrent mark and sweep), which has markedly increased performance for higher values of JVM heap sizes
- Hints are stored in files and replay has been improved

 Apart from these, there have been a plethora of operational improvements. You can take a look at them at `https://docs.datastax.com/en/cassandra/3.x/cassandra/features.html`.

# Summary

In this chapter, you explored the reasons to choose Cassandra from among the many databases available, and having determined that Cassandra is a great choice, you installed it on your development machine.

You had your first taste of the Cassandra Query Language when you issued your first few commands via the CQL shell in order to create a keyspace table, and insert and read data. You're now ready to begin working with Cassandra in earnest.

In the next chapter, we'll begin building the MyStatus application, starting out with a simple table to model users. We'll cover a lot more CQL commands, and before you know it, you'll be reading and writing data like a pro.

# 2
# The First Table

For the next few chapters, we'll be building the persistence layer for an application called **MyStatus**, which allows its users to post status updates for their friends to see. In this chapter, we'll make the first table of that persistence layer, which will store user profiles.

In Chapter 1, *Getting Up and Running with Cassandra*, you set up a local Cassandra installation, started the cqlsh, and ran some CQL commands. Now we're prepared to hit the ground running. This chapter will provide a whirlwind tour of many core Cassandra concepts such as the following:

- How to configure keyspaces
- How Cassandra tables are structured
- Cassandra's type system
- How to create a table
- How to insert rows into a table
- How to retrieve rows by primary key
- How to query for all rows in a table
- How to page through large result sets

## How to configure keyspaces

In the previous chapter, we learned a little bit about keyspaces. A **keyspace** is essentially a namespace for various tables in a cluster. It is somewhat analogous to a database in the relational world. All data will reside within some keyspace. The main function of declaring keyspaces over declaring tables directly is not to serve as a mapping layer, but to control the replication of closely related tables.

Let's create the keyspace for our MyStatus application by executing the following command in CQL shell:

```
CREATE KEYSPACE "my_status"
WITH REPLICATION = {
      'class': 'SimpleStrategy', 'replication_factor': 1
};
```

When creating a keyspace, you have to specify certain configuration parameters such as the replication strategy and the replication factor. The replication strategy tells the Cassandra cluster how to distribute various copies of the same data across the different data centers and racks of cluster. The replication factor specifies how many copies of each record to store. There is another configuration parameter called durable writes, which we will learn about later.

For now, we will use SimpleStrategy and a replication factor of 1 since we have a single node cluster running. This keyspace will serve as the namespace for all the tables we create in the rest of the book.

In CQL, you select the keyspace to use via the USE command. To ensure all the future tables reside within the my_status keyspace, we enter the following statement:

```
USE "my_status";
```

Another way to select a keyspace is to prefix a table name with the keyspace name wherever we use it, such as <keyspace_name> and <table_name>.

# Creating the users table

Our first table will store basic user account information: username, email, and password. To create the table, fire up the CQL shell (don't forget to use the USE  my_status; statement if you are starting a fresh session) and enter the following CQL statement:

```
CREATE TABLE "users" (
  "username" text PRIMARY KEY,
  "email" text,
  "encrypted_password" blob
);
```

In the preceding statement, we created a new table called users, which has three columns: username and email, which are the text columns, and encrypted_password, which has the type blob. The username column acts as the primary key for the table.

Another way to declare this table is as follows:

```
CREATE TABLE "my_status"."users" (
  "username" text,
  "email" text,
  "encrypted_password" blob,
  primary key (username)
);
```

Later, we will learn that the second way of declaring tables is often the only way.

# Structuring of tables

Cassandra structures tables in rows and columns, just like a relational database. Also like a relational database, the columns available to a table are defined in advance. New columns cannot be added on the fly when inserting data, although it's possible to update an existing table's schema.

Every table defines one or more columns to act as the `primary key`; each row is uniquely identified by the value(s) in its primary key column(s), and those columns cannot be left blank in any row. Cassandra does not offer auto-incrementing primary keys; each row, when created, must be explicitly assigned a primary key by the client. One good way to structure the primary key is to use a `natural key`, which is a value that is fundamentally unique for each row you want to store. That's what we do in the `users` table by making `username`, a naturally unique identifier, the `primary key`.

 Before we continue, I should emphasize the importance of using the latest version of Cassandra. Cassandra and CQL have changed substantially over the past few years, and the current CQL version 3.4 is not backward compatible with older versions of the language. The examples in this book target the latest Cassandra version (at the time of writing, 3.0.9); make sure you're running this version or a newer one.

# Table and column options

The table creation statement given in the previous section is very simple: little more than a list of column names and their respective types. In contrast, an SQL `CREATE TABLE` statement will often look quite complex, with multiple options set on each column, such as defaults, constraints, and nullability flags. What sorts of bells and whistles can we add to a CQL table?

At the table level, Cassandra does have quite a few configuration options known as **table properties**. These properties allow you to tune a wide range of under-the-hood aspects of the table, such as caching, compression, garbage collection, and read repair. Table properties do not, however, bear on the table's behavior from the application's standpoint. For this reason, we won't go into detail about them in this book.Columns, on the other hand, have very few knobs to turn. In fact, outside of the type, each column is pretty much the same. There are several column options you may be accustomed to from SQL databases that don't carry over to Cassandra, such as the following:

- Cassandra doesn't have a concept of null values; columns either have data, or they don't. Primary key columns are always required to have a value; non-key columns are always optional. You will see the word null appear in the `cqlsh` output, but that simply means there is no data in this column and should not be confused with the concept of null in a relational database.
- Cassandra doesn't support default values for columns. If a row is inserted without a value for a certain column, that column just doesn't have a value.
- Cassandra doesn't provide data validations such as length limits or other more complex column constraints. As long as a value is of the right type for the column you're putting it in, it's valid.

Fortunately, most modern applications do not need to rely on the sorts of aforementioned constraints; domain modeling libraries and object mappers typically allow you to easily apply these constraints at the application level.

# The type system

Each column defined for a table has a defined type. In the `users` table, we used the `text` and `blob` types, but those are only two of the many types built into Cassandra.

## Strings

Cassandra has two types that store string data:

- The `text` type stores the UTF-8 encoded strings. It's also aliased as the `varchar` type; you can use these interchangeably
- The `ascii` type stores strings of ASCII characters (bytes 0-127)

Neither of the previous string types has a limit on the length of strings that can be stored. In CQL, string literals are surrounded by single quotes, 'like this'.

# Integers

Cassandra has five types that store integers:

- The int type stores 32-bit integers, which can store values ranging from approximately -2.1 billion to 2.1 billion
- The bigint type stores 64-bit integers, which can store values from about -9 quintillion to 9 quintillion
- The smallint type stores 16-bit integers, which can store values from -32,768 to 32,767
- The tinyint type stores 8-bit integers, which can store values from -128 to 127
- The varint type stores integers of arbitrary size; it has no minimum or maximum value

All integer types are signed, meaning they can hold positive or negative integers. There are no unsigned numeric types in Cassandra. Integer literals in CQL, like in most languages, consist of an optional minus sign followed by one or more digits, such as 3,549.

# Floating point and decimal numbers

Cassandra has three types that store non-integer numbers:

- The float type stores 32-bit IEEE-754 floating point numbers.
- The double type stores 64-bit IEEE-754 floating point numbers.
- The decimal type stores variable-precision decimal numbers, with no upper bound on size. Unlike a floating point number, a variable-precision decimal will never suffer from base 10 rounding errors in the fractional part of the number.

Like the integer types, the floating point and decimal types are always signed. In CQL, floating point and decimal literals are represented by an optional minus sign, followed by a series of digits, followed by a period, followed by another series of digits, such as 7,152.6846. You can also write them using exponential notation, such as 9.021e14.

# Timestamp

Date and time can be stored using the `timestamp` type, which holds date/time data with millisecond precision. Timestamp literals are enclosed in single quotation marks like string literals, and they take the `yyyy-mm-dd HH:mm:ssZ` format, for example `2014-05-18 15:49:31-0400`. There is no type that stores the date without the time, although the time portion of a timestamp literal can be omitted, which defaults the time to midnight in the given time zone. To represent timestamps with millisecond precision, you may also use an integer literal with the number of milliseconds since midnight UTC on January 1, 1970, for instance 1,400,442,761,830.

# UUIDs

Cassandra has two types that store Universally Unique Identifiers:

- The `uuid` type stores Version 1 and Version 4 UUIDs
- The `timeuuid` type stores Version 1 UUIDs and has special functionality for conversion between UUIDs and timestamps

A **Universally Unique Identifier (UUID)**, is essentially a very large number generated in a specific way, designed to guarantee that the same UUID will never be generated anywhere in the world at any time. Version 1 UUIDs are generated using a high-precision timestamp and the generating computer's MAC address; the timestamp can be extracted from the UUID. Version 4 UUIDs use random or pseudo-random numbers.

CQL uses the canonical representation of UUIDs, which is a sequence of hexadecimal digits broken up in specific places by dashes, in the form *8-4-4-4-12*. A CQL UUID literal is not surrounded by quotation marks or any other delimiter; for example, *550e8400-e29b-41d4-a716-446655440000* is a valid UUID literal. Most languages have UUID libraries available that will generate UUIDs and output them in the canonical format.

# Booleans

The `boolean` type stores simple true/false values. A boolean literal is either `true` or `false`, with no surrounding quotation marks.

# Blobs

The `blob` type stores unstructured binary data. Blobs are a good choice for images, audio, and encrypted data. In CQL, the blob literal is a sequence of hexadecimal digits, prefixed with *0x*, for instance, *0x1d4375023013dba2d5f9a*. Blob literals are not surrounded by quotation marks.

# Collections

Cassandra provides three major collection data types to bundle up multiple objects into a single column without having to declare multiple keys for each of the objects. Here are the three types:

- `List`: A non-unique ordered collection of one or more elements
- `Set`: A unique collection of one or more elements
- `Map`: A collection of key value pairs

# Other data types

Cassandra provides other data types used for convenience purposes such as the following:

- `Counter`: A coun64-bit a 64-bit integer used as a distributed counter value
- `Date`: Date is a string formatted as `yyyy-mm-dd` such as 2016-11-02
- `Inet`: Inet is an IP address string in `IPv4` or `IPv6` format
- `Time`: Time is a string formatted as `HH:MM:SS.XXXXXXXXX`, which lets time values be stored with nanosecond precision

# The purpose of types

Now that you know the full range of types available in Cassandra, you may be wondering what purpose those types serve. In fact, the type system in Cassandra plays a few roles:

- Types are used for input validation. If you attempt to put a string value in an integer column, for instance, Cassandra will return an error.
- Type information is made available to client libraries; most adapters will return the results of queries with values represented using the appropriate data type for the language.

- In some scenarios, rows can be ordered by the value of a certain column. In that case, the type of the column determines the order of values in the column. For instance, in a `text` column, 2 is larger than 10, but in an `int` column, 10 is larger than 2.

 You can find a full list of all the CQL data types in the DataStax CQL documentation at
`http://www.datastax.com/documentation/cql/3.1/cql/cql_reference/`
`cql_data_types_c.html`.

Now that we've got a firm grasp of how to create a Cassandra table and what options are available to us when creating columns, it's time to put the table to use.

# Inserting data

For our status-sharing application, the first thing we'll want any user to do is to create an account. We'll ask them to choose a `username` column, enter their `email` column, and pick a `password` column; our business logic will be responsible for ensuring that the entries are valid and for encrypting the password appropriately. At that point, we'll be ready to insert the account information as a new row in the `users` table:

```
INSERT INTO "users"
("username", "email", "encrypted_password")
VALUES (
    'alice',
    'alice@gmail.com',
    0x8914977ed729792e403da53024c6069a9158b8c4
);
```

In the previous statement, which should be familiar to anyone who has used an SQL database, we provide the following information:

- We want to add a row to the `users` table
- We'll be adding data to three columns in that row: `username`, `email`, and `encrypted_password`
- Finally, we provide the values to insert into those columns in the same order that the column names were listed previously

**Does whitespace matter?**
CQL is agnostic about whitespace. The query as written uses a lot of newlines for readability, but the query would be just as valid written on a single line.

Type the preceding CQL statement into your Cassandra shell (don't forget about the semicolon at the end!) Did it work? At first glance, it may be hard to tell.

# Writing data does not yield feedback

If the INSERT statement worked, you should not see any response in the shell whatsoever; it should simply provide you with a new command prompt. This is not simply a quirk of the CQL shell, but a fundamental fact about writing data in Cassandra; writing data does not normally result in any information about the operation from the database, other than an error message if the write failed. Most client libraries will return a null value, or the equivalent in the language in question, when you perform a successful write query.

This may come as a surprise if you're used to working with an SQL database, which will typically give you a detailed feedback when you write data, such as returning the primary key of the new row or simply telling you how many rows were affected by the operation.

We'll see some exceptions to this rule when we explore lightweight transactions in Chapter 7, *Expanding Your Data Model*.

# Partial inserts

You are not, of course, required to provide values for all columns—other than primary key columns—when inserting a row. If, for instance, we decide to allow users to register without providing an email, we may issue this perfectly valid query:

```
INSERT INTO "users"
("username", "encrypted_password")
VALUES (
  'bob',
  0x10920941a69549d33aaee6116ed1f47e19b8e713
);
```

In the preceding query, we only insert values for the `username` and `encrypted_password` fields; the row will have no value in the `email` field.

**Do empty columns take up space?**

Only columns with values take up storage space in Cassandra. This is in contrast to relational databases, in which every row has space allocated for every column, whether or not that column has a value. So, there's little downside to defining columns in Cassandra that you expect to rarely populate; they'll only take up space where they have values. For a full reference on the `INSERT` statement in CQL, consult the DataStax CQL documentation at `http://www.datastax.com/documentation/cql/3.1/c ql/cql_reference/insert_r.html`.

We haven't explored all of the possibilities for `INSERT` statements yet, but we'll cover many of them in future chapters.

# Selecting data

We now know how to retrieve data from the database, but that isn't much good unless we can get it back again. Let's say we now want to build an account settings page for MyStatus; we've got the user's username stored in a persistent session, but we will retrieve the other profile fields from the database to display in the settings form:

```
SELECT * FROM "users"
WHERE "username" = 'alice';
```

This query tells Cassandra we want to retrieve the rows where the value for `username` (the primary key) is `alice`. The * wildcard simply says we would like all the columns in that row, saving us from having to type them all out. You'll see the rows we requested nicely formatted in the CQL shell as follows:

```
username | email           | encrypted_password
---------+-----------------+-----------------------------------------------
   alice | alice@gmail.com | 0x8914977ed729792e403da53024c6069a9158b8c4
```

In other scenarios, we don't need all the columns. When a user tries to log in to MyStatus, we want to retrieve their password and compare it to the one the user provided us with, but we don't care about the email. Avoiding unnecessary columns reduces the amount of data that needs to be transferred between Cassandra and our application, thus making the queries faster. Instead of using the (*) wildcard, we can instead type a list of columns we are interested in:

```
SELECT "username", "encrypted_password" FROM "users"
WHERE "username" = 'alice';
```

```
 username | encrypted_password
----------+-----------------------------------------------
    alice | 0x8914977ed729792e403da53024c6069a9158b8c4
```

You'll see that in the results, the email column no longer appears since it wasn't in the list of columns that we specified.

# Missing rows

What happens when we ask for a primary key that doesn't exist? Let's try it out:

```
SELECT * FROM "users"
WHERE "username" = 'bogus';
```

You'll see that Cassandra simply returns no results; it is not an error to try to retrieve a primary key that does not exist.

# Selecting more than one row

Let's say we'd like to build an administrative interface that allows employees to access data for several users on one screen. We could, of course, simply perform a query for each username specified, but Cassandra gives us a more efficient way to do this:

```
SELECT * FROM "users"
WHERE "username" IN ('alice', 'bob');
```

This query will return two rows: one with the `alice` primary key and the other with the `bob` primary key:

```
 username | email            | encrypted_password
----------+------------------+------------------------------------------------
    alice | alice@gmail.com  | 0x8914977ed729792e403da53024c6069a9158b8c4
      bob |            null  | 0x10920941a69549d33aaee6116ed1f47e19b8e713
```

Note that while this will be faster than performing two queries, it does require Cassandra to perform two seeks for the two rows, so querying for the additional row comes at some cost.

# Retrieving all the rows

Perhaps we'd like to expand our administrative interface to show a list of all the users who've signed up for MyStatus. To do this, we'll want to simply ask Cassandra for all the user records:

```
SELECT * FROM "users";
```

Since we omitted the `WHERE` portion of the query, Cassandra will simply return all rows in the `users` table:

```
 username | email            | encrypted_password
----------+------------------+------------------------------------------------
      bob |            null  | 0x10920941a69549d33aaee6116ed1f47e19b8e713
    alice | alice@gmail.com  | 0x8914977ed729792e403da53024c6069a9158b8c4
```

If you've been following along with the examples, you'll see that the latest query returns both rows that we've inserted into the database. However, had we inserted over 10,000 rows, we'd notice that only 10,000 rows would be returned. This is a limit built into `cqlsh`; using a language driver, you can retrieve result sets of arbitrary size.

You'll also notice that `bob` is returned before `alice`. Clearly, rows are not returned in lexical order of their primary key. As it happens, in a table with a single primary key column, row ordering is deterministic but not defined from a client standpoint. Deterministic ordering is enough, however, to allow us to page through very large result sets.

 You'll find a full reference for the `SELECT` statement in the DataStax CQL documentation at
`http://www.datastax.com/documentation/cql/3.1/cql/cql_reference/`
`select_r.html`.

# Paginating through results

In most situations, we will want to avoid displaying an arbitrary number of results to a user in a single response. Instead, we will display a fixed number of results, and give the user an interface to load additional pages of the same size. In an SQL database, pages are typically specified using the `OFFSET` keyword, but CQL does not have this capability. Instead, we'll use the natural ordering of primary keys to put a lower bound on the key values displayed on a given page.

Let's insert a couple more rows into our table to get a sense of how pagination works using the following `INSERT` statements:

```
INSERT INTO "users"
("username", "email", "encrypted_password")
VALUES (
  'carol',
  'carol@gmail.com',
  0xed3d8299b191b59b7008759a104c10af3db6e63a
);

INSERT INTO "users"
("username", "email", "encrypted_password")
VALUES (
  'dave',
  'dave@gmail.com',
  0x6d1d90d92bbab0012270536f286d243729690a5b
);
```

Now that we've got four users in our system, we can paginate over them. To save ourselves the trouble of adding numerous additional entries by hand, we'll just use a page size of two to demonstrate the process. We'll start by retrieving the first page as follows:

```
SELECT * FROM users
LIMIT 2;
```

The LIMIT part of the query simply tells Cassandra to return no more than two results:

```
 username | email           | encrypted_password
----------+-----------------+-------------------------------------------
      bob |            null | 0x10920941a69549d33aaee6116ed1f47e19b8e713
     dave | dave@gmail.com  | 0x6d1d90d92bbab0012270536f286d243729690a5b
```

Now that we have our first page, we want to get the second. It would be nice if we could simply ask for the next primary key in order after dave using the following SELECT statement:

```
SELECT * FROM "users"
WHERE "username" > 'dave'
LIMIT 2;
```

Unfortunately, this will give an error:

```
[Invalid query] message="Only EQ and IN relation are supported on the partition key (unless you use the token() function)"
```

The message is a bit cryptic, and we don't know what exactly a partition key is yet, but it does contain a helpful hint: we can use the token() function to do what we want. The reason that our attempted query doesn't work is that, as we noticed before, the primary keys in our users table are not stored in lexical order; Cassandra can only return rows in the order in which they are stored.

The actual ordering is determined by the token of the primary key—the way the token is calculated is opaque to us, but Cassandra lets us use the token() function to retrieve the token for a given value:

```
SELECT "username", token("username")
FROM "users";
```

Now we can see why the rows are returned in the order they are; they ascend by token:

```
username | system.token(username)
---------+------------------------
     bob |    -5396685590450884643
    dave |    -4493667438046306776
   carol |    -3169904368870211108
   alice |     5699955792253506986
```

Armed with this function, we can retrieve the next page of results as follows:

```
SELECT * FROM "users"
WHERE token("username") > token('dave')
LIMIT 2;
```

And just as we'd hoped, the next two rows are returned as shown next:

```
username | email            | encrypted_password
---------+------------------+---------------------------------------------
   carol | carol@gmail.com  | 0xed3d8299b191b59b7008759a104c10af3db6e63a
   alice | alice@gmail.com  | 0x8914977ed729792e403da53024c6069a9158b8c4
```

Using this technique, we can paginate over arbitrarily large tables using multiple queries.

 It bears emphasizing that retrieving large result sets from tables structured like `users` is a relatively expensive operation for Cassandra. In `Chapter 3`, *Organizing Related Data*, we'll begin to develop a more advanced table structure that will allow us to retrieve batches of rows very efficiently.

# Inserts are always upserts

Suppose you try to insert data into a table with a primary key, which already exists; the data doesn't get updated in place. Rather, a new copy of the data is written, and the old copy is kept until it is deleted by some internal Cassandra mechanism. To demonstrate how this works, let's update one of the records using the `INSERT` statement.

Let's change Alice's email by running the following `INSERT` statement:

```
INSERT INTO "users"
("username", "email")
VALUES ('alice', 'alice@yahoo.com');
```

Let's query for the updated row and see what we get:

```
SELECT * FROM "users" where "username"   = 'alice';
```

```
username | email          | encrypted_password
---------+----------------+------------------------------------------
   alice | alice@yahoo.com | 0x8914977ed729792e403da53024c6069a9158b8c4
```

You can see that the e-mail column has been updated even if you use the INSERT statement with a primary key that already exists.

Next, we will delete the row and insert a non-existing row using the UPDATE command and look at the behavior.

First, let's delete the row and verify that it got deleted. To delete the row, execute the following statement:

```
DELETE FROM "users" WHERE "username"   = 'alice';
```

To check whether it worked, run the preceding SELECT query:

```
SELECT * FROM "users" where "username"   = 'alice';
```

You will get an empty result set or 0 rows. Next, let's try to use the UPDATE command to update non-existing rows with primary key (username) alice:

```
UPDATE "users"
SET "email" = 'alice@gmail.com',
"encrypted_password" = 0x8914977ed729792e403da53024c6069a9158b8c4
WHERE "username" = 'alice';
```

Now to verify, run the aforementioned SELECT query again, and you will see that the data got inserted successfully:

```
username | email          | encrypted_password
---------+----------------+------------------------------------------
   alice | alice@yahoo.com | 0x8914977ed729792e403da53024c6069a9158b8c4
```

This tells us that the UPDATE statement has the same effect as an INSERT statement.

# Developing a mental model for Cassandra

Any time you learn a new tool, you will naturally begin to develop a mental model for how that tool works. So far, our model for how Cassandra tables works is fairly simple; we will expand upon it throughout the book.

For now, we can think of a Cassandra table as a collection of keys, each of which points to a row. Each row contains data in some subset of its columns.

We also know that, at least in the users table, rows are stored non-contiguously; accessing each row requires Cassandra to seek a different place in storage. So we may imagine the current state of our users table to look something like this:

Essentially, we can think of our Cassandra table as a key-value store, where each value consists of one or more predefined columns containing data of a predefined type.

# Summary

In this chapter, you're off to a running start with your MyStatus application, having created our first table, inserted data into it, and learned a few ways to retrieve that data. We developed a model for how Cassandra tables are structured and took a deep dive into Cassandra's type system.

We now have experience with the INSERT and SELECT statements, two of the core operations in CQL. You learned that primary keys, at least the ones we've seen so far, determine the order in which rows are returned, but that ordering is opaque to an application. We can only rely on it being consistent. We saw some of the limitations of simple tables in Cassandra, and we know that the types of multirow retrieval we know so far aren't the most efficient.In Chapter 3, *Organizing Related Data*, we'll introduce a new way to structure a table that lets us overcome many of the limitations we encountered here.

# 3
# Organizing Related Data

In Chapter 2, *The First Table*, we created our first table, which stores user accounts. We discussed how to insert data into the table and how to retrieve it. However, we also encountered several significant limitations in the tasks we can perform with the table we created.

In this chapter, we'll introduce the concept of compound primary keys, which are simply primary keys comprising more than one column. Although this might, at first glance, seem like a trivial addition to our understanding of Cassandra tables, a table with compound primary keys, in fact, is a considerably richer data structure that opens up substantial new data access patterns.

Our introduction to compound primary keys will help us build a table that stores a timeline of users' status updates. In this chapter, we'll focus on defining the table and understanding how it works. Chapter 4, *Beyond Key-Value Lookup*, will introduce new patterns to query compound primary key tables.

We'll explore two different approaches to design schemas with compound primary keys. In the first approach, the primary key encodes a parent-child relationship implicitly; in this case, a user's status updates are children of the user record itself. We'll also look at an alternative schema design using static columns; this design allows us to store information about users and their status updates in a single table without duplication. This makes the relationship between users and status updates explicit in the structure of the table.

By the end of this chapter, you'll know the following:

- How to create a table with a compound primary key
- The difference between a partition key and a clustering column
- How Cassandra organizes data in a compound key table
- When to use UUIDs for primary key components
- How to use static columns to associate data with partition keys
- When static columns are useful for schema design

# A table for status updates

In the MyStatus application, we'll begin by creating a timeline of status updates for each user. Users can view their friends' status updates by accessing the timeline of the friend in question.

The user timeline requires a new level of organization, which we didn't see in the `users` table that we created in the previous chapter. Specifically, we have two requirements:

- Rows (individual status updates) should be logically grouped by a certain property (the user who created the update)
- Rows should be accessible in a sorted order (in this case, by creation date)

Fortunately, compound primary keys provide exactly these qualities.

# Creating a table with a compound primary key

The syntax for creating tables with compound primary keys is a bit different from the single-column primary key syntax we saw in the previous chapter. We create a `user_status_updates` table with a compound primary key, as follows:

```
CREATE TABLE "user_status_updates" (
  "username" text,
  "id" timeuuid,
  "body" text,
  PRIMARY KEY ("username", "id")
);
```

In particular, instead of appending a single-column definition with a `PRIMARY KEY` modifier, we make a separate `PRIMARY KEY` declaration at the end of the list of columns, which itself specifies the two columns that make up the compound primary key.

While this is the only way to declare a compound primary key, it's also a perfectly valid way to declare a single-column primary key. So, our `users` table from the previous chapter could have been declared like this:

```
CREATE TABLE "users" (
  "username" text,
  "email" text,
  "encrypted_password" blob,
  PRIMARY KEY ("username")
);
```

Here, we simply move the `PRIMARY KEY` declaration to the end of the column list. It's a little less concise, but it has the exact same effect as a single-column definition with a `PRIMARY KEY` modifier.

# The structure of the status updates table

The most notable aspect of `user_status_updates` is that it has two columns for a primary key. This means that each row is identified uniquely by the combination of its `username` and `id` columns. It also means that every row must have a value in both of these columns.

In addition to this, our `user_status_updates` table is the first time we've seen a `timeuuid` column in the wild. As you can recollect from the previous chapter, a **UUID** is essentially a very large number that is generated using an algorithm that guarantees that the identifier is unique across time and space.

You will also recollect that Cassandra does not have the ability to generate auto-incrementing sequences for use in primary keys as this would require an unacceptably high level of coordination between nodes in the cluster. In the `users` table, we used a natural key; we want each user to have a unique `username`, so the `username` column makes a perfectly good unique identifier for rows.

In the case of a status update, however, there is no obvious natural key. The only user-generated data associated with a status update is the body, but a free text field doesn't make a very good primary key, and anyway, there's no guarantee that status update bodies will be unique. This is where UUIDs come in handy. Since they're guaranteed to be unique, we can use them as a **surrogate key**—a unique identifier that isn't derived from the data in the row. Auto-incrementing primary keys in relational databases are also surrogate keys.

## UUIDs and timestamps

While there are several algorithms that can be used to generate UUIDs, the Version 1 UUID has an additional useful property: part of the UUID encodes the timestamp at which the UUID is generated. This timestamp can be extracted from the full UUID, meaning that it's possible to know exactly when any Version 1 UUID was generated.

Cassandra's `timeuuid` type lets us capitalize on that property. Cassandra is aware of the structure of a `timeuuid` and is able to both convert timestamps into UUIDs and extract the creation timestamp from a UUID. As we'll soon see, Cassandra can also sort our rows by their creation time using the timestamps encoded in the UUIDs.

# Working with status updates

Now that we've got our status updates table ready, let's create our first status update:

```
INSERT INTO "user_status_updates"
("username", "id", "body")
VALUES (
  'alice',
  76e7a4d0-e796-11e3-90ce-5f98e903bf02,
  'Learning Cassandra!'
);
```

This will look pretty familiar; we specify the table we want to insert data into, the list of columns we're going to provide data for, and the values for these columns in the given order.

Let's give `bob` a status update too by inserting the following row in the `user_status_updates` table:

```
INSERT INTO "user_status_updates"
("username", "id", "body")
VALUES (
  'bob',
  97719c50-e797-11e3-90ce-5f98e903bf02,
  'Eating a tasty sandwich.'
);
```

Now we have two rows, each identified by the combination of the `username` and `id` columns. Let's take a look at the contents of our table using the following `SELECT` statement:

```
SELECT * FROM "user_status_updates";
```

We'll be able to see the two rows that we inserted, as follows:

```
username | id                                   | body
---------+--------------------------------------+-------------------------
     bob | 97719c50-e797-11e3-90ce-5f98e903bf02 | Eating a tasty sandwich.
   alice | 76e7a4d0-e796-11e3-90ce-5f98e903bf02 |       Learning Cassandra!
```

Note that, as we saw in the `users` table, the rows are not returned in lexical order of `username`; indeed, they're in the same order as the user records themselves are. Recall from the *Paginating through results* section of Chapter 2, *The First Table*, that the `username` column is ordered by an internally generated token, which is deterministic but meaningless from the application's perspective.

# Extracting timestamps

As we previously mentioned, Cassandra has special capabilities for the `timeuuid` type, which includes extracting the timestamp that's encoded in these UUIDs. We can see this in action using the `DATEOF` function:

```
SELECT "username", "id", "body", DATEOF("id")
FROM "user_status_updates";
```

The `DATEOF` function instructs Cassandra to return a result column containing the timestamp at which the given column's UUID value was created. We now have access to information encoded in the `id` column that was previously obscure:

```
username | id                                   | body                     | DATEOF(id)
---------+--------------------------------------+--------------------------+--------------------------
     bob | 97719c50-e797-11e3-90ce-5f98e903bf02 | Eating a tasty sandwich. | 2014-05-29 21:13:21-0400
   alice | 76e7a4d0-e796-11e3-90ce-5f98e903bf02 |       Learning Cassandra! | 2014-05-29 21:05:17-0400
```

If you're following along with your CQL shell, you'll notice that the dates do not tell you when the rows were created but when the UUIDs in the `id` column were generated. Since we're using UUIDs that I generated when writing this book, we'll see that the creation timestamp shows an older time.

While the `DATEOF` output is very readable, the timestamps only offer precision at the second level. For a more precise representation of the timestamp at which the UUIDs were generated, use the `UNIXTIMESTAMPOF` function instead:

```
SELECT "username", "id", "body", UNIXTIMESTAMPOF("id")
```

```
FROM "user_status_updates";
```

The UNIXTIMESTAMPOF function returns the timestamp represented as the number of milliseconds since January 1, 1970 at midnight UTC:

```
username | id                                   | body                    | UNIXTIMESTAMPOF(id)
---------+--------------------------------------+-------------------------+--------------------
     bob | 97719c50-e797-11e3-90ce-5f98e903bf02 | Eating a tasty sandwich.|       1401412401813
   alice | 76e7a4d0-e796-11e3-90ce-5f98e903bf02 |       Learning Cassandra!|       1401411917725
```

# Looking up a specific status update

In our status update application, we'll want to allow direct linking to status updates, in which case we'll need to be able to retrieve a specific status update from the table. So far, we've issued an open-ended SELECT statement to see all the rows we've inserted in user_status_updates, but we haven't seen how to return one particular row.

Since the user_status_updates table has a compound primary key, we need new CQL syntax to allow us to specify values for multiple columns in order to form a unique identifier. CQL provides the AND construct for this purpose:

```
SELECT * FROM "user_status_updates"
WHERE "username" = 'alice'
AND "id" = 76e7a4d0-e796-11e3-90ce-5f98e903bf02;
```

By specifying both the username and the id, we identify exactly one row:

```
username | id                                   | body
---------+--------------------------------------+--------------------
   alice | 76e7a4d0-e796-11e3-90ce-5f98e903bf02 | Learning Cassandra!
```

We now have all the tools we need to interact with the user_status_updates table in the same way as we interact with the users table; let's move on to explore some of the things that make a compound primary key table different.

# Automatically generating UUIDs

In the status updates we've created so far, we used predetermined UUIDs that were generated on May 29, 2014. For this reason, the timestamp encoded in the UUIDs doesn't really tell us anything useful about when the rows were created. However, in the general case, we would like to encode useful data in the UUID, and in particular, the timestamp at which the row itself was created.

Libraries that generate Version 1 UUIDs are available for just about any programming language, but Cassandra also gives us a built-in CQL function to generate a UUID from the current time, the NOW function. Let's use that function to insert a few new status updates:

```
INSERT INTO "user_status_updates" ("username", "id", "body")
VALUES ('alice', NOW(), 'Alice Update 1');
INSERT INTO "user_status_updates" ("username", "id", "body")
VALUES ('bob', NOW(), 'Bob Update 1');
INSERT INTO "user_status_updates" ("username", "id", "body")
VALUES ('alice', NOW(), 'Alice Update 2');
INSERT INTO "user_status_updates" ("username", "id", "body")
VALUES ('bob', NOW(), 'Bob Update 2');
INSERT INTO "user_status_updates" ("username", "id", "body")
VALUES ('alice', NOW(), 'Alice Update 3');
INSERT INTO "user_status_updates" ("username", "id", "body")
VALUES ('bob', NOW(), 'Bob Update 3');
```

Instead of explicitly specifying a UUID constant for the id field, we used the NOW function to generate a new and unique UUID for each row we inserted.

While the NOW function is quite convenient, particularly in the CQL shell, it comes with one major downside. Since a CQL INSERT statement does not give any feedback on the results of the operation, you won't actually know what UUID the NOW function generates. Sometimes, this is fine; but in many cases, your application would want to perform further business logic that requires knowing the primary key of the record that was just created. In these cases, it's better to use a library to generate UUIDs at the application level and provide them explicitly as literals in the INSERT statement.

Now that we've got a handful of rows in the user_status_updates table, let's take a look at its contents:

```
SELECT "username", "id", "body", UNIXTIMESTAMPOF("id")
FROM "user_status_updates";
```

As we did previously, we'll ask Cassandra to return the millisecond-precision timestamp of the UUIDs in the table along with the data in all columns. Let's take a look at the results:

```
username | id                                   | body                  | UNIXTIMESTAMPOF(id)
---------+--------------------------------------+-----------------------+--------------------
     bob | 97719c50-e797-11e3-90ce-5f98e903bf02 | Eating a tasty sandwich. |   1401412401813
     bob | 3f9d81e0-e8f7-11e3-9211-5f98e903bf02 |          Bob Update 1 |      1401563437310
     bob | 3f9e9350-e8f7-11e3-9211-5f98e903bf02 |          Bob Update 2 |      1401563437317
     bob | 3f9f56a0-e8f7-11e3-9211-5f98e903bf02 |          Bob Update 3 |      1401563437322
   alice | 76e7a4d0-e796-11e3-90ce-5f98e903bf02 |    Learning Cassandra! |     1401411917725
   alice | 3f9b5f00-e8f7-11e3-9211-5f98e903bf02 |        Alice Update 1 |      1401563437296
   alice | 3f9df710-e8f7-11e3-9211-5f98e903bf02 |        Alice Update 2 |      1401563437313
   alice | 3f9ee170-e8f7-11e3-9211-5f98e903bf02 |        Alice Update 3 |      1401563437319
```

We notice a couple of interesting things here. First, we can see that the results are grouped by username: all the status updates of `bob` appear first, followed by all the status updates of `alice`. This is despite the fact that we interleaved the status updates of `alice` and `bob` when we inserted them.

Second, within each user's status updates, the updates are returned in ascending order of the timestamp of the row's `id` column. Looking at the rightmost column in the results, we see that the timestamps monotonically increase for each user. This is no coincidence; the `id` column determines the ordering of rows in the `user_status_updates` table, and since it's a `timeuuid` column, the timestamp encoded in the UUID determines the semantic ordering of the rows.

# Anatomy of a compound primary key

At this point, it's clear that there's some nuance in the compound primary key that we're missing. Both the `username` column and the `id` column affect the order in which rows are returned; however, while the actual ordering of `username` is opaque, the ordering of `id` is meaningfully related to the information encoded in the `id` column.

In the lexicon of Cassandra, `username` is a **partition key**. A table's partition key groups rows together into logically related bundles. In the case of our MyStatus application, each user's timeline is a self-contained data structure, so partitioning the table by user is a sound strategy.

We call the `id` column a clustering column. The job of a clustering column is to determine the ordering of rows within a partition. This is why we observed that within each user's status updates, the rows were returned in a strictly ascending order by timestamp of the `id`. This is a very useful property since our application will want to display status updates ordered by the creation time.

**Is sorting by clustering column efficient?**

Sorting any collection at read time is expensive for a non-trivial number of elements. Fortunately, Cassandra stores rows in a clustering order; so when you retrieve them, it simply returns them in the order they're stored in. There's no expensive sorting operation at read time.

All of the rows that share the same primary key are stored in a contiguous structure on disk. It's within this structure that rows are sorted by their clustering column values. Because each partition is tightly bound at the storage level, there is an upper bound on the number of rows that can share the same partition key. In theory, this limit is about 2 billion total column values. For instance, if you have a table with 10 data columns, your upper bound would be 200 million rows per partition key.

For further information on data modeling using compound primary keys, the DataStax CQL documentation has a good explanation at `http://www.datastax.com/documentation/cql/3.1/cql/ddl/ddl_compou nd_keys_c.html`.

# Anatomy of a single-column primary key

Now that you understand the distinction between a partition key and a clustering column, you might be wondering which role the username column plays in the users table.

As it turns out, it's a partition key. All Cassandra tables must have a partition key; clustering columns are optional. In the users table, each row is its own tiny partition; no row is grouped with any other.

# Beyond two columns

We've now seen a table with two columns in its primary key: a partition key and a clustering column. As it turns out, neither of these roles is limited to a single column. A table can define one or more partition key columns and zero or more clustering columns.

# Multiple clustering columns

Clustering columns are not limited to one field as specified before. Let's take a look at how multiple clustering columns work and facilitate data ordering. To illustrate this, we will recreate our status updates table so that it is clustered by the date and time when the user updated their status:

```
CREATE TABLE "user_status_updates_by_datetime" (
  "username" text,
  "status_date" date,
  "status_time" time,
  "body" text,
  PRIMARY KEY ("username", "status_date", "status_time")
);
```

We have created a new table `user_status_updates_by_datetime` as shown next:

- **Partition key**: `username`, which is a text field.
- **Clustering columns**: `status_date` and `status_time`. Rows for a particular username are clustered by both columns, first by `status_date` and then by `status_time`.

Since our primary goal is to figure out how a primary key with multiple clustering columns behaves, we will be inserting updates for a single user, `alice`.

Let's insert a few records as follows:

```
INSERT INTO "user_status_updates_by_datetime" ("username",
"status_date", "status_time", "body")
VALUES ('alice', '2016-11-18', '08:30:55.123', 'Alice Update 1');

INSERT INTO "user_status_updates_by_datetime" ("username",
"status_date", "status_time", "body")
VALUES ('alice', '2016-11-18', '14:40:25.123456789', 'Alice Update 2');

INSERT INTO "user_status_updates_by_datetime" ("username",
"status_date", "status_time", "body")
VALUES ('alice', '2016-11-19', '08:25:25', 'Alice Update 3');

INSERT INTO "user_status_updates_by_datetime" ("username",
"status_date", "status_time", "body")
VALUES ('alice', '2016-11-21', '08:35:55.123456', 'Alice Update 4');

INSERT INTO "user_status_updates_by_datetime" ("username",
"status_date", "status_time", "body")
VALUES ('alice', '2016-11-21', '14:30:15.123', 'Alice Update 5');
```

```
INSERT INTO "user_status_updates_by_datetime" ("username",
"status_date", "status_time", "body")
VALUES ('alice', '2016-11-23', '14:50:45.123456', 'Alice Update 6');
```

You will notice that status_date and status_time, which are date and time data types respectively, are inserted as strings similar to text data type.

As mentioned earlier, date should be of the format YYYY-MM-DD, and time should be of the format HH:MM:SS.

The CQL protocol enforces strict rules on values you can enter for any field, be it year, month, day, hour, minute, or second. Time is specified with nanosecond precision. It isn't necessary to specify all nine digits of the nanoseconds as we saw in the preceding INSERT statements.

Let's try to insert a few records with erroneous input:

```
INSERT INTO "user_status_updates_by_datetime" ("username",
"status_date", "status_time", "body")
VALUES ('alice', '2016-14-23', '14:50:45.123456', 'Alice Update 7');
```

The response is as follows:

```
InvalidRequest: code=2200 [Invalid query] message="Unable to coerce '2016-14-23' to a formatted date (long)"
```

```
INSERT INTO "user_status_updates_by_datetime" ("username",
"status_date", "status_time", "body")
VALUES ('alice', '2016-11-23', '14:65:45.123456', 'Alice Update 8');
```

The response is as follows:

```
InvalidRequest: code=2200 [Invalid query] message="(TimeType) Unable to coerce '14:65:45.123456' to a formatted time (long)"
```

We notice that both of the preceding queries failed. The first insert failed because of an invalid value for status_date, which has a wrong value for month. The second insert failed because of an invalid value for status_time, which has a wrong value for minutes. Underneath, CQL protocol converts both status_date and status_time to a long format and checks for correctness of different values within the data types, date, and time.

Now, if we want to fetch all the status updates by username alice regardless of status_date or status_time, we simply run the following query:

```
SELECT * FROM "user_status_updates_by_datetime";
```

The response is as follows:

```
username | status_date | status_time          | body
---------+-------------+----------------------+----------------
   alice |  2016-11-18 | 08:30:55.123000000   | Alice Update 1
   alice |  2016-11-18 | 14:40:25.123456789   | Alice Update 2
   alice |  2016-11-19 | 08:25:25.000000000   | Alice Update 3
   alice |  2016-11-21 | 08:35:55.123456000   | Alice Update 4
   alice |  2016-11-21 | 14:30:15.123000000   | Alice Update 5
   alice |  2016-11-23 | 14:50:45.123456000   | Alice Update 6
```

You will notice that all the status updates for the user `alice` are ordered by `status_date` first and then by `status_time` for a particular `status_date` value. The order in which the inserts were performed doesn't matter. The results would still have been ordered by date and time.

Let's try to run some queries on clustering columns and see which queries are supported and which are not. First, we will fetch all status updates before `2016-11-20` regardless of the time:

```
SELECT * FROM "user_status_updates_by_datetime"
WHERE "username" = 'alice' AND "status_date" < '2016-11-20';
```

The response is as follows:

```
username | status_date | status_time          | body
---------+-------------+----------------------+----------------
   alice |  2016-11-18 | 08:30:55.123000000   | Alice Update 1
   alice |  2016-11-18 | 14:40:25.123456789   | Alice Update 2
   alice |  2016-11-19 | 08:25:25.000000000   | Alice Update 3
```

You will see that the query returns three status updates, which were posted before `2016-11-20`. Always make sure your query contains an equality relation on the partition key. Clustering columns support both equality and inequality relations although there are certain limitations.

Let's try to get status updates that were posted after `2016-11-20` and after noon or `12:00:00`. This can be done by running the following query:

```
SELECT * FROM "user_status_updates_by_datetime"
WHERE "username" = 'alice' AND "status_date" > '2016-11-20' AND
"status_time" > '12:00:00';
```

The response is as follows:

```
InvalidRequest: code=2200 [Invalid query] message="Clustering column "status_time" cannot be restricted (preceding column "status_date" is restricted by a non-EQ relation)"
```

This throws a cryptic error saying it is an invalid query. This is one of the limitations when querying is based on multiple clustering columns. This simply means that if you are using an inequality relation on a clustering column, all the preceding clustering columns need to have an equality relation. Let's test this by fetching status updates that were posted on 2016-11-21 and after 12:00:00:

```
SELECT * FROM "user_status_updates_by_datetime"
WHERE "username" = 'alice' AND "status_date" = '2016-11-21' AND
"status_time" > '12:00:00';
```

```
 username | status_date | status_time          | body
----------+-------------+----------------------+----------------
    alice |  2016-11-21 | 14:30:15.123000000   | Alice Update 5
```

# Composite partition keys

There might be cases where a partition size might grow well beyond the disk size of a Cassandra instance, or a partition might have more than 100,000 cells, which will reduce the performance of some of the internal operations of Cassandra as well as read queries on that partition. To ensure you don't face this situation, Cassandra provides a concept of composite partition keys. Composite partition keys contain more than one column as part of the partition key. So, data is distributed based on a combination of values of both the columns. A composite partition key can split up a very large internal partition into multiple internal partitions.

# Composite partition key table

So far, we have only worked with tables that have a single column partition key. Let's try working with multiple columns in the partition key. For instance, in our status application, we might want to allow users to reply to other users' status updates. In this case, each status update would have a stream of replies; replies would be partitioned by the full primary key of the original status update, and each reply would get its own timestamped UUID:

```
CREATE TABLE "status_update_replies" (
  "status_update_username" text,
  "status_update_id" timeuuid,
  "id" timeuuid,
```

```
    "author_username" text,
    "body" text,
    PRIMARY KEY (
      ("status_update_username", "status_update_id"),
      "id"
    )
);
```

Note the extra set of parentheses around the `status_update_username` and `status_update_id` columns in the `PRIMARY KEY` declaration. This tells Cassandra that we want those two columns together to form the partition key. Without the extra parentheses, Cassandra assumes, by default, that only the first column in the primary key is a partition key, and the remaining columns are clustering columns.

Let's try inserting some data into the table:

```
INSERT INTO "status_update_replies" ("status_update_username",
"status_update_id", "id", "author_username", "body")
VALUES ('alice', 76e7a4d0-e796-11e3-90ce-5f98e903bf02, NOW(), 'bob',
'Reply1');

INSERT INTO "status_update_replies" ("status_update_username",
"status_update_id", "id", "author_username", "body")
VALUES ('alice', 97719c50-e797-11e3-90ce-5f98e903bf02, NOW(), 'bob',
'Reply2');
```

Now, let's try fetching the replies first by just the `status_update_username` column and second by the `status_update_username` and `status_update_id` columns:

```
SELECT * FROM "status_update_replies"
WHERE "status_update_username" = 'alice';
```

The response is as follows:

```
InvalidRequest: code=2200 [Invalid query] message="Partition key parts: status_update_id must be restricted as other parts are"
```

```
SELECT * FROM "status_update_replies"
WHERE "status_update_username" = 'alice' AND
"status_update_id" = 97719c50-e797-11e3-90ce-5f98e903bf02;
```

You will notice that the first query fails because you failed to specify the equality relation for both parts of the partition key in the where clause. Since you are trying to fetch all the replies associated with the status updates made by the username `alice` and this could be spread across multiple partitions, Cassandra doesn't support it as it will have a poor performance.

# Structure of composite partition key tables

The structure of a composite partition key is similar to a single column partition key. The partitioning is based on a hash generated on the combination of values specified for columns in the partition key. So, every unique combination of the partition key columns value will belong to a different partition. This necessitates us to specify values for all the partition key columns when querying a table with a composite partition key. This is what it looks like for the previously specified table:

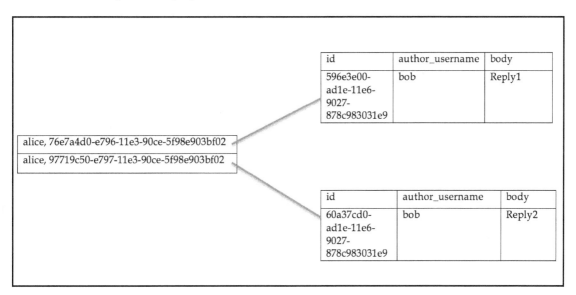

# Composite partition key with multiple clustering columns

It is also possible to declare a table that has both a composite partition key as well as multiple clustering columns. Suppose we wish to model a status update replies table to be clustered by the reply date first and then the reply time; we would have a table like this:

```
CREATE TABLE "status_update_replies" (
  "status_update_username" text,
  "status_update_id" timeuuid,
   "status_date" date,
   "status_time" time,
  "id" timeuuid,
  "author_username" text,
  "body" text,
```

```
      PRIMARY KEY (
        ("status_update_username", "status_update_id"),
        "status_date", "status_time", "id"
      )
    );
```

In the preceding table, the partition key is a combination of `status_update_username` and `status_update_id`.

The replies are clustered by `status_date`, `status_time` and `id`.

# Compound keys represent parent-child relationships

In the *What is Cassandra and why Cassandra?* section of `Chapter 1`, *Getting Up and Running with Cassandra*, you learned that Cassandra is not a relational database despite some surface similarities. Specifically, this means that Cassandra does not have a built-in concept of the relationships between data in different tables. There are no foreign key constraints and there's no `JOIN` clause available in the `SELECT` statements; in fact, there is no way to read from multiple tables in the same query whereas relational databases are designed to explicitly account for the relationships between data in different tables, whether they're one-to-one, one-to-many, or many-to-many. Cassandra has no built-in mechanism for describing or traversing inter-table relationships.

That being said, Cassandra's compound primary key structure provides an ample affordance for a particular kind of relationship—the parent-child relationship. This is a specific type of one-to-many relationship in which the one side plays a unique role with respect to the many side; we can say that the one is a parent or a container for the many. We've already seen two examples of this: a user's status updates are children of the user themselves, and the comments about a status update are children of that status update.

This relationship is represented quite transparently in the compound primary key structure. The partition key acts as a reference to the parent, and the clustering column uniquely identifies the row among its siblings. This is why we used both the `status_update_username` and `status_update_id` columns for the partition key in our `status_update_replies` table; these columns together provide a full reference to the reply's parent, namely the status update to which it's a reply.

It's worth emphasizing that not every one-to-many relationship is a parent-child relationship. For instance, on a blogging platform, we'd expect a blog post to have at least a couple of many-to-one relationships, namely an author relation and a blog relation. Only one of these can be a parent-child relationship; in the blog example, it seems natural to think of the parent of a blog post as the blog.

Our Cassandra data models can only accommodate a single parent relation for a given table because the parent relation is expressed as the partition key column(s) of the table. Not all table schemas fit this line of reasoning; sometimes a partition key is just a partition key, such as a time-series table that partitions by date. However, parent-child relationships provide a fruitful framework for Cassandra data modeling across a wide variety of applications.

# Coupling parents and children using static columns

The parent-child relationships we've encoded in our schema thus far are implicit in the structure of the primary keys but not explicit from Cassandra's standpoint. While we know that the `user_status_updates.username` column corresponds to the parent primary key `users.username`, Cassandra itself has no concept of the relationship between the two.

In a relational database, we might make the relationship explicit in the schema using foreign key constraints, but Cassandra doesn't offer anything like this. In fact, if we want to use two different tables for `users` and `user_status_updates`, there isn't anything we can do to explicitly encode their relationship in the database schema. However, there is a way to combine user profiles and status updates into a single table while still maintaining the one-to-many relationship between them. To achieve this merger, we'll use a feature of Cassandra tables that we haven't seen before—static columns.

## Defining static columns

To see how static columns work, we'll create a new table called `users_with_status_updates`. Our goal for this table is to contain both user profiles and users' status updates; however, we only want one copy of a user profile even though each user might have many status updates. To accomplish this, we'll add all of the columns from both `users` and `user_status_updates` to our new table, but we'll declare the user profile columns as `STATIC`:

```
CREATE TABLE "users_with_status_updates" (
```

```
    "username" text,
    "id" timeuuid,
    "email" text STATIC,
    "encrypted_password" blob STATIC,
    "body" text,
    PRIMARY KEY ("username", "id")
);
```

Since the `email` and `encrypted_password` columns are properties of a user and not of a specific status update, we declare them `STATIC`. Any column that is declared `STATIC` has one value per partition key. In other words, there will be exactly one `email` value associated with a given `username` in our table.

The goal of static columns is to allow rows that share a partition key value to share other data as well. For this to be useful, there must be multiple rows per partition key, which is another way of saying that there must be at least one clustering column. It's illegal to declare a static column in a table with no clustering columns.

# Working with static columns

Let's say that we've decided, in our MyStatus application, that when a user creates a new account, we also require them to create an initial status update. In this workflow, we'll end up creating a new user record at the same time as when we create their first status update, which is to say that we'll be populating all the columns of the `users_with_status_updates` table in a single statement:

```
INSERT INTO "users_with_status_updates"
("username", "id", "email", "encrypted_password", "body")
VALUES (
  'alice',
  76e7a4d0-e796-11e3-90ce-5f98e903bf02,
  'alice@gmail.com',
  0x8914977ed729792e403da53024c6069a9158b8c4,
  'Learning Cassandra!'
);
```

It's worth emphasizing that even though this is a single `INSERT` statement, we're actually doing two separate things:

- Assigning the `email` and `encrypted_password` values to every row whose `username` value is `alice`
- Creating a new row in the `alice` partition, with `Learning Cassandra!` as the value of `body`

```
SELECT * FROM "users_with_status_updates";
```

Looking at the output, we'll observe that it's just what we'd expect (I've omitted the `encrypted_password` column to save space):

```
username | id                                   | email           | body
---------+--------------------------------------+-----------------+----------------------
   alice | 76e7a4d0-e796-11e3-90ce-5f98e903bf02 | alice@gmail.com | Learning Cassandra!

(1 rows)
```

The single row shown in the preceding figure is precisely what we wrote with the `INSERT` statement earlier. So far, we haven't seen any special behavior for static columns. To see static columns in action, let's add another status update to the table:

```
INSERT INTO "users_with_status_updates"
("username", "id", "body")
VALUES ('alice', NOW(), 'Another status update');
```

Note that in this case, we did not specify values for either of the static columns; we provided the partition key, the clustering column, and a value for the non-static data column `body`. Now, let's take a look at the contents of the table:

```
SELECT * FROM "users_with_status_updates";
```

The output is as follows:

```
username | id                                   | email           | body
---------+--------------------------------------+-----------------+----------------------
   alice | 76e7a4d0-e796-11e3-90ce-5f98e903bf02 | alice@gmail.com |   Learning Cassandra!
   alice | c5eeb290-7345-11e4-a0e6-5f98e903bf02 | alice@gmail.com | Another status update

(2 rows)
```

Now, the effect of the `STATIC` column declaration is clear: both rows have the e-mail address we assigned to the first row even though we did not specify an `email` value in our second `INSERT` query.

# Interacting only with the static columns

We've seen that static columns give us the ability to associate data with all rows that share the same partition key. However, what if we want to treat the data associated with that partition key as a discrete value rather than some extra information attached to each clustering column value?

More concretely, if we want to display an interface for alice to edit her user profile, all we really need to do is get the information associated with her partition key. We don't care if there are one, 10, or 1,000 status updates; we just need a single row with her username, e-mail address, and so on. With users as a separate table, this is trivial; we just select the single row with the partition key value alice. Let's see what happens when we do the equivalent in users_with_status_updates:

```
SELECT "username", "email", "encrypted_password"
FROM "users_with_status_updates"
WHERE "username" = 'alice';
```

Note that we've omitted the id and body fields, which contain distinct values in each row; we only select the partition key, username, and the static columns, email and encrypted_password. Unfortunately, we don't quite get what we're looking for:

```
 username | email             | encrypted_password
----------+-------------------+-----------------------------------------
    alice | alice@gmail.com   | 0x8914977ed729792e403da53024c6069a9158b8c4
    alice | alice@gmail.com   | 0x8914977ed729792e403da53024c6069a9158b8c4

(2 rows)
```

The result is two rows; the rows contain identical data because all of the selected columns are per-partition-key, but we still get duplicate results when we only want one. Fortunately, the DISTINCT keyword allows us to retrieve a result in the format that we'd like:

```
SELECT DISTINCT "username", "email", "encrypted_password"
FROM "users_with_status_updates"
WHERE "username" = 'alice';
```

Now, the result takes the form we'd like—a single row containing the information specific to the `alice` partition key:

```
username | email             | encrypted_password
---------+-------------------+------------------------------------------
   alice | alice@gmail.com   | 0x8914977ed729792e403da53024c6069a9158b8c4

(1 rows)
```

By formulating our SELECT statement correctly, we can basically ignore the fact that there's a clustering column at all; the result here is exactly the same as it would have been if we had selected `alice`'s row out of the `users` table. To complete this analogy, we'd also like to be able to write static columns to our table without thinking about the non-static columns.

## Static-only inserts

As it turns out, inserting a row that consists only of static data is perfectly valid. Let's say, we relax our rule that upon signing up, a user must also write their first status update. If `bob` wishes to sign up, he may simply enter a username, e-mail, and password:

```
INSERT INTO "users_with_status_updates"
("username", "email", "encrypted_password")
VALUES (
  'bob',
  'bob@gmail.com',
  0x10920941a69549d33aaee6116ed1f47e19b8e713
);
```

Now, we have an `email` and an `encrypted_password` associated with the partition key `bob` but no clustering column values forming rows under that partition key. So, can we retrieve the information about `bob` that we just inserted? As it turns out, we can. Here's the updated state of the table that can be retrieved using the SELECT * FROM "users_with_status_updates"; statement:

```
username | id                                   | email           | body
---------+--------------------------------------+-----------------+----------------------
     bob |                                 null | bob@gmail.com   |                 null
   alice | 76e7a4d0-e796-11e3-90ce-5f98e903bf02 | alice@gmail.com | Learning Cassandra!
   alice | c5eeb290-7345-11e4-a0e6-5f98e903bf02 | alice@gmail.com | Another status update

(3 rows)
```

We do, indeed, see `username` and `email` of `bob`, but we also notice something odd: the `id` column—part of the table's primary key—is `null`! This is because the row with the `username` value `bob` is essentially a synthetic row, representing the data associated with a partition key that has no actual rows. To satisfy ourselves of this fact, let's add a status update for `bob`:

```
INSERT INTO "users_with_status_updates"
("username", "id", "body")
VALUES ('bob', NOW(), 'Bob status update');
```

Now, let's take a look at the table again with the help of the `SELECT * FROM "users_with_status_updates";` statement:

```
username | id                                   | email           | body
---------+--------------------------------------+-----------------+----------------------
     bob | 0b899e60-734a-11e4-a0e6-5f98e903bf02 |   bob@gmail.com |    Bob status update
   alice | 76e7a4d0-e796-11e3-90ce-5f98e903bf02 | alice@gmail.com |   Learning Cassandra!
   alice | c5eeb290-7345-11e4-a0e6-5f98e903bf02 | alice@gmail.com | Another status update

(3 rows)
```

The row with the `id` value `null` has disappeared since the synthetic construct is no longer necessary. We now have access to static column values of `bob` via a real row.

 For more information about static columns, visit the page in the DataStax CQL reference at
`http://www.datastax.com/documentation/cql/3.1/cql/cql_reference/refStaticCol.html`.

## Static columns act like predefined joins

Now that we've explored the behavior of static columns, it's rather striking how similar the data model in `users_with_status_updates` is to the data model represented by `users` and `user_status_updates` taken together. In particular, both representations do the following:

- Associate multiple status updates with a single user
- Associate a single e-mail address and password with a single user
- Allow creating and accessing discrete user records, with or without associated status updates

The difference is simply the interface to the data model: are we working with one table, or two? It turns out that `users_with_status_updates` behaves very much like the result of an SQL `LEFT JOIN` of `users` and `user_status_updates`. Cassandra, of course, does not support `JOIN` clauses when reading data; instead, this join is baked into the schema itself through the use of static columns.

# When to use static columns

We've now seen two ways to model users, each of whom has many status updates. The first approach was simply to define a table for users and a table for their status updates; the relationship between the two is encoded in the key structure of `user_status_updates`. The second approach is to store all of the information in one `users_with_status_updates` table using static columns to associate user-level data with the username partition key rather than having a different value for each clustering column. Which is better?

The answer largely depends on how closely coupled the related data types are. If we expect that most of our interactions with user profile information will also involve interacting with the user's status updates, and vice versa, then it makes a lot of sense to store them together in one table. The reasoning is similar to the parent-child conceptual framework discussed earlier, but in reverse. Not only is the user a special relationship from the standpoint of the status update, but also the status update is a special relationship from the standpoint of the user.

In the case of MyStatus, on balance, the relationship between users and status updates doesn't quite pass this test. In subsequent chapters, we'll expand our schema to accommodate several different one-to-many relationships where the user plays the role of *parent*. It's not clear that the relationship between users and status updates is more fundamental than the other relationships that we will model for users.

For this reason, we'll continue to work with the `users` and `user_status_updates` tables and leave behind the `users_with_status_updates` table as an interesting exercise.

# Refining our mental model

In the previous chapter, we began to develop a mental model of a Cassandra table that looked like a key-value store where each value is a collection of columns with values. Now that we have seen compound primary keys, we can refine that mental model to take into account the more complex structures we now know how to build, as follows:

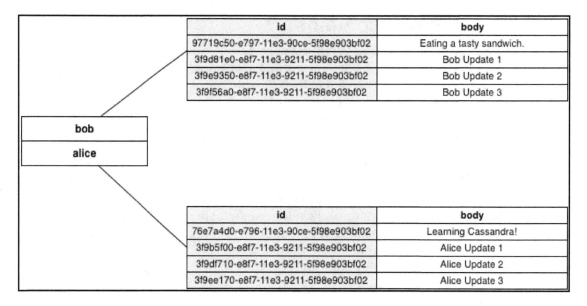

| id | body |
|---|---|
| 97719c50-e797-11e3-90ce-5f98e903bf02 | Eating a tasty sandwich. |
| 3f9d81e0-e8f7-11e3-9211-5f98e903bf02 | Bob Update 1 |
| 3f9e9350-e8f7-11e3-9211-5f98e903bf02 | Bob Update 2 |
| 3f9f56a0-e8f7-11e3-9211-5f98e903bf02 | Bob Update 3 |

bob

alice

| id | body |
|---|---|
| 76e7a4d0-e796-11e3-90ce-5f98e903bf02 | Learning Cassandra! |
| 3f9b5f00-e8f7-11e3-9211-5f98e903bf02 | Alice Update 1 |
| 3f9df710-e8f7-11e3-9211-5f98e903bf02 | Alice Update 2 |
| 3f9ee170-e8f7-11e3-9211-5f98e903bf02 | Alice Update 3 |

We can envision the `user_status_updates` table as a more robust key-value structure. Our keys are still usernames, but the values are now ordered collections of rows, both identified and ordered by the `id` clustering column. As with our earlier model, each partition key's data stands alone; to get data from multiple partitions, we have to go looking in multiple places.

# Summary

In this chapter, we were introduced to the concept of compound primary keys and learned that a primary key consists of one or more partition keys and, optionally, one or more clustering columns. We saw how partition keys—the only type of key we had previously encountered—can group related rows together and how clustering columns provide an order for these rows within each partition.

Compound primary keys allow us to build a table containing users' status updates because they expose two important structures: grouping of related rows and ordering of rows. In the `user_status_updates` table, we encoded the relationship between users and their status updates implicitly in the structure of the primary key; the partition key refers to the parent row in the `users` table. We also explored the use of static columns to make this relationship explicit, storing all the information about users and their status updates in a single table.

In `Chapter 4`, *Beyond Key-Value Lookup*, we will dive into new ways of interacting with data that is organized using compound primary keys, allowing us to build functionality in our application for viewing users' timelines in a variety of interesting ways.

# 4
# Beyond Key-Value Lookup

In the last chapter, we explored a powerful data organization concept in Cassandra - the compound primary key. This allowed us to construct a table for status updates that satisfies two important requirements: related data is grouped together, and records have a built-in ordering within each group. So far, however, we only have two tools for querying data: either retrieve a single row using its full primary key, or retrieve all the rows in a table. In this chapter, we will dive into the more sophisticated queries that are available on tables with clustering columns, and use these queries to build the main reading interface for our MyStatus application. By the end of this chapter, you'll know:

- How to retrieve all rows within a single partition
- How to retrieve rows within a range of clustering column values
- How to paginate over rows in a single partition
- How to change the order of results
- How to store rows in descending order of clustering column
- How to paginate over all rows in a compound primary key table
- How to construct autocomplete functionality using a compound primary key table

## Looking up rows by partition

The core reading experience of the MyStatus application will be an interface to read a given user's status updates. In order to do this, we need to be able to retrieve status updates for a given user from the user_status_updates table. As you might expect, this follows naturally from the CQL syntax we've seen in previous chapters:

```
SELECT * FROM "user_status_updates"
WHERE "username" = 'alice';
```

Previously, we've used the WHERE keyword to specify an exact value for a full primary key. In the preceding query, we only specify the partition key part of the primary key, which allows us to retrieve only those rows that we've asked for the partition:

```
 username | id                                     | body
----------+----------------------------------------+---------------------
    alice | 76e7a4d0-e796-11e3-90ce-5f98e903bf02   | Learning Cassandra!
    alice | 3f9b5f00-e8f7-11e3-9211-5f98e903bf02   |       Alice Update 1
    alice | 3f9df710-e8f7-11e3-9211-5f98e903bf02   |       Alice Update 2
    alice | 3f9ee170-e8f7-11e3-9211-5f98e903bf02   |       Alice Update 3
```

In the results, we only see the rows whose **username** is alice. To emphasize what we discussed in the previous chapter, in the *Looking up a specific status update* section, this is a very efficient query. Cassandra stores all of alice's status updates together, already in order; so returning this view of the table is quite inexpensive.

# The limits of the WHERE keyword

At this point, we've seen that you can look up rows by partition key alone, or by a combination of a partition key and a clustering column. We can easily imagine other ways to use WHERE, but it's not as flexible as we might hope.

# Restricting by clustering column

In Chapter 3, *Organizing Related Data,* you learned that any row in a table is uniquely identified by the combined values of its primary key columns. However, in the case of user_status_updates, the role of the *username* column is superfluous for the purposes of uniqueness; since *id* is a UUID, we know that it alone will uniquely identify the row on its own.

So, can we skip the username partition key and just look up rows by the id clustering column? Let's give it a shot:

```
SELECT * FROM "user_status_updates"
WHERE id = 3f9b5f00-e8f7-11e3-9211-5f98e903bf02;
```

This query is a syntactically valid CQL, and the WHERE clause identifies an existing row in the table - specifically, the status update whose body reads alice Update 1.

This is not, however, a legal query. Instead, we see an error message, as follows:

```
Bad Request: Cannot execute this query as it might involve data filtering
 and thus may have unpredictable performance. If you want to execute this
 query despite the performance unpredictability, use ALLOW FILTERING
```

Recalling our mental model for compound primary key tables, Cassandra organizes status updates like a key-value store, where the partition key acts as the lookup key. Without the partition key, Cassandra can't efficiently get to the row(s) you've specified. Instead, it would simply need to iterate internally over all the rows in the table, looking for rows that meet the conditions in the query. This sort of full table scan is extremely expensive for any table of non-trivial size, and Cassandra won't let you perform one unless you indicate with the `ALLOW FILTERING` directive appended to the end of the query that you know what you're getting yourself into.

# Restricting by part of a partition key

The `Our status_update_replies` table has a two-column partition key consisting of `status_update_username` and `status_update_id`. In some cases, we may want to, for instance, retrieve all the replies to a certain user's status updates. It would be nice if we could query by part of the partition key.

Let's insert a row into `status_update_replies`, and then try to retrieve it using only the `status_update username` column:

```
INSERT INTO "status_update_replies"
("status_update_username", "status_update_id", "id", "body")
VALUES( 'alice', 76e7a4d0-e796-11e3-90ce-5f98e903bf02, NOW(), 'Good
luck!');
```

Let's take a look at the table contents:

```
SELECT * FROM "status_update_replies"
WHERE "status_update_username" = 'alice';
```

As it turns out, this is also illegal:

```
Bad Request: Partition key part status_update_id must be restricted
since preceding part is
```

This error message tells us that if we're going to restrict any part of the partition key, we need to restrict all of it. This constraint is necessary because the layout of partition keys in a table is not related to their semantic ordering: instead, they're organized using the hash-like token of each key that we encountered in `Chapter 2`, *The First Table*. So, rows that contain `alice` in the `status_update_username` column will be distributed evenly through the partition key space; Cassandra doesn't have any way of knowing where to find them.

If we decide that retrieving all replies to a given user's status updates is an important access pattern, we can choose a different primary key arrangement for status update replies. If we made `status_update_username` alone the partition key, with `status_update_id` and `id` together forming the clustering column, then the resulting table would be ideally suited for the query in question. It would still be possible to look up the replies to a single status update, although it would not be quite as efficient as in our original formulation. This sort of reasoning, known as query-driven schema design, is critical to designing efficient Cassandra schemas; we will discuss it at length in the *Designing around queries* section of `Chapter 5`, *Establishing Relationships*.

# Retrieving status updates for a specific time range

Having explored the limits of the `WHERE` keyword in CQL, let's return to the `user_status_updates` table. Suppose we'd like to build an archive feature for MyStatus that displays all of the user's status updates for a requested month. In CQL terms, we want to select a range of clustering columns; for instance, let's get back all of `alice`'s status updates created in May 2014:

```
SELECT "id", DATEOF("id"), "body"
FROM "user_status_updates"
WHERE "username" = 'alice'
AND "id" >= MINTIMEUUID('2014-05-01')
AND "id" <= MAXTIMEUUID('2014-05-31');
```

Before diving into the mechanics of this query, we can confirm that the only status update is the one with a UUID that was provided in the previous chapter, and was generated on May 29:

| id | DATEOF(id) | body |
|---|---|---|
| 76e7a4d0-e796-11e3-90ce-5f98e903bf02 | 2014-05-29 21:05:17-0400 | Learning Cassandra! |

# Creating time UUID ranges

In the preceding query, we encounter two new CQL functions: MINTIMEUUID and MAXTIMEUUID. These functions form perhaps the most powerful components of Cassandra's toolkit for working with timestamp-based UUIDs.

As you learned in Chapter 1, *Getting Up and Running with Cassandra*, version 1 UUIDs are generated using a timestamp, and this timestamp is the highest order consideration in how UUIDs are ordered. However, for each timestamp, there are about three hundred trillion possible UUIDs.

Since UUIDs are just numbers, it follows that for any given timestamp, there is a smallest UUID and a largest UUID. This is what the MINUUID and MAXUUID functions tell us. Cassandra doesn't give us a way to directly see the output of MINTIMEUUID and MAXTIMEUUID, but we can use them in the WHERE clauses, as shown in the preceding query.

> For a complete account of the UUID-related functions available in CQL, refer to the DataStax CQL reference: http://docs.datastax.com/en/cql /3.3/cql/cql_reference/timeuuid_functions_r.html.

# Selecting a slice of a partition

With a solid understanding of the UUID functions we're using in this query, we can now break down exactly what we're asking Cassandra to give us:

- Rows in the alice partition
- With an *id* that is greater than or equal to the minimum possible UUID generated on May 1, 2014
- With an *id* that is less than or equal to the maximum possible UUID generated on May 31, 2014

This is a very common query pattern in Cassandra and is referred to as a **range slice query**. A range slice query selects a single partition key and a range of clustering column values. Like a query that is purely restricted by partition key, range slice queries are very efficient, as they take advantage of the underlying layout of the data in the table.

# Paginating over rows in a partition

As our users create more and more status updates, we'll build pagination functionality into MyStatus so that the information on the page doesn't overwhelm readers. For the sake of convenience, let's say that each page will only contain three status updates.

To retrieve the first page, we'll use the LIMIT keyword that we first encountered in Chapter 2, *The First Table*:

```
SELECT "id", DATEOF("id"), "body"
FROM "user_status_updates"
WHERE "username" = 'alice'
LIMIT 3;
```

As expected, Cassandra will give us the first three rows in ascending order of id:

```
 id                                   | DATEOF(id)               | body
--------------------------------------+--------------------------+---------------------
 76e7a4d0-e796-11e3-90ce-5f98e903bf02 | 2014-05-29 21:05:17-0400 | Learning Cassandra!
 3f9b5f00-e8f7-11e3-9211-5f98e903bf02 | 2014-05-31 15:10:37-0400 |       Alice Update 1
 3f9df710-e8f7-11e3-9211-5f98e903bf02 | 2014-05-31 15:10:37-0400 |       Alice Update 2
```

Now, we'll ask for the collection of rows where the id value is strictly greater than the last id we saw:

```
SELECT "id", DATEOF("id"), "body"
FROM "user_status_updates"
WHERE "username" = 'alice'
AND id > 3f9df710-e8f7-11e3-9211-5f98e903bf02
LIMIT 3;
```

This is similar to the pagination query for users that we made in Chapter 2, *The First Table*, but in some ways it's simpler. We keep the restriction of rows to alice's partition and then add a simple greater than restriction for id.

Unlike in the users table, we don't need to use the TOKEN function, because id is not a partition key. Since clustering columns are stored in semantic order rather than token order, we just require the next set of logically greater id values. The result is the fourth and final row in alice's status updates:

| id | DATEOF(id) | body |
|----|-----------|------|
| 3f9ee170-e8f7-11e3-9211-5f98e903bf02 | 2014-05-31 15:10:37-0400 | Alice Update 3 |

# Counting rows

While, in some cases, it might be fine to simply keep requesting pages until no more records are encountered, it's often nice to give the user a sense of how many records they're dealing with up front. Happily, we can use the COUNT function to do just this:

```
SELECT COUNT(1) FROM "user_status_updates"
WHERE "username" = 'alice';
```

Instead of requesting a list of columns or a wildcard to get all columns, we select COUNT(1) to get a total count of rows matching the WHERE condition:

```
 count
-------
     4

(1 rows)
```

We could have also used COUNT(*), which behaves in the same way as COUNT(1). There are, however, no other valid ways to use the COUNT function in CQL.

While the COUNT function is convenient, it's of dubious utility in production applications. Under the hood, performing a COUNT query requires the same work for Cassandra that actually returning the rows would; by using the COUNT function, you're mostly saving network bandwidth. If you need to efficiently track the number of rows stored in a given table or partition, you're better off using a counter cache. We'll introduce a good way to do this in Chapter 9, *Aggregating Time-Series Data*.

> For more information on COUNT queries, refer to the DataStax Cassandra documentation for SELECT: http://docs.datastax.com/en/cql/3.3/cql /cql_reference/select_r.html?scroll=reference_ds_d35_v2q_xj__c ounting-returned-rows.

# Reversing the order of rows

We're on our way to building great data access logic for displaying a user's timeline of status updates. There's one minor problem though: if I'm viewing `alice`'s status updates, I'm probably interested in reading her most recent ones first. So far, we've always gotten the status updates in ascending order of id, meaning the oldest ones come first. Fortunately, we've got a couple of ways to change this, reversing the order of rows.

# Reversing clustering order at query time

Using our `existing user_status_updates` table, we can instruct Cassandra to return results in reverse order of `id`:

```
SELECT "id", DATEOF("id"), "body"
FROM "user_status_updates"
WHERE "username" = 'alice'
ORDER BY "id" DESC;
```

This is the first time we've seen an ORDER BY in CQL, but it should be familiar to anyone who's worked with a SQL database: the DESC tells Cassandra that we want to order rows by descending values in the `id` column:

| id | DATEOF(id) | body |
|---|---|---|
| 3f9ee170-e8f7-11e3-9211-5f98e903bf02 | 2014-05-31 15:10:37-0400 | Alice Update 3 |
| 3f9df710-e8f7-11e3-9211-5f98e903bf02 | 2014-05-31 15:10:37-0400 | Alice Update 2 |
| 3f9b5f00-e8f7-11e3-9211-5f98e903bf02 | 2014-05-31 15:10:37-0400 | Alice Update 1 |
| 76e7a4d0-e796-11e3-90ce-5f98e903bf02 | 2014-05-29 21:05:17-0400 | Learning Cassandra! |

You might assume that the ORDER BY gives us a lot of flexibility in ordering rows - you might think that `id` can just as well be replaced by any other column. Let's see for ourselves:

```
SELECT "id", DATEOF("id"), "body"
FROM "user_status_updates"
WHERE "username" = 'alice'
ORDER BY "body" DESC;
```

Here, we're trying to sort our rows by descending (Z-A) values in the body field. Alas, it is not to be:

```
Bad Request: Order by is currently only supported on the clustered
columns of the PRIMARY KEY, got body
```

As it turns out, the only valid argument to the ORDER BY clause is the name of the first clustering column. Effectively, the entire ORDER BY clause exists purely to allow you to reverse the order of rows from their natural clustering order.

# Reversing clustering order in the schema

While it's useful to be able to show the newest status updates first using ORDER BY, it would be even better if the rows were naturally ordered newest first. Although we can't change the clustering order of an existing table, we can make a new table that has the same structure as user_status_updates, but with id ordered newest first:

```
CREATE TABLE "reversed_user_status_updates" ("username" text,
  "id" timeuuid, "body" text, PRIMARY KEY ("username", "id")) WITH
CLUSTERING ORDER BY ("id" DESC);
```

The CLUSTERING ORDER BY property tells Cassandra that we want to store columns in descending order by id, rather than the default ascending order. Adding a few quick rows to our table, we can see the reversed clustering order in action:

```
INSERT INTO "reversed_user_status_updates"("username", "id", "body")
VALUES ('alice', NOW(), 'Reversed status 1');
INSERT INTO "reversed_user_status_updates"("username", "id", "body")
VALUES ('alice', NOW(), 'Reversed status 2');
INSERT INTO "reversed_user_status_updates"
("username", "id", "body")
VALUES ('alice', NOW(), 'Reversed status 3');
SELECT * FROM "reversed_user_status_updates"
WHERE "username" = 'alice';
```

Even though we did not specify a descending order, the rows are naturally returned with the newest records first:

```
username | id                                   | body
---------+--------------------------------------+-------------------
   alice | 64e9cc20-f03a-11e3-995c-5f98e903bf02 | Reversed status 3
   alice | 64e956f0-f03a-11e3-995c-5f98e903bf02 | Reversed status 2
   alice | 64e670c0-f03a-11e3-995c-5f98e903bf02 | Reversed status 1
```

# Limitations of ORDER BY

There are a couple of reasons for which you might want to specify an explicit clustering order at table creation time. First, reversing the clustering order at query time has a slight performance penalty; you don't need to avoid it but, all things being equal, it's best to create the table with the clustering order corresponding to your most frequent access pattern. In the case of status updates, our second table with the reversed clustering order is better, since in most cases we'll want to see the newest status updates first.

Secondly, if you have multiple clustering columns, you might want to order by a mixture of ascending and descending columns. For instance, you might want to store a list of products in ascending order by manufacturer name, and then in descending order by the date on which the product was added within each manufacturer. In this case, you would need to set the CLUSTERING ORDER at table creation time, since ORDER BY does not allow you to reverse the clustering order of one column without reversing the order of all columns. To illustrate this, let us consider our user_status_updates_by_datetime table, which has username as the partition key and is clustered by status_date and status_time. By default, the records are fetched in the following way:

```
ORDER BY status_date ASC, status_time ASC;
```

Let us try both of the queries to verify that they produce the same output.

```
SELECT * FROM "user_status_updates_by_datetime";

SELECT * FROM "user_status_updates_by_datetime"
 WHERE "username" = 'alice'
 ORDER BY "status_date" ASC, "status_time" ASC;
```

The result is as follows:

```
 username | status_date | status_time          | body
----------+-------------+----------------------+-----------------
    alice | 2016-11-18  | 08:30:55.123000000   | Alice Update 1
    alice | 2016-11-18  | 14:40:25.123456789   | Alice Update 2
    alice | 2016-11-19  | 08:25:25.000000000   | Alice Update 3
    alice | 2016-11-21  | 08:35:55.123456000   | Alice Update 4
    alice | 2016-11-21  | 14:30:15.123000000   | Alice Update 5
    alice | 2016-11-23  | 14:50:45.123456000   | Alice Update 6
```

You will notice that the result is the same in both cases. The records are ordered by status_date and status_time in ascending order. The status updates are ordered with the oldest statuses showing up first. By default, clustering is done in an ascending order on all the clustering columns.

Suppose you want to fetch the latest status updates first. To do this, you will have ORDER BY status_date DESC, status_time DESC. Let us try this out:

```
SELECT * FROM "user_status_updates_by_datetime"
WHERE "username" = 'alice'
ORDER BY "status_date" DESC, "status_time" DESC;
```

The result is:

```
 username | status_date | status_time          | body
----------+-------------+----------------------+-----------------
    alice | 2016-11-23  | 14:50:45.123456000   | Alice Update 6
    alice | 2016-11-21  | 14:30:15.123000000   | Alice Update 5
    alice | 2016-11-21  | 08:35:55.123456000   | Alice Update 4
    alice | 2016-11-19  | 08:25:25.000000000   | Alice Update 3
    alice | 2016-11-18  | 14:40:25.123456789   | Alice Update 2
    alice | 2016-11-18  | 08:30:55.123000000   | Alice Update 1
```

You will notice that the ordering has been reversed from the default query. The latest status updates are displayed first. Thus, reversing the ORDER of both the clustering columns together seems to have worked.

Next, let us try to fetch the updates by ascending order on one column and descending order on the other column. The queries will be:

```
SELECT * FROM "user_status_updates_by_datetime"
WHERE "username" = 'alice'
ORDER BY "status_date" ASC, "status_time" DESC;
SELECT * FROM "user_status_updates_by_datetime"
WHERE "username" = 'alice'
ORDER BY "status_date" DESC, "status_time" ASC;
```

You will see that both queries will fail due to a limitation in Cassandra in the ORDER BY functionality:

```
InvalidRequest: code=2200 [Invalid query] message="Unsupported order by relation"
```

To achieve the earlier queries, we would have to recreate our table to support both of the earlier queries. This can be done by having opposite orders for both of the clustering columns.

```
CREATE TABLE "reversed_user_status_updates_by_datetime" ( "username" text,
"status_date" date, "status_time" time, "body" text, PRIMARY KEY
("username", "status_date", "status_time")) WITH CLUSTERING ORDER BY
("status_date" ASC, "status_time" DESC);
```

This will support the earlier queries but will fail for the following ones:

```
ORDER BY status_date ASC, status_time ASC;
```

```
ORDER BY status_date DESC, status_time DESC;
```

# ORDER BY summary

The ORDER BY option allows selecting the order of the returned results. It takes as argument a list of column names, along with the order for the column (ASC for ascendant and DESC for descendant, omitting the order being equivalent to ASC). Currently, the possible orderings are limited (which depends on the table CLUSTERING ORDER):

- If the table has been defined without any specific CLUSTERING ORDER, then allowed orderings are the order induced by the clustering key and the reverse of that one
- Otherwise, the orderings allowed are the order of the CLUSTERING ORDER option and the reversed one

# Paginating over multiple partitions

Returning to our original `user_status_updates` table, we might in certain situations, for an administrative interface, for instance display all of the status updates in the system. In this case, we will certainly want the ability to paginate, as the total collection of status updates will get very large.

As in our previous example, let's use a page size of three. The query for the first page is simple enough:

```
SELECT * FROM "user_status_updates"
LIMIT 3;
```

As expected, we'll get back `bob`'s first three status updates:

```
 username | id                                   | body
----------+--------------------------------------+-------------------------
      bob | 97719c50-e797-11e3-90ce-5f98e903bf02 | Eating a tasty sandwich.
      bob | 3f9d81e0-e8f7-11e3-9211-5f98e903bf02 |             Bob Update 1
      bob | 3f9e9350-e8f7-11e3-9211-5f98e903bf02 |             Bob Update 2
```

For the second page, things get a bit more complicated. We know that the last row we retrieved was from `bob`'s partition, but we're not sure if there are any more status updates for `bob`. In case there are, we will ask for the next page of `bob`'s partition:

```
SELECT * FROM "user_status_updates"
WHERE "username" = 'bob'
AND id > 3f9e9350-e8f7-11e3-9211-5f98e903bf02;
```

In this query, we ask for any status updates in `bob`'s partition that have an `id` that is greater than the last `id` we saw in the previous page. As it turns out, there is one more row:

```
 username | id                                   | body
----------+--------------------------------------+--------------
      bob | 3f9f56a0-e8f7-11e3-9211-5f98e903bf02 | Bob Update 3
```

Since we want to display pages of three, we should try to fetch more results before displaying this page to the user. Knowing that we've reached the end of `bob`'s partition, let's see if we can find two more results in partitions that are situated after `bob`'s:

```
SELECT * FROM "user_status_updates"
```

```
WHERE TOKEN("username") > TOKEN('bob')
LIMIT 2;
```

By asking for usernames whose partition token is greater than the bob token, we guarantee that we get back results we haven't seen yet. The rows returned are the first two in alice's status updates:

| username | id | body |
|---|---|---|
| alice | 76e7a4d0-e796-11e3-90ce-5f98e903bf02 | Learning Cassandra! |
| alice | 3f9b5f00-e8f7-11e3-9211-5f98e903bf02 | Alice Update 1 |

Since we requested two rows and retrieved two rows, we know that there might be more rows in alice's partition. Once again, we ask for id values greater than the last one that we saw in alice's status updates:

```
SELECT * FROM "user_status_updates"
WHERE "username" = 'alice'
AND id > 3f9b5f00-e8f7-11e3-9211-5f98e903bf02
LIMIT 3;
```

The query returns two remaining status updates for alice:

| username | id | body |
|---|---|---|
| alice | 3f9df710-e8f7-11e3-9211-5f98e903bf02 | Alice Update 2 |
| alice | 3f9ee170-e8f7-11e3-9211-5f98e903bf02 | Alice Update 3 |

Since we asked for three rows and only got back two, we know that we've now seen all the status updates in alice's partition. Now, we should check whether there are any more partitions to iterate over; we'll just ask for one, since we already have the first two rows of this page:

```
SELECT * FROM "user_status_updates"
WHERE TOKEN("username") > TOKEN('alice')
LIMIT 1;
```

When we run this query, we'll find that no rows are returned. This tells us that we've reached the last page.

This sort of two-step pagination might seem a bit arduous, but the process can be expressed concisely. We followed these steps until no more rows were returned:

1. Ask for the first rows in the table.
2. Ask for the next rows in the same partition as the last row that was returned. Repeat until no more rows are returned for this partition.
3. Ask for rows in the next partition.
4. Go back to step 2.

# JSON support

**JSON** is short for **JavaScript Object Notation** and is a way to store information in an organized, easy-to-access manner. In a nutshell, it gives us a human-readable collection of data that we can access in a really logical manner. It is the most commonly used data format for client/server communication.

Starting with Cassandra 2.2, JSON support was added to the features list of Cassandra. This is an extension of CQL, which makes it easier to work with JSON documents. The SELECT and INSERT statements now include a JSON-focused variant, and two new native functions have been added to convert to and from JSON.

# INSERT JSON

The INSERT statement accepts a JSON variant. Suppose we want to insert some JSON data into our user_status_updates_by_datetime table, we can do it in the following way:

```
INSERT INTO "user_status_updates_by_datetime"
JSON '{"username": "alice", "status_date": "2016-11-24", "status_time":
"13:35:20.123456", "body": "Alice Update 7"}';
```

Now, if you run the query `SELECT * FROM "user_status_updates_by_datetime";` you will get the new column that you added using the JSON variant of `INSERT` as well:

```
username | status_date | status_time          | body
---------+-------------+----------------------+----------------
   alice | 2016-11-18  | 08:30:55.123000000   | Alice Update 1
   alice | 2016-11-18  | 14:40:25.123456789   | Alice Update 2
   alice | 2016-11-19  | 08:25:25.000000000   | Alice Update 3
   alice | 2016-11-21  | 08:35:55.123456000   | Alice Update 4
   alice | 2016-11-21  | 14:30:15.123000000   | Alice Update 5
   alice | 2016-11-23  | 14:50:45.123456000   | Alice Update 6
   alice | 2016-11-24  | 13:35:20.123456000   | Alice Update 7
```

The JSON-encoded map is simply a CQL string literal that is a JSON encoding of a map, where keys are column names and values are column values. When Cassandra types have a sensible native JSON equivalent, such as int, float, boolean, and lists, those native types are accepted. For Cassandra types that don't have a clear JSON equivalent, such as UUIDs, a string representation matching the normal CQL literal format should be used.

# SELECT JSON

The `SELECT` statement has also been extended to support retrieval of rows in a JSON-encoded map format. The results for `SELECT JSON` will only include a single column named `[json]`. This column will contain the same JSON-encoded map representation of a row that is used for `INSERT` JSON.

Let us try to fetch all status updates that were made by `alice` after the date `2016-11-20` in JSON format:

```
SELECT JSON * FROM "user_status_updates_by_datetime"
WHERE "username" = 'alice'
AND status_date > '2016-11-20';
```

You will get each CQL row as a separate JSON-encoded string:

```
[json]
-----------------------------------------------------------------------------------------------------------------
{"username": "alice", "status_date": "2016-11-21", "status_time": "08:35:55.123456000", "body": "Alice Update 4"}
{"username": "alice", "status_date": "2016-11-21", "status_time": "14:30:15.123000000", "body": "Alice Update 5"}
{"username": "alice", "status_date": "2016-11-23", "status_time": "14:50:45.123456000", "body": "Alice Update 6"}
{"username": "alice", "status_date": "2016-11-24", "status_time": "13:35:20.123456000", "body": "Alice Update 7"}
```

# Building an autocomplete function

So far, we've been focused on storing users and their status updates, but we can use our knowledge of compound primary keys to make it a bit easier to write status updates too. Let's introduce a hashtagging function into the status update composition interface and then autocomplete hashtags as users type them.

First, we'll set up a table to store hashtags using the following query:

```
CREATE TABLE "hash_tags" ( "prefix" text, "remaining" text, "tag" text,
PRIMARY KEY ("prefix", "remaining"));
```

The structure of our table is a bit unusual, but it will work very well for our purposes. The partition key is a prefix, which we'll use to store the first two letters of each hashtag. The clustering column, `remaining`, will store the remaining letters of the `hashtag`, and `tag` will contain the entire hashtag start to finish.

By partitioning the table this way, we'll make things easy for Cassandra by immediately narrowing down the list of possible autocomplete tags to those in the partition identified by the two-letter prefix. This does, of course, mean that we can't autocomplete entries of fewer than two letters, but this is a pretty standard limitation.

To see how the autocomplete works, let's add some seed data into the table:

```
INSERT INTO "hash_tags" ("prefix", "remaining", "tag")
VALUES ('ca', 'ssandra', 'cassandra');

INSERT INTO "hash_tags" ("prefix", "remaining", "tag")
VALUES ('ca', 'ssette', 'cassette');

INSERT INTO "hash_tags" ("prefix", "remaining", "tag")
VALUES ('ca', 'sual', 'casual');

INSERT INTO "hash_tags" ("prefix", "remaining", "tag")
VALUES ('ca', 'ke', 'cake');
```

Now, let's say the user starts typing a hashtag and has so far typed `ca`. That's easy: we can just ask for the `ca` partition in our table:

```
SELECT "tag" FROM "hash_tags"
WHERE "prefix" = 'ca';
```

Just as we want, we'll get tags starting with the letters `ca`:

```
tag
-----------
      cake
 cassandra
  cassette
    casual
```

So far, so good! Now, let's say the user has typed `cas`. In this case; we want to return all the words starting with `cas`, but CQL doesn't have a starting-with operator. Instead, we'll use a range slice query to describe the rows we're looking for. From the standpoint of lexical string ordering, we're looking for strings that are lexically greater than `cas`, but lexically smaller than `cat`, since `t` is the next letter after `s`. Translated into a CQL query, it looks like this:

```
SELECT "tag" FROM "hash_tags"
WHERE "prefix" = 'ca' AND "remaining" >= 's' AND "remaining" < 't';
```

The remaining range slice will cover strings such as `ssete`, `sual`, and `ssandra`, because those are all lexically greater than s and lexically smaller than t. So, we get just the results we're looking for:

```
tag
-----------
 cassandra
  cassette
    casual
```

Supposing the user typed a couple more letters, for a total entry of `cassa`, we'd narrow the range further:

```
SELECT "tag" FROM "hash_tags"
WHERE "prefix" = 'ca' AND "remaining" >= 'ssa' AND "remaining" < 'ssb';
```

Again, we construct the upper bound for the range slice by simply replacing the last character of the input with the following character in the alphabet, giving us the right lexical upper bound. Now we've narrowed our results to a single `hashtag`:

```
tag
-----------
cassandra
```

While compound primary keys are an intuitively good fit storing timestamped data partitioned into logical groups, with a little creativity the data structure can be applied to a wide range of other problems. The autocomplete implementation we built here might not be the simplest one you've come across, but it can efficiently store and autocomplete billions of hashtags, which isn't anything to sneeze at!

# Summary

In this chapter, we've explored data access patterns for compound primary key tables, and used our new knowledge to expose a paginated view of a user's most recent status updates. We discussed how to query range slices of clustering column values, and how to reverse the clustering order at both table creation time and query time. We reinforced our understanding of the CQL `SELECT` queries by performing the intricate task of paginating over all the rows in our status updates table, and then applied our new compound primary key toolkit to a totally different problem, the autocompletion of hashtags.

In `Chapter 5`, *Establishing Relationships*, we will apply our techniques for compound primary key data modeling to the task of describing relationships that do not have the clear parent-child structure of users and status updates. We'll also go beyond primary key-based data access, exploring the use of secondary indexes to look up data using any column we wish.

# 5
# Establishing Relationships

At this point, we might declare our MyStatus application a minimum viable product. Users can create accounts and post status updates, and those status updates can be viewed in their authors' timelines. And, of course, since we're storing the data in Cassandra, we don't need to worry about scaling up to plenty of users and status updates.

As our service grows, however, it would be nice for users to be able to view all their friends' status updates in one place. The first step of that, of course, would be to know who a user's friends are. So, we'll build a feature that allows one user to follow another.

We've already seen a good way to use Cassandra to model a specific type of relationship. Compound primary keys are a natural fit for parent-child associations, but a follow relationship is many-to-many: I follow many users, and, hopefully, many users follow me.

In this chapter, we'll build on our knowledge of Cassandra data modeling and introduce new patterns to model relationships. We'll explore two ways to model relationships. First, we will explicitly create a table whose role is to represent the relationship between two other entities. Second, we'll look at how secondary indexes can help us represent relationships without the need for an extra lookup table. Third, we will use materialized views instead of secondary indexes to avoid denormalization.

By the end, we'll have two alternative data structures to capture followers in the database, and you'll have learned the following:

- How to model many-to-many relationships in Cassandra
- Data modeling in Cassandra
- How query-driven design can produce denormalized data structures
- How to delete rows from a Cassandra table
- How to create secondary indexes
- The limitations and disadvantages of secondary indexes
- How to create materialized views
- Performance of materialized views

# Modeling follow relationships

A data model for follow relationships should be able to answer two questions on behalf of a user:

- Who do I follow?
- Who follows me?

In Chapter 3, *Organizing Related Data*, you learned to design our table structures so that all important data access can be accomplished by querying a single partition. For this reason, we're better off considering the aforementioned questions separately and designing the right table schema for each.

# Outbound follows

We'll start with the question *Who do I follow?*. We'll want a partition per user, with each partition containing all the other users they follow:

```
CREATE TABLE "user_outbound_follows" (
  "follower_username" text,
  "followed_username" text,
  PRIMARY KEY ("follower_username", "followed_username")
);
```

Simple enough, but there's something unusual here: there are only two columns in the table, and they're both part of the primary key. As it turns out, this is a perfectly valid way to construct a table schema; non-key columns are optional in Cassandra tables. Since all we need to know is who's at the other end of the follow relationship, which is available via the clustering column `followed_user_id`, no additional data columns are needed.

# Inbound follows

Our new `user_outbound_follows` table allows us to efficiently find out who a user follows; since the partition key is the username of the following user, we'll only be accessing a single partition to answer the question. It does not, however, provide any way to find out who follows a certain user. In order to broadcast users' status updates to their followers, we'll certainly need to be able to find out who their followers are.

To accomplish this, we'll create a new table, which is the mirror image of `user_outbound_follows`:

```
CREATE TABLE "user_inbound_follows" (
  "followed_username" text,
  "follower_username" text,
  PRIMARY KEY ("followed_username", "follower_username")
);
```

The new `user_inbound_follows` table looks exactly like the `user_outbound_follows` table, except that the order of the keys is reversed; now the followed user's username is the partition key, and each row within the partition is identified by the follower user's username. Like `user_outbound_follows`, our new table does not have any non-key columns.

# Storing follow relationships

We've now created two tables, each of which allows us to answer two important questions about follow relationships: first, whom a user follows; and second, who follows a user. Now let's establish some follow relationships.

For now, let's have `alice` follow a couple of other users, `bob` and `carol`:

```
INSERT INTO "user_outbound_follows"
  ("follower_username", "followed_username")
VALUES ('alice', 'bob');
INSERT INTO "user_inbound_follows"
  ("followed_username", "follower_username")
VALUES ('bob', 'alice');
INSERT INTO "user_outbound_follows"
  ("follower_username", "followed_username")
VALUES ('alice', 'carol');
INSERT INTO "user_inbound_follows"
  ("followed_username", "follower_username")
VALUES ('carol', 'alice');
```

For each follow relationship, we have to insert two rows: one in the `user_outbound_follows` table to store the relationship from the perspective of the follower, and one in the `user_inbound_follows` table to store the relationship from the perspective of the followed user.

# Cassandra data modelling

**Cassandra data modeling** is the process of designing tables. This could involve drawing up an entity-relationship diagram, designing tables based on queries, and finally, making optimizations based on the features supported by Cassandra. Ideally, the data model can be split into three levels of abstraction:

- **Conceptual data model:** A conceptual data model represents a high level view of the data. It is technology agnostic and not specific to Cassandra or any other database system. The purpose of creating a conceptual data model is to understand the data. We get a clear idea of the entities involved and the relationships between different entities. For our case, we will be using the entity relationship model as the conceptual data model.
- **Logical data model**: A logical data model will act as a bridge between the business case and the final table design. We will use the conceptual model and apply query-driven design rules to get a logical data model.
- **Physical data model**: A physical data model will add certain optimizations relevant to the database being used. This will be the final stage of data modeling, and we should be ready with the final table design.

# Conceptual data model (entity relationship model)

For those with a background in relational systems, the ER model should be quite familiar. An entity-relationship model is used to describe relationships between inter-related entities. There are two major components of the entity relationship model:

- **Entity**: An entity is a thing or object involved in an information system
- **Attribute**: Entities are represented by properties known as attributes
- **Relationship**: A relationship is an association or interaction between entities

ER models/diagrams can be quite useful in designing tables for Cassandra. They are useful in Cassandra data modeling in most cases except for a few special scenarios. So, we will be taking a look at some of the concepts of the ER model and how they apply to data modeling within Cassandra.

An entity can be represented in the following ways:

- **Name**: This denotes the name of the entity
- **Attributes**: These can be atomic, set-valued, or composite
- **Key**: This denotes the minimum set of attributes that uniquely identify an entity

Please refer the following figure for a better understanding:

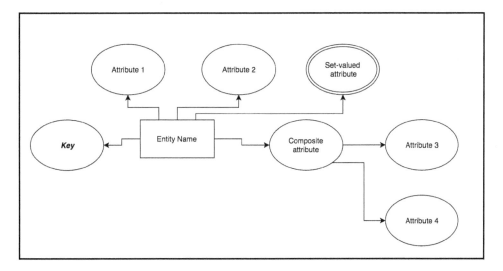

Suppose that we want to created an ER representation of `user` type for our MyStatus application; it might look like this:

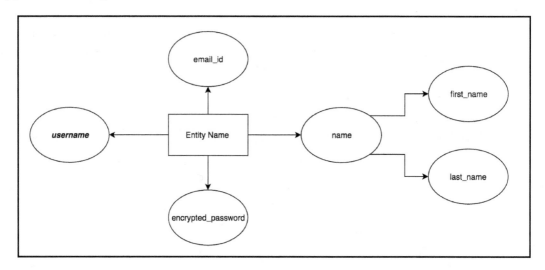

A relationship can be represented as follows:

- Name
- Attributes
- Key
- Cardinality constraints: This denotes the number of times an entity can appear in a relationship

Please refer the following figure for a better understanding:

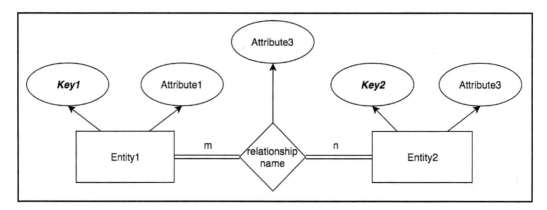

There are three major relationships possible between entities in an ER model. We will quickly gloss over all three of these along with an example:

- **One-to-one relationship (1:1 relationship):** In this relationship, each entity appears only once. For example, let's consider a person and a passport as two separate entities. We wish to store the passport information of different people:

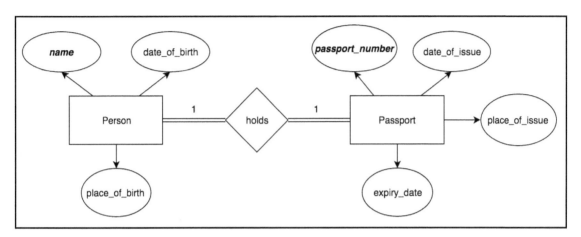

Here, each person holds exactly one passport at a time. Also, a passport is held by only one person. We assume name is unique for every person, which might not be the case in reality. You can consider a combination of name and other attributes such as date and place of birth as the key. The keys for this relationship are name for the Person entity and passport_number for the Passport entity.

- **One-to-many (or many-to-one) relationship (1:m relationship)**: In this relationship, one of the entities appears only once, whereas the cardinality of the other entities is more than one. We have already come across this scenario in our `user_status_updates` table. Let's consider a user and a status update as the entities. The ER diagram for the relationship looks like this:

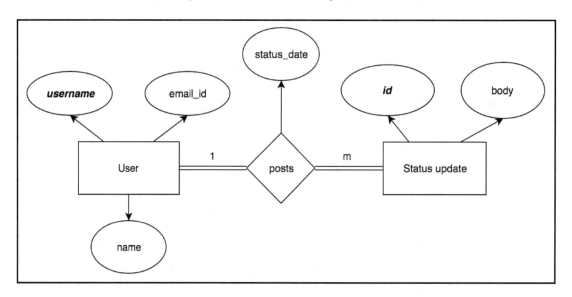

Each user can post multiple status updates whereas each status update is posted by only one user. The keys for this relationship that uniquely identify the entities as well as the relationship itself are `username`, `id` (status update id), and `status_date`.

- **Many-to-many relationship (m:n relationship)**: In this relationship, each of the entities will have a cardinality higher than one. Each entity will appear more than once. Both `user_outbound_follows` and `user_inbound_follows` are examples of this relationship:

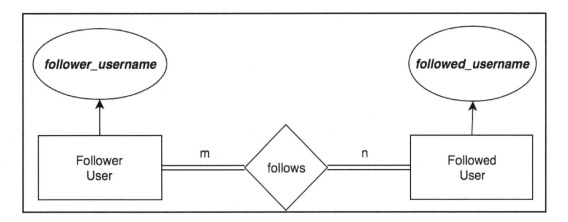

Each user can follow multiple users, and each user can be followed by multiple users as well.

ER diagrams can tend to be much more complex than what we have seen so far. One entity type can be a subtype of another entity type. Subtypes inherit attributes of a parent type. There are different constraints possible such as the following:

- **Covering constraint**: Union of subtypes is equal to the supertype
- **Disjoint constraint**: Set of subtypes are disjoint

# Logical data model (query-driven design)

Our choice to store two representations of a single follow relationship is a prime example of **query-driven design**: the practice of designing table schemas to accommodate the data access patterns of our application rather than simply building structures to naturally represent the underlying data. In the case of follow relationships, either the `user_outbound_follows` or `user_inbound_follows` table is sufficient on its own to store the data about follow relationships; were we using a relational database, it is likely that we would only use one of these tables, with secondary indexes on the non-key columns for efficient lookup. But when using Cassandra, neither table is able to satisfy all of the query needs our application will have; so query-driven design instructs us to include both in our database.

When thinking about the best way to satisfy the data access needs of our application, it's helpful to think of our Cassandra tables in terms of a core data structure: a map of values to a collections of values. If we want to know whom a given user follows, we want a map of usernames to the collection of users they follow. This abstract representation of the ideal data structure instructs us to build a table whose primary key is a username and whose rows consist of usernames of users they follow.

Let's build a simple logical data model for our `user_status_updates` table. Suppose that we wish to get all the status updates for a particular user and order them by status ID. We do this by creating a table with `username` and `id` as part of the primary key.

Since there can be multiple values of `id` belonging to the same `username`, `username` will be our partition key, and `id` will be the clustering column.

| Partition key | username |
|---|---|
| **Clustering column** | id |
| **Non-primary key columns** | name (static)<br>email_id (static)<br>status_date<br>body |

There are certain rules you should follow whenever designing schema based on queries. These will help you design an optimal data model for your use case:

- Make sure your schema is designed in such a way that each query requires accessing only one partition. Partitions could be single row or multi-row, but it is generally desirable to have small partitions ( < 100 MB in size).
- For queries requiring you to access multiple partitions such as getting status updates for two users, always make sure you run asynchronous queries and do a client-side merge.
- Use various data nesting techniques to ensure a partition-per-query paradigm.
- Data nesting mechanisms should include the use of clustering columns as well as collection columns to store related data within a single partition.
- Duplicate data if your queries demand it. Data can be duplicated across tables, partitions, and/or rows.

# Physical data model

Finally, you might want to make further optimizations to the table design to speed up the queries. These optimizations could include the following:

- Splitting partitions in a table to keep their size manageable
- Merging partitions to speed up queries
- Adding columns for efficient querying

Querying non-primary key columns is either not supported or very expensive. In certain situations, it might be useful to create secondary indexes or materialized views to facilitate efficient querying on non-primary key columns. Some scenarios also require us to use distributed counters or lightweight transactions. We will take a look at all of the aforementioned features in the following chapters.

# Denormalization

Our follow tables are also the first example we've seen of denormalization, which is the practice of storing the same data in more than one place. **Denormalization** is typically frowned upon in relational database schemas, although from a practical standpoint it's often a useful optimization even in that scenario. In non-relational databases, denormalization is often a critical tool in query-driven designs.

The downside of denormalization is exemplified by our preceding insert pattern: we have to make two INSERT statements to fully represent one fundamental fact. From a standpoint of performance, this is acceptable: Cassandra is optimized for efficient write operations, so we're happy to make verbose writes in order to allow efficient reads. This does, of course, add more complexity at the application level: the application is responsible for ensuring that any modification to the user_outbound_follows table is accompanied by an equivalent modification to the user_inbound_follows table. If there is a flaw in the application's logic, the two tables may not contain consistent information.

# Looking up follow relationships

Now that we've studiously designed our follow tables to efficiently support our application's data access patterns, let's do some data access. To start, we'll want to give `alice` an interface to manage the list of users she follows; this interface will, of course, need to show her who she currently follows:

```
SELECT "followed_username"
FROM "user_outbound_follows"
WHERE "follower_username" = 'alice';
```

Here, we ask for all of the outbound follows in the partition of `alice`: an efficient query since it only looks up a single partition's worth of data. As expected, we see that `alice` follows `bob` and `carol`:

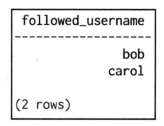

```
 followed_username
-------------------
              bob
            carol

(2 rows)
```

Note that the usernames returned are in alphabetical order: this is not a coincidence. Since `followed_username` is the clustering column in the `user_outbound_follows` table, the rows are stored in string order of the followed user's username. While this isn't critical to the functionality of our application, it's a happy *bonus* feature of the data structure we've chosen.

Now let's explore the other side of the relationship—*Who follows bob?* To reinforce our earlier discussion of query-driven design, let's first try to answer that question using the `user_outbound_follows` table:

```
SELECT "follower_username"
FROM "user_outbound_follows"
WHERE "followed_username" = 'bob';
```

When we attempt this query, we see an error that is familiar from the previous chapter: Cassandra is unable to efficiently perform the lookup we're asking for, so we're required to include the `ALLOW FILTERING` directive as a *waiver* indicating that we know the query may be expensive:

```
Bad Request: Cannot execute this query as it might involve data filtering
 and thus may have unpredictable performance. If you want to execute this
 query despite the performance unpredictability, use ALLOW FILTERING
```

Having assured ourselves that our denormalized structure is justified, we'll use the `user_inbound_follows` table to find out who follows `bob`:

```
SELECT "follower_username"
FROM "user_inbound_follows"
WHERE "followed_username" = 'bob';
```

Since we're doing the lookup using the `follower_username` partition key, Cassandra has no complaints, and the result is what we expect:

Poor `bob` has only one follower. Keep posting those funny cat pictures, `bob`, and you'll have more in no time!

# Unfollowing users

It's conceivable that `bob` may end up posting too many funny cat pictures for `alice`'s taste, in which case, she may decide to unfollow him. For `alice` to do that, we'll need to remove the rows representing the follow relationship from both the inbound and outbound follow tables:

```
DELETE FROM "user_outbound_follows"
WHERE "follower_username" = 'alice'
  AND "followed_username" = 'bob';

DELETE FROM "user_inbound_follows"
```

```
WHERE "followed_username" = 'bob'
  AND "follower_username" = 'alice';
```

This is our first encounter with CQL's DELETE statement, although it should look quite familiar to anyone who's worked with SQL. To delete a row, we specify the full primary key of the row, that is, both the partition key(s) and the clustering column(s). The WHERE...AND syntax is the same as that used in SELECT queries, introduced in Chapter 3, *Organizing Related Data*.

To check the effects of the deletion, we can query again for the list of users alice follows:

```
SELECT "followed_username"
FROM "user_outbound_follows"
WHERE "follower_username" = 'alice';
```

As expected, alice no longer follows bob:

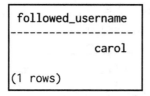

```
 followed_username
-------------------
             carol

(1 rows)
```

Were we to check the user_inbound_follows table for bob, we would find that he no longer has any followers.

For more on the DELETE statement, see the DataStax CQL reference at htt p://docs.datastax.com/en/cql/3.3/cql/cql_reference/delete_r.ht ml.

# Using secondary indexes to avoid denormalization

So far, we've exclusively used primary key columns to look up rows—either the full primary key when we're looking for a specific row, or just the partition key when retrieving multiple rows in a single partition. We know that these kinds of lookups are very efficient because Cassandra can satisfy the query by accessing the single region of storage that holds the partition's data in order.

This is the motivation for the denormalized follow structure we've built in this chapter: whether we want to answer the question *Who does alice follow?* or the question *Who follows alice?*, we can construct a query that only needs to access a single partition. However, we're accepting additional complexity in the form of storing two versions of the same information in `user_inbound_follows` and `user_outbound_follows`.

As it happens, Cassandra does provide us with a way to answer both questions in a reasonably efficient way using a single table with a single representation of each follow relationship. By adding a **secondary index**, we can enable lookup of rows using columns other than the primary key.

# The form of the single table

To demonstrate this approach, we'll start by creating a new table, `user_follows`, that has an identical structure to our `user_inbound_follows` table:

```
CREATE TABLE "user_follows" (
  "followed_username" text,
  "follower_username" text,
  PRIMARY KEY ("followed_username", "follower_username")
);
```

As with `user_outbound_follows`, this new table uses a followed user as its partition key and the follower as its clustering column. At a higher level, for each user, *U*, this table stores a partition of rows representing the users that follow *U*. So, if we'd like to find out who follows a given user, we can do so very efficiently using this table.

However, we've said that we want to use the same table for both inbound and outbound follows; that is to say, we'd like this table to be able to answer the question, *Who does Alice follow?* Let's recall what happens if we naively try a query to answer that question on the `user_follows` table:

```
SELECT * FROM "user_follows"
WHERE "follower_username" = 'alice';
```

Of course, Cassandra won't allow us to perform this query:

```
code=2200 [Invalid query] message="Cannot execute this query as it might
  involve data filtering and thus may have unpredictable performance. If
you want to execute this query despite the performance unpredictability,
  use ALLOW FILTERING"
```

The structure of Cassandra's primary keys requires us to strictly adhere to a set of rules for what columns we may specify in the WHERE clause of a query. In particular, if we want to look up rows by a given column or columns, we can use the following:

- Exact values for all partition key columns
- Exact values for all partition key columns, and an exact value for the first clustering column
- Exact values for all partition key columns and for the first two clustering columns

Most importantly, if we're going to specify values for any columns, we must specify values for the partition key columns. This is because the partition key is the top-level lookup key for rows in any table; recall our mental model from the *Refining our mental model* section at the end of Chapter 3, *Organizing Related Data*.

# Adding a secondary index

There is one exception to this rule, and that is when a secondary index is in use. A secondary index should be a familiar concept to anyone who has worked with a relational database; in the relational world, they're often just referred to as indexes. Put simply, secondary indexes allow us to perform a reasonably efficient lookup of rows using columns other than the partition key.

In our case, we'd like to look up rows in user_follows by providing a value for the follower_username row but omitting a value for the followed_username partition key. To do this, we can use the CREATE INDEX statement:

```
CREATE INDEX ON "user_follows" ("follower_username");
```

The syntax here is pretty straightforward: we simply provide Cassandra with the name of a table and the name of a column within the table that we'd like to create an index on.

To see our index in action, let's add a few follow relationships to our new table:

```
INSERT INTO "user_follows"
  ("followed_username", "follower_username")
VALUES ('alice', 'bob');

INSERT INTO "user_follows"
  ("followed_username", "follower_username")
VALUES ('alice', 'carol');

INSERT INTO "user_follows"
  ("followed_username", "follower_username")
VALUES ('carol', 'bob');

INSERT INTO "user_follows"
  ("followed_username", "follower_username")
VALUES ('dave', 'bob');
```

Now let's say we'd like to answer the question *Who does bob follow?* We can construct a query of the same form that caused us an error before we had created the index:

```
SELECT * FROM "user_follows"
WHERE "follower_username" = 'bob';
```

But this time, we'll get the results we're looking for:

```
 followed_username | follower_username
-------------------+-------------------
              dave |               bob
             carol |               bob
             alice |               bob

(3 rows)
```

This is the first time we've been able to construct a query that looks up rows by a column value without specifying the partition key. Secondary indexes give a significant new tool when designing our data models and access patterns.

In this case, we created a secondary index on a clustering column, but there's no restriction on the kind of column that can be used for a secondary index. We'll explore more examples here and in `Chapter 8`, *Collections, Tuples, and User-Defined Types*.

# Other uses of secondary indexes

We've seen that secondary indexes neatly allow us to turn a denormalized relationship structure into a normalized one: the `user_follows` table is able to answer all the important questions about follow relationships without any duplication of data. This is but one of the many use cases for which secondary indexes are well suited.

Secondary indexes are best suited for **low-cardinality** columns, that is, columns that contain the same value for many rows. An example might be a `location` column on the `users` table; if this is restricted to city and state, many users will share the same location. In fact, we will add a `location` column to the `users` table in the *Adding columns to tables* section in `Chapter 7`, *Expanding Your Data Model*. If we wanted to be able to answer questions such as *Who are all of the users that live in New York?*, that index would be quite useful.

Secondary indexes can also be used for columns whose values are unique, such as the `email` column in the `users` table. If, for instance, we wanted to build a *forgot password* feature in which the user enters their e-mail address, we'd be able to use an index on `email` to look up the user's record.

Use caution when creating indexes on unique or high-cardinality columns; these indexes can only handle moderate query volume. The DataStax Cassandra reference warns us:

 For columns containing unique data, it is sometimes fine performance-wise to use an index for convenience as long as the query volume to the table having an indexed column is moderate and not under constant load.

Another interesting use case for secondary indexes would be for easier lookup of status updates from the `user_status_updates` table. Recall that that table's partition key is the username of the user who wrote the status update, and the clustering column is a UUID column. In order to look up a specific status update, we would normally have to specify both `username` and `id` values. But the `id` column alone uniquely identifies each status update because UUIDs are globally unique. So, if we place a secondary index on the `id` column, we can look up status updates more tersely, which is useful to generate URLs and the like.

For more information on secondary indexes, take a look at the DataStax CQL reference for the CREATE INDEX statement at http://docs.datasta x.com/en/cql/3.3/cql/cql_reference/create_index_r.html.

# Limitations of secondary indexes

We've seen that secondary indexes are useful in a range of scenarios, and we'll explore more in Chapter 8, *Collections, Tuples, and User-Defined Types*. However, indexes are not without limitations and downsides.

## Secondary indexes can only have one column

One major limitation of secondary indexes is that they can only target one column. It would not be legal, for instance, to specify a secondary index such as follows:

```
CREATE INDEX ON "users" ("email", "encrypted_password");
```

We'll explore one workaround to this limitation in the *Working with tuples* section of Chapter 8, *Collections, Tuples, and User-Defined Types*.

## Secondary indexes can only be tested for equality

In the section on *Retrieving status updates for a specific time range* in Chapter 4, *Beyond Key-Value Lookup*, we explored the use of inequality operators to select ranges of columns. Secondary indexes can only be queried for equality; queries such as the following are not possible:

```
SELECT * FROM "user_follows"
WHERE "follower_username" > 'alice';
```

## Secondary index lookup is not as efficient as primary key lookup

Although secondary indexes give us a reasonably efficient way to look up rows using a non-partition key column, they're not as efficient as queries based on the primary key we've explored in the previous chapters. This is because lookup by a secondary index is a two-step process. First, Cassandra will access the secondary index to find the primary keys of all rows matching the query. Second, it will access the table itself to retrieve the matched rows.

The second step will generally involve querying over many partitions or at least over disjoint ranges of a single partition. These random reads over the data can never be as efficient as a single focused read of one range of one partition.

For this reason, it's best to avoid using secondary indexes for the core data access patterns of your application. Our structure in the `user_follows` table bears this out: answering the question *Who follows alice?* is central to the process of broadcasting her status updates to her followers. On the other hand, the question *Who does alice follow?* is only necessary when `alice` or another user wishes to see a list of those users. By structuring the table with the `followed_username` column as the partition key, we ensure that super-efficient partition key lookup is available for the most important question and use secondary index lookup for less essential queries.

 For more on when to use secondary indexes and when not to, see the chapter from the DataStax Cassandra documentation at: `http://www.data stax.com/documentation/cql/3.1/cql/ddl/ddl_when_use_index_c.ht ml#concept_ds_sgh_yzz_zj__when-no-index`.

# Materialized views

While we were modeling our follow relationships, we noted that different access patterns required us to store the same data in multiple tables with different schema. To avoid this denormalization, we created a secondary index on one of the columns. But adding a secondary index on a non-partition key column has a performance impact on read latency. This is especially the case when the column on which the index was created has a high cardinality. Thus, secondary indexes should be used in cases of low cardinality columns or you specify the partition key as well within your queries so the queries don't scale across multiple partitions. To avoid client-side denormalization and the use of secondary indexes for high cardinality columns, materialized views were introduced in Cassandra 3.0. Materialized views handle server-side denormalization ensuring eventual consistency between the base and view data. This provides very fast lookups of data in materialized views even when the cardinality is high. Additionally, you can create a view on multiple columns.

# Adding a view

To avoid confusion, let's recreate the `user_follows` table with a different name:

```
CREATE TABLE "user_follows_base" (
  "followed_username" text,
```

```
"follower_username" text,
PRIMARY KEY ("followed_username", "follower_username")
);
```

Primarily, the preceding table lets us query the list of followers of a person. To query a list of persons someone is following, we created a secondary index earlier. Let's create a materialized view for the same:

```
CREATE MATERIALIZED VIEW "user_follows_view"
AS SELECT followed_username, follower_username
FROM "user_follows_base"
WHERE follower_username IS NOT NULL AND followed_username IS NOT NULL
PRIMARY KEY (follower_username, followed_username);
```

This CREATE MATERIALIZED VIEW statement has several features:

- The CREATE MATERIALIZED VIEW phrase creates a materialized view with the given name
- The AS SELECT phrase identifies the columns copied from the base table to the materialized view
- The FROM phrase identifies the base table from which Cassandra will copy the data to the view
- The WHERE clause must include all primary key columns with the IS NOT NULL phrase so that only rows with data for all the primary key columns are copied to the materialized view
- Finally, the PRIMARY KEY is specified for the view as well, similar to the base table (specify the primary key according to the access pattern)
- Since user_follows_base, the source table, uses followed_username and follower_username as its primary key, both must be present in the materialized view's primary key

> In this materialized view, follower_username is used as the partition key and followed_username is a clustering column. In Cassandra 3.0 and earlier, you cannot use a column as a clustering column if any of its values are larger than 64 KB.

Let's try inserting a few records into our user_follows_base table:

```
INSERT INTO "user_follows_base"
  ("followed_username", "follower_username")
VALUES ('alice', 'bob');

INSERT INTO "user_follows_base"
```

```
    ("followed_username", "follower_username")
  VALUES ('alice', 'carol');

  INSERT INTO "user_follows_base"
    ("followed_username", "follower_username")
  VALUES ('carol', 'bob');

  INSERT INTO "user_follows_base"
    ("followed_username", "follower_username")
  VALUES ('dave', 'bob');
```

Now, let's try to fetch the users who are following the user `alice`:

```
  SELECT * FROM "user_follows_base"
  WHERE "followed_username" = 'alice';
```

We get the result as expected:

```
 followed_username | follower_username
-------------------+-------------------
             alice |               bob
             alice |             carol
```

Let's try to fetch the list of users `bob` has followed:

```
  SELECT * FROM "user_follows_base"
  WHERE "follower_username" = 'bob';
```

This returns the same error as before:

```
InvalidRequest: code=2200 [Invalid query] message="Cannot execute this query as it might involve data filtering and thus may have unpredictable
 performance. If you want to execute this query despite the performance unpredictability, use ALLOW FILTERING"
```

To fetch the list of users `bob` follows, you would have to query from the view rather than the base table. The syntax to query from the `user_follows_view` view is similar to a query on a base table:

```
  SELECT * FROM "user_follows_view"
  WHERE "follower_username" = 'bob';
```

Since the data that gets written to the base table is also written to the view, we get the results as expected:

```
follower_username | followed_username
------------------+------------------
             bob |             alice
             bob |             carol
             bob |              dave
```

Now suppose `bob` decides to unfollow the user `dave`. We can do this by deleting the particular record from the base table:

```
DELETE FROM "user_follows_base"
WHERE "followed_username" = 'dave'
AND "follower_username" = 'bob';
```

Let's try to fetch the users `bob` follows from the view `user_follows_view` just like we did before. You will notice that the user `dave` no longer exists within the list of users `bob` follows. When the delete statement on the `user_follows_base` table was issued, the corresponding row was removed from the view `user_follows_view` as well. Thus, we get the result as follows:

```
follower_username | followed_username
------------------+------------------
             bob |             alice
             bob |             carol
```

The requirements for a materialized view are as follows:

- The columns of the base table's primary key must be part of the materialized view's primary key
- Only one new column can be added to the materialized view's primary key; static columns are not allowed

Materialized views are not an ideal solution to avoid denormalization. The write throughput goes down drastically as you increase the number of views on a table. Materialized views also cause hotspots when low cardinality data is inserted.

# Summary

In this chapter, we looked at ways to model relationships between objects that go beyond the straightforward parent-child relationships, which are captured elegantly by a compound primary key. We found that query-driven schema design motivated us to create multiple representations of the follow relationship; each representation was optimized to answer a specific question about follows. This led us to a denormalized schema, wherein each follow has multiple representations in our database.

While our denormalized schema requires more write operations than a normalized one and extra care at the application level to ensure the different representations of follows are consistent with one another, we end up with a better overall performance because writing data to Cassandra is cheaper than reading it. By designing our schema to allow Cassandra to efficiently access data in a single partition to answer any question the application needs, we ensure that Cassandra can continue efficiently serving the application's needs even at a massive scale.

As an alternative to denormalization, we introduced secondary indexes and materialized views as ways to avoid storing the same follow relationship in two places. We explored the uses and limitations of secondary indexes as well as materialized views and recognized that while it is convenient to only have a single table for follow relationships, we do lose some performance using the said features.

Based on the data and the access patterns, we can decide on using secondary indexes, materialized views, or simply denormalization (maintaining the same data in multiple tables).

Finally, we introduced deletion of rows, our first foray into modifying data that we've stored in Cassandra.

In the next chapter, we'll continue our explanation of denormalized data structures when we create home timelines for each user, which will allow us to broadcast a user's status updates to all of their followers.

# 6
# Denormalizing Data for Maximum Performance

In the previous chapter, we created a structure that allows a user to follow other users. The goal of the follow system was to allow users to see all of their followed users' status updates in one place, which we'll call the home timeline. In this chapter, we will build a table to store users' home timelines.

The follow structures in Chapter 5, *Establishing Relationships*, introduced the concept of denormalization, the practice of storing the same piece of data in more than one place in order to optimize read performance. The denormalization we used for follows was fairly mild; however, each follow relationship is stored in exactly two places. For home timelines, we will create a much more aggressively denormalized data structure: a given piece of data will be stored in an arbitrary number of places.

While this highly denormalized structure will be the end result of our work in this chapter, we'll explore several approaches along the way, starting with a fully normalized data structure, proceeding through a partially denormalized approach, and finally settling on a fully denormalized design. We'll discuss the advantages and disadvantages of each, both in terms of implementation complexity and runtime performance. By the end of this chapter, you'll have learned the following:

- How to retrieve data from more than one specific partition
- How to order and paginate in multipartition queries
- How to apply different denormalization strategies to a problem
- How to group multiple write statements into a single operation using logged batches

# A normalized approach

Before we proceed down the path of denormalization, let's first try an approach that requires adding no new tables to our schema. Our goal is to display to a user all the status updates of all the users they follow, the most recent first. So, the simplest approach would be to simply look up the followed users and then retrieve their status updates.

If you've been following along with the code examples so far, you should currently have a single follow relationship in the database, such as `alice` follows `carol`. To make things more interesting, let's also have `alice` follow `dave`:

```
INSERT INTO "user_outbound_follows"
  ("follower_username", "followed_username")
VALUES ('alice', 'dave');

INSERT INTO "user_inbound_follows"
  ("followed_username", "follower_username")
VALUES ('dave', 'alice');
```

Now that `alice` is following a couple of users, we can build a meaningful home timeline for her. Let's have `carol` and `dave` write some updates:

```
INSERT INTO "user_status_updates" ("username", "id", "body")
VALUES ('dave', NOW(), 'dave update one');

INSERT INTO "user_status_updates" ("username", "id", "body")
VALUES ('carol', NOW(), 'carol update one');

INSERT INTO "user_status_updates" ("username", "id", "body")
VALUES ('dave', NOW(), 'dave update two');

INSERT INTO "user_status_updates" ("username", "id", "body")
VALUES ('carol', NOW(), 'carol update two');
```

# Generating the timeline

We now have all the data we need to generate a home timeline for `alice`. First, we require a list of users that `alice` follows:

```
SELECT "followed_username"
FROM "user_outbound_follows"
WHERE "follower_username" = 'alice';
```

This is a straightforward single-partition query, simply looking up all of the rows in the `alice` partition in the `user_outbound_follows` table. We'll get back the usernames of those users whose updates `alice` is interested in:

```
followed_username
-------------------
            carol
             dave

(2 rows)
```

Now we need to retrieve all of the status updates for these users:

```sql
SELECT "id", UNIXTIMESTAMPOF("id"), "body"
FROM "user_status_updates"
WHERE "username" IN ('carol', 'dave');
```

We briefly looked at the `WHERE...IN` syntax in the *Selecting more than one row* section of `Chapter 2`, *The First Table*, where we used it to select multiple specific rows from a table with a single column primary key. Here, we generalize this approach to select rows from multiple specific partitions: in this case, we retrieve all the status updates in the `carol` and `dave` partitions. The result is all of the status updates for both users:

```
 id                                   | UNIXTIMESTAMPOF(id) | body
--------------------------------------+---------------------+------------------
 3a597500-28cf-11e4-8069-5f98e903bf02 |      1408583123024  | carol update one
 3a5a3850-28cf-11e4-8069-5f98e903bf02 |      1408583123029  | carol update two
 3a58d8c0-28cf-11e4-8069-5f98e903bf02 |      1408583123020  | dave update one
 3a59c320-28cf-11e4-8069-5f98e903bf02 |      1408583123026  | dave update two
```

One thing we might notice right away is that, while we have the right status updates in the results, they're not in the right order. This, of course, is because results that comprise multiple partitions are returned in the order of the token of the partition key; as a result, we'll see all status updates of `carol` before we see any of `dave`. In the case where the entire timeline comprises only four status updates, it's entirely reasonable to just sort them on the client side.

# Ordering and pagination

If our service is even slightly successful, a user's timeline is going to contain thousands or tens of thousands of status updates. We will, of course, want to show only a few most recent by default and allow the user to paginate through older ones. Fortunately, Cassandra allows us to use the ORDER BY clause in a query that specifies multiple partitions using the IN keyword; under the hood, Cassandra will perform an ordered merge of the rows from the specified partitions.

Let's assume that we only want to show two status updates per page. Accordingly, we'll add the LIMIT and ORDER BY clauses to our query:

```
SELECT "username", "id", UNIXTIMESTAMPOF("id"), "body"
FROM "user_status_updates"
WHERE "username" IN ('carol', 'dave')
ORDER BY "id" DESC
LIMIT 2;
```

Note that, as always, the column given to ORDER BY is the first clustering column; this remains the only valid argument to ORDER BY.

Just as we hoped, we now receive the results in descending order of creation time, regardless of partition key. This is a powerful feature of Cassandra as it allows us to break out of the narrow constraints of single-partition range queries:

| username | id | UNIXTIMESTAMPOF(id) | body |
|----------|------------------------------------------|---------------------|-----------------|
| carol | 3a5a3850-28cf-11e4-8069-5f98e903bf02 | 1408583123029 | carol update two |
| dave | 3a59c320-28cf-11e4-8069-5f98e903bf02 | 1408583123026 | dave update two |

If we want to retrieve the second page, we can use the same strategy that we used to paginate over slices in a single partition: simply look for the next newest ID values following the ones we've already seen:

```
SELECT "username", "id", UNIXTIMESTAMPOF("id"), "body"
FROM "user_status_updates"
WHERE "username" IN ('carol', 'dave')
AND "id" < 3a59c320-28cf-11e4-8069-5f98e903bf02
ORDER BY "id" DESC
LIMIT 2;
```

In this query, our WHERE clause plays two roles. As earlier, we specify multiple partitions using the IN keyword, but now we also use a range query on id to ensure that we get the second page of results. This is among the most complex WHERE statements that are legal in CQL without resorting to ALLOW FILTERING. As expected, the resulting rows comprise the second page:

| username | id | UNIXTIMESTAMPOF(id) | body |
|---|---|---|---|
| carol | 3a597500-28cf-11e4-8069-5f98e903bf02 | 1408583123024 | carol update one |
| dave | 3a58d8c0-28cf-11e4-8069-5f98e903bf02 | 1408583123020 | dave update one |

# Multiple partitions and read efficiency

In the real world, most users will likely follow dozens or hundreds of other users. In this case, our WHERE...IN clause will specify hundreds of partitions. Remember from Chapter 3, *Organizing Related Data*, that each partition is stored separately by Cassandra; querying hundreds of partitions would require hundreds of random accesses. In fact, Cassandra's official documentation warns us against using WHERE...IN in most circumstances.

> Under most conditions, using IN in the WHERE clause is not recommended. Using IN can degrade performance because usually, many nodes must be queried.

Furthermore, in this particular case, Cassandra has to retrieve one page of rows from each partition, perform an ordered merge, and throw away all but the last handful. For instance, if I follow 100 users and have a page size of 10, Cassandra must retrieve 1,000 rows just to figure out which 10 are the most recent. While this approach technically works, its read performance characteristics aren't going to cut it for a production application. We'll need to explore different strategies.

# Partial denormalization

Our initial approach to home timelines, which used the existing, fully-normalized data structure that we've already built, is technically viable but will perform very poorly at scale. If I follow $F$ users and want a page of size $P$ for my home timeline, Cassandra will need to do the following:

- Query $F$ partitions for $P$ rows, each
- Perform an ordered merge of $FxP$ rows in order to retrieve only the most recent $P$

The most distressing part of this is the fact that both operations grow in complexity proportionally with the number of people I follow. Let's start by trying to fix this.

The basic goal of the home timeline is to show me the most recent status updates that matter to me. Instead of doing all the work to find out what status updates matter to me, based on whom I follow, at read time, let's shift some of the work to write time.

I'll create a table that stores references to status updates that I care about. Whenever someone I follow creates a new status update, I'll add a reference to that update to my home timeline list; this way, when I want to view my home timeline, I'll know exactly what status updates to return.

Let's create our new table:

```
CREATE TABLE "home_status_update_ids" (
  "timeline_username" text,
  "status_update_id" timeuuid,
  "status_update_username" text,
  PRIMARY KEY ("timeline_username", "status_update_id")
)
WITH CLUSTERING ORDER BY ("status_update_id" DESC);
```

Note that there's something subtle going on here with the primary key. In the user_status_updates table, the username column of the author is the partition key, and the timestamp UUID, id, is the clustering column. In order to retrieve a specific row from this table, we need to provide both the username and the id columns.

However, our home_status_update_ids table does not include the author's username in the primary key: the status_update_username column is just a normal data column. This is because the status_update_id column alone, being a UUID, uniquely identifies the status update, even though it is insufficient on its own to retrieve the status update from the database. We store status_update_username as data only so that we know what partition to look at when we go to retrieve the status update.

Now, let's insert some data into our new table. To keep things moving forward, let's ignore the status updates that have already been created; we'll just start using our new timeline structure with new status updates. Let's say `carol` writes a new status update. Now, along with inserting the status update into her user timeline, we'll need to add a reference to it to all her followers' home timelines. So, the first thing we'll need to do is check who follows her:

```
SELECT "follower_username"
FROM "user_inbound_follows"
WHERE "followed_username" = 'carol';
```

We'll find that `carol`'s only follower is `alice`:

```
 follower_username
-------------------
              alice

(1 rows)
```

While this part of the process might seem simple, we should not take it lightly. Recall that Cassandra is optimized for write performance; because of this, we should strive to avoid reading data during write operations, whenever possible. In this case, we are performing a very efficient read operation at write time—retrieving all the rows from a single partition—in order to write a data structure that makes other read operations far more efficient. It's a good trade-off.

Now we will write all of the data we need to for `carol`'s new status update:

```
INSERT INTO "user_status_updates"
("username", "id", "body")
VALUES (
   'carol', 65cd8320-2ad7-11e4-8069-5f98e903bf02,
   'carol update 3');

INSERT INTO "home_status_update_ids"
   ("timeline_username", "status_update_id",
   "status_update_username")
VALUES
   ('alice', 65cd8320-2ad7-11e4-8069-5f98e903bf02, 'carol');
```

One difference from the previous status update creations jumps out: we're specifying the id column explicitly instead of using the NOW() function to generate a timeuuid on the fly. As you'll recall from Chapter 2, *The First Table*, the INSERT statements do not give us any feedback: so, if we were to use NOW(), we wouldn't know the UUID that had just been generated. We could try to find out after the fact by reading the most recent id out of carol's partition in the table, but if another process had concurrently created another status update, we'd get the wrong answer.

We need to know with certainty the id column of the new status update so that we can use it to create a reference to the status update in carol's followers' home timelines. So, instead of using NOW(), we'll generate a UUID in our application. Most languages have perfectly good built-in or third-party libraries for generating UUIDs; in a pinch, you can use a CQL query to do it:

```
SELECT NOW() FROM "user_status_updates" LIMIT 1;
```

Our choice of user_status_updates is arbitrary. We could use any non-empty table here since we're not actually reading any data from the table; rather, we're just exploiting CQL's willingness to generate UUIDs for us, as shown here:

```
NOW()
------------------------------------
aeebe5d0-2ada-11e4-8069-5f98e903bf02
```

Returning to our earlier status update creation statements, let's examine the second one. Here, we're storing a row that contains three pieces of information: username of a user who is interested in this status update, id of the status update, and username of the author of the status update.

To make things more interesting for alice, let's also have dave create a new status update:

```
INSERT INTO "user_status_updates"
  ("username", "id", "body")
VALUES
  ('dave', a05b90b0-2ada-11e4-8069-5f98e903bf02, 'dave update 3');

INSERT INTO "home_status_update_ids"
  ("timeline_username", "status_update_id",    "status_update_username")
VALUES
  ('alice', a05b90b0-2ada-11e4-8069-5f98e903bf02, 'dave');
```

As with `carol`'s status update earlier, we add a reference to the status update to the home timeline of each of `dave`'s followers; in this case, it's only `alice`'s.

# Displaying the home timeline

Now, let's say `alice` wants to view her home timeline. In the `home_status_update_ids` table, we have a partition that contains exactly what we need: references to status updates that `alice` is interested in, in descending order of creation time. So, to know what status updates we want to display to `alice`, we simply perform a range query on her partition:

```
SELECT "status_update_username", "status_update_id"
FROM "home_status_update_ids"
WHERE "timeline_username" = 'alice';
```

Note that we don't need an explicit ORDER BY clause because we created the table with descending clustering order; as long as we're working within a single partition, results will, by default, be returned in the order we want:

```
 status_update_username | status_update_id
------------------------+-----------------------------------
                   dave | a05b90b0-2ada-11e4-8069-5f98e903bf02
                  carol | 65cd8320-2ad7-11e4-8069-5f98e903bf02

(2 rows)
```

So now we know what the `primary` keys of the status updates we want are, but we don't have the actual status updates; those live in the `user_status_updates` table. To actually display `alice`'s home timeline, we need to go to that table to retrieve the status update's content:

```
SELECT * FROM "user_status_updates"
WHERE "username" IN ('dave', 'carol')
AND "id" IN (
  a05b90b0-2ada-11e4-8069-5f98e903bf02,
  65cd8320-2ad7-11e4-8069-5f98e903bf02
);
```

The form that this query takes might be a bit surprising. In reality, we have a collection of compound primary key-pairs consisting of `username` and `id` that we would like to retrieve from the table. However, the semantics of the `WHERE` clause in our query are different: here, we are giving a list of username values and a list of id values, and asking for any row that has any arbitrary pair of the given values as a primary key.

This works in the preceding case because the `id` column, as a UUID, is a globally unique identifier for the row. We only specify the `username` column so that Cassandra knows which partitions to go looking for the rows in; as far as identifying the row goes, the `username` column is redundant information. If our data structure was such that it was possible for rows with different partition key values to have the same clustering column value, a query of the preceding form would be incorrect.

In this case, though, we get the results we're looking for:

```
 username | id                                   | body
----------+--------------------------------------+----------------
     dave | a05b90b0-2ada-11e4-8069-5f98e903bf02 |   dave update 3
    carol | 65cd8320-2ad7-11e4-8069-5f98e903bf02 |  carol update 3

(2 rows)
```

# Read performance and write complexity

Let's now examine the performance characteristics of our new data. In the first query, against the `home_status_update_ids` table, we are performing a range query across a single partition; we know that this is an extremely efficient query and in the form we should strive to always use in our application. The second query, however, accesses several partitions, one for each status update author in the result set. If we're using a page size of ten, we might read updates from as many as ten partitions, although it might be fewer if more than one of the updates comes from the same author.

This is an improvement over our previous approach: the number of partitions that we need to access is no longer proportional to the number of followers a user has; it is only proportional to the page size.

The cost of improved read-time performance characteristics is additional write-time complexity. Now any time a status update is created, the application must determine who follows the author and write a row to the `home_status_update_ids` table for each follower. If the author later gains additional followers, the application might need to go through all of the author's old status updates and add them to the new follower's home timeline.

We also need to ensure that deletions are propagated to the `home_status_update_ids` table. If a status update is deleted, references to it should also be deleted from the home timeline of anyone who follows its author. Let's say that `dave` decides to delete his most recent status update:

```
DELETE FROM "user_status_updates"
WHERE username = 'dave'
AND id = a05b90b0-2ada-11e4-8069-5f98e903bf02;

DELETE FROM "home_status_update_ids"
WHERE timeline_username IN ('alice')
AND status_update_id = a05b90b0-2ada-11e4-8069-5f98e903bf02;
```

In the second query, we use an `IN` query even though there is only a single `timeline_username` in play to demonstrate that this is possible: if `dave` had many followers, we could simply add more usernames to that clause and still accomplish the deletion with a single query.

In general, the `WHERE` clause of a `DELETE` query can take any form that encodes a list of discrete primary key values. Thus, the equality and `IN` operators are allowed; range operators are not. Performing a `DELETE` query without a `WHERE` clause is also not allowed as it also fails to specify discrete primary key values.

# Fully denormalizing the home timeline

The partially denormalized structure we built using the `home_status_update_ids` table certainly improves read-time performance, but we're still not at the sweet spot of querying exactly one partition to display the home timeline. In order to do this, we'll need to take the denormalization one step further.

Instead of storing references to status updates in the home timeline, we'll store actual copies of the status updates. Each user's timeline will contain its own copy of the status updates of all the users they follow. We create the following table:

```
CREATE TABLE "home_status_updates" (
```

```
  "timeline_username" text,
  "status_update_id" timeuuid,
  "status_update_username" text,
  "body" text,
  PRIMARY KEY ("timeline_username", "status_update_id")
) WITH CLUSTERING ORDER BY ("status_update_id" DESC);
```

This table looks very much like the `home_status_update_ids` table, except it contains an additional `body` column. By adding `body`, we now have a table that will hold a copy of all the data in a given status update; if `user_status_updates` had ten columns, we would put all ten columns on `home_status_updates` too, along with a partition key for the user who owns the timeline.

# Creating a status update

Now let's say `carol` and `dave` each creates a new status update. As earlier, we will not attempt to backfill `home_status_updates` with status updates that were written prior to its creation; we'll just propagate new status updates to the `home_status_updates` table:

```
SELECT "followed_username"
FROM "user_inbound_follows"
WHERE "followed_username" = 'carol';

INSERT INTO "user_status_updates"
  ("username", "id", "body")
VALUES
  ('carol',
  cacc7de0-2af9-11e4-8069-5f98e903bf02,
  'carol update 4'
);

INSERT INTO "home_status_updates"
  ("timeline_username", "status_update_id",    "status_update_username",
"body")
VALUES (
  'alice',
  cacc7de0-2af9-11e4-8069-5f98e903bf02,
  'carol',
  'carol update 4'
);

SELECT "followed_username"
FROM "user_inbound_follows"
WHERE "followed_username" = 'dave';
```

```
INSERT INTO "user_status_updates"
  ("username", "id", "body")
VALUES
  ('dave', 16e2f240-2afa-11e4-8069-5f98e903bf02, 'dave update 4');

INSERT INTO "home_status_updates"
  ("timeline_username", "status_update_id",    "status_update_username",
"body")
VALUES (
  'alice',
  16e2f240-2afa-11e4-8069-5f98e903bf02,
  'dave',
  'dave update 4'
);
```

The flow of the write operation looks pretty much the same as the partially denormalized version:

1. Look up the author's followers.
2. Write the status update to the author's user timeline.
3. Write a copy of the status update to each of the followers' home timelines.

The only difference between partial and full denormalization is that, in the final step, we write all the data from the status update to the home timeline, not just the primary key values.

# Displaying the home timeline

Now let's display `alice`'s home timeline. All the work we did at write time has paid off; we can now get all the data we need in a single query:

```
SELECT "status_update_username", "status_update_id", "body"
FROM "home_status_updates"
WHERE "timeline_username" = 'alice';
```

Simple as that, we've got `alice`'s home timeline:

```
 status_update_username | status_update_id                      | body
------------------------+---------------------------------------+----------------
                   dave | 16e2f240-2afa-11e4-8069-5f98e903bf02  |  dave update 4
                  carol | cacc7de0-2af9-11e4-8069-5f98e903bf02  | carol update 4

(2 rows)
```

# Write complexity and data integrity

The amount of work we need to do to write data in the fully normalized strategy is basically equal to what we needed to do with a partially normalized layout. Our storage needs to increase by a bit; now we're storing one full copy of each status update for every follower the author has. However, storage is cheap, and writing data in Cassandra is cheap, so we've managed to make our timeline read pattern far more efficient at a low cost.

One concern in any sort of denormalized scenario is data integrity. At the Cassandra level, the only thing stopping us from adding a status update to the `user_status_updates` table is forgetting to add copies as appropriate to the `home_status_updates` table, or vice versa. Even worse, if a user deletes a status update and we don't properly remove copies from all the `home_status_updates` table, the user's followers might see status updates that they aren't supposed to.

For the most part, the responsibility for maintaining data integrity falls on the application, and there's no magic formula—just well-factored data access logic and lots of tests. However, there is one scenario that is outside the application's control: what if part of the write operation succeeds but another part fails?

In our example, it's possible that, although writing `dave`'s status update to the `user_status_updates` table works fine, the write to the `home_status_updates` table fails because the required nodes are unavailable. By the time the application knows something is wrong, it has already written data to `user_status_updates`, leaving the data in an invalid state.

One approach would be for the application to delete the row from `user_status_updates` if it encounters an error on a subsequent write. However, this sort of manual rollback is error-prone and burdensome, particularly as write operations become more complex.

Fortunately, Cassandra gives us a cleaner way to ensure that write failures don't lead to a breakdown of data integrity. Multiple write statements can be sent in a single batch; Cassandra will guarantee that if any statement in a batch succeeds, all of it will. So, we can perform all the write operations to store dave's status update without worry:

```
BEGIN BATCH
  INSERT INTO "user_status_updates"
    ("username", "id", "body")
  VALUES (
    'dave',
    16e2f240-2afa-11e4-8069-5f98e903bf02,
    'dave update 4'
);

  INSERT INTO "home_status_updates" (
    "timeline_username",
    "status_update_id",
    "status_update_username",
    "body")
  VALUES (
    'alice',
    16e2f240-2afa-11e4-8069-5f98e903bf02,
    'dave',
    'dave update 4'
  );
APPLY BATCH;
```

This operation has only two possible outcomes: either it's successful and rows are written to both user_status_updates and home_status_updates, or it fails and no data is written at all. In either case, our data is consistent.

If you typed the earlier query into cqlsh, you might have noticed that a new prompt did not appear until after APPLY BATCH. This is because even though it contains multiple write statements, a batch must be sent as a single query to Cassandra. This is in contrast to SQL in which it is valid to open a transaction by sending a BEGIN TRANSACTION statement to the database and to close it with a latter statement.

# Batching in Cassandra

In Cassandra, a client can batch multiple statements, which may or may not be related to be executed as a single statement. Earlier, we got a first look at how to use batches in Cassandra. Here, we will dig a bit deeper into the different types of batches and how batches have evolved over time to accommodate more nuanced features, such as atomic batching, batches with custom timestamps, and so on.

Prior to Cassandra 1.2, batches were somewhat resilient. If an update within a batch failed, the coordinator would just hint that particular update. This ensured that all the updates within a batch were eventually committed assuming the coordinator node doesn't go down in between. In the case of the failure scenario where the coordinator node fails mid-batch execution, the client can retry the same batch on a different coordinator. This shouldn't cause any data integrity issues since all the operations within a batch (insert, update, or delete) as well as the entire batch itself are idempotent operations. But if the coordinator and the client fail at the same time, there is no way to recover other than manually crawling through your records and reconciling inconsistencies. Some clients have implemented sophisticated ways such as client-side commit logs to deal with these failure cases, but the server, rather than the client, should handle such cases. So, atomic batches were introduced in Cassandra 1.2.

# Logged batches

Batches are atomic by default, also known as logged batches. Running a batch with logging enabled ensures that if any of the batch succeeds, all of it will.

Atomic batches use a new system table, `batchlog`, defined as follows:

```
CREATE TABLE batchlog (
id uuid PRIMARY KEY,
written_at timestamp,
data blob
);
```

When an atomic batch is written, the serialized batch is first written to the `batchlog` table as a `data blob`. After the rows in the batch have been successfully written (or hinted at), the `batchlog` entry is removed. The batchlog table is node-local, along with the rest of the system keyspace.

# Unlogged batches

There is a performance penalty associated with the batchlog as it is written to two other nodes. If you do not want to incur this penalty, run the batch operation without using the `batchlog` table using the `UNLOGGED` keyword. So, to execute the earlier batch statement as an unlogged batch, you would have to execute the following command:

```
BEGIN UNLOGGED BATCH
    INSERT INTO "user_status_updates"
        ("username", "id", "body")
    VALUES (
        'dave',
        16e2f240-2afa-11e4-8069-5f98e903bf02,
        'dave update 4'
);

    INSERT INTO "home_status_updates" (
        "timeline_username",
        "status_update_id",
        "status_update_username",
        "body")
    VALUES (
        'alice',
        16e2f240-2afa-11e4-8069-5f98e903bf02,
        'dave',
        'dave update 4'
    );
APPLY BATCH;
```

Unlogged batches don't ensure atomicity. Some operations within a batch might fail, while others might succeed.

Note that we mean atomic in the database sense that if any part of the batch succeeds, all of it will. No other guarantees are implied; in particular, there is *no isolation*; other clients will be able to read the first updated rows from the batch while others are in progress. However, updates within a single row are isolated.

# When to use unlogged batches

As we saw earlier, logged batches or atomic batches can be used to keep multiple tables in sync. Unlogged batches can be used when you are making updates to the same partition. For example, you are trying to add multiple status update replies to the `status_update_replies` table for a user on a particular `status_update_id`:

```
BEGIN UNLOGGED BATCH
INSERT INTO "status_update_replies" ("status_update_username",
"status_update_id", "id", "author_username", "body")
VALUES ('alice',
 76e7a4d0-e796-11e3-90ce-5f98e903bf02, NOW(), 'bob',
'Bob Reply1');
INSERT INTO "status_update_replies" ("status_update_username",
"status_update_id", "id", "author_username", "body")
VALUES ('alice', 76e7a4d0-e796-11e3-90ce-5f98e903bf02, NOW(), 'carol',
'Carol Reply1');
APPLY BATCH;
```

# Misuse of BATCH statements

One common anti-pattern when using batches is as follows:

```
BEGIN UNLOGGED BATCH
  INSERT INTO "user_status_updates"
    ("username", "id", "body")
  VALUES (
    'dave',
    NOW(),
    'dave update 5'
);

  INSERT INTO "user_status_updates"
    ("username", "id", "body")
  VALUES (
    'ellen',
    NOW(),
    'ellen update 6'
);
APPLY BATCH;
```

Since the batch update is performed on multiple partitions (dave and ellen), this has serious performance implications. Unlogged batches require the coordinator to do all the work of managing these inserts, and they will make a single node do more work. It's worse if the partition keys are owned by other nodes because then the coordinator node has an extra network hop to manage as well. The data is not delivered in the most efficient path.

Logged batches add a fair amount of work to the coordinator. However, they have an important role in maintaining consistency between tables. When a batch is sent out to a coordinator node, two other nodes are sent batchlogs so that, if that coordinator fails, both the other nodes retry the batch. This obviously puts a fair amount of work on the coordinator node and cluster as a whole. Therefore, the primary use case of a logged batch is when you need to keep tables in sync with one another, and *not* performance.

# Summary

In this chapter, we explored three different approaches to displaying a user's home timeline. The first approach had the advantage of requiring no additional tables in our database; it was fully normalized. The downside was that reading all the data to display a user's home timeline was prohibitively expensive. The next approach, partial denormalization, kept references to the status updates in each user's home timeline and allowed us to avoid the worst performance characteristics of the normalized approach. Partial denormalization did not, however, allow us to get to the point where a home timeline could be displayed with only a single query to a single partition.

By storing a full copy of every status update in the home timeline of every follower of the update's author—a fully denormalized approach—we achieved the ideal read-time access pattern, namely selecting a slice of a single partition in a single table. While read performance increased as we denormalized, write complexity and data integrity concerns also increased. You learned to be vigilant about ensuring that application logic is watertight in keeping denormalized data consistent, and you also learned how to use batches to guarantee that a low-level failure does not leave our data in an inconsistent state. You also learned about the different types of batches available in Cassandra and when to use them.

In the first six chapters, we explored the Cassandra schema design and data access from a high level, focusing on questions such as the following:

- What tables should my application have?
- How should I structure my primary keys?
- How do I retrieve the data I need?
- When does it make sense to store multiple copies of the same data?

In the next few chapters, we will transition away from these questions and begin to explore the full breadth of Cassandra's functionality. You'll learn how to store collections of data in a single column, how to add new columns to an existing table, how to ensure that an INSERT statement doesn't clobber existing data, and quite a bit more.

# 7
# Expanding Your Data Model

In the preceding chapters, we focused largely on the high-level structure of Cassandra tables and particularly on the forms and uses of primary keys. Now we will turn our focus to the data that's stored within tables, exploring advanced techniques to add, change, and remove data.

Previously, we created several tables in the MyStatus application, but so far, we haven't made any changes to those tables' schemas. In this chapter, we'll introduce the `ALTER TABLE` statement, which enables us to add and remove columns from the tables in our `keyspace`.

We'll move on to the `UPDATE` statement, which is used to change the data in existing rows. You'll learn that `INSERT` and `UPDATE` have more in common than our experience with relational databases might lead us to believe, and that `INSERT`, in particular, can have unexpected and undesirable effects if not used carefully. We'll also expand our understanding of the `DELETE` statement, using it to remove data from specific columns in a row rather than deleting the entire row, as we have so far.

We will also take a brief look at the `TRUNCATE` statement, which is used to delete data from a table without deleting the schema. We will also take a look at the `DROP` command, which is used to delete `keyspaces` or tables along with the data, as well as the schema.

Finally, we'll introduce lightweight transactions as a way to ensure data integrity when modifying data. We'll use transactional inserts to make sure that we don't accidentally overwrite a user record when a different user wants the same username, and transactional updates to avoid writing stale data to existing rows. We'll delve into the ways in which Cassandra's lightweight transactions differ from traditional transactions in a relational database.

By the end of this chapter, you'll know the following:

- How to view a `keyspace` schema using `cqlsh`
- How to view a table's schema in `cqlsh`
- How to add and remove columns from an existing table
- How to update data in a row
- How to remove the data from a single column
- How to remove data from a table
- How to delete an entire `keyspace` or table (along with the schema)
- How to ensure that a newly inserted row doesn't conflict with an existing row's key
- How to perform conditional updates to existing rows

# Viewing a keyspace schema

Suppose we lost a local copy of the schema we created and wish to retrieve the schema from Cassandra. In such situations, we can use the `cqlsh` functions to fetch the `keyspace` schema as well as the schema of any particular table. To get a list of `keyspaces` that were created on the local node within Cassandra, we can simply run the following statement:

```
DESCRIBE KEYSPACES;
```

This will return the list of `keyspaces`. This also contains several system `keyspaces`, which are used by Cassandra for internal purposes. As we can see, this will also contain the `my_status` keyspace we created:

```
system_schema  system_auth  system  system_distributed  system_traces  my_status
```

To view the schema of a particular `keyspace`, you can run either of the following statements:

```
DESCRIBE KEYSPACE "my_status";
```

You could also use the following:

```
DESCRIBE "my_status";
```

Both of these commands will return the `keyspace` schema followed by the schemas of all the tables that are present within the `keyspace` schema:

```
CREATE KEYSPACE my_status WITH replication = {'class': 'SimpleStrategy', 'replication_factor': '1'}  AND durable_writes = true;

CREATE TABLE my_status.user_status_updates (
    username text,
    id timeuuid,
    body text,
    PRIMARY KEY (username, id)
) WITH CLUSTERING ORDER BY (id ASC)
```

# Viewing a table schema in cqlsh

In this chapter, we'll be working with the users table, which we haven't had much
interaction with since the early chapters. Before we start making changes to the users table,
it would be helpful to have a reminder of what its schema looks like.

One option would be to simply issue a SELECT statement and look at the row headers;
however, cqlsh gives us a more elegant way to view the schema, namely the DESCRIBE
TABLE statement:

```
DESCRIBE TABLE "users";
```

The output is a CREATE TABLE statement showing the table's schema, as well as all
properties for the table:

```
CREATE TABLE users (
  username text,
  email text,
  encrypted_password blob,
  PRIMARY KEY (username)
) WITH
  bloom_filter_fp_chance=0.010000 AND
  caching='KEYS_ONLY' AND
  comment='' AND
  dclocal_read_repair_chance=0.000000 AND
  gc_grace_seconds=864000 AND
  index_interval=128 AND
  read_repair_chance=0.100000 AND
  replicate_on_write='true' AND
  populate_io_cache_on_flush='false' AND
  default_time_to_live=0 AND
  speculative_retry='99.0PERCENTILE' AND
  memtable_flush_period_in_ms=0 AND
  compaction={'class': 'SizeTieredCompactionStrategy'} AND
  compression={'sstable_compression': 'LZ4Compressor'};
```

The part of the output beginning with WITH tells us the table properties for the users table; in this case, the properties are all set to their default values. We can ignore this part of the output as working with table properties goes beyond the scope of this book.

The important part of the output is at the top, listing the columns in the table and telling us which comprise the primary key. We're now reminded that the users table has the username column as its primary key, and email and encrypted_password are data columns in the table.

> DESCRIBE is not a core CQL command; if you were to try to use it from a language driver, you would see an error stating that it is unrecognized. Instead, it is part of an extension to the CQL language that is provided by cqlsh. A list of all cqlsh extensions to CQL is available at http://www.da tastax.com/documentation/cql/3.3/cql/cql_reference/cqlshComman dsTOC.html.

# Adding columns to tables

Let's say we want to allow our users to enter their location in the profile. To store a user's location, we need a new column in the users table; fortunately, it's perfectly straightforward to add a new column to an existing table:

```
ALTER TABLE "users" ADD "city_state" text;
```

This query instructs Cassandra that we'd like to add a column named city_state, of type text, to the users table. It's identical to the equivalent operation in SQL, although the CQL ALTER TABLE statement is much more constrained in the operations it can perform.

Now let's check our table schema again:

```
DESC TABLE "users";
```

Here, we have used the command DESC, which is a short version of the DESCRIBE command. As we hoped, we've got a city_state column in the schema. I've omitted the table properties for brevity:

```
CREATE TABLE users (
  username text,
  city_state text,
  email text,
  encrypted_password blob,
  PRIMARY KEY (username)
) WITH
```

# Deleting columns

Upon further consideration, we may decide that location is a better column name than city_state. Cassandra does not allow us to rename existing data columns; however, since we haven't put any data in the city_state column yet, we can achieve our goals simply by dropping the city_state column and adding a location column instead:

```
ALTER TABLE "users" DROP "city_state";
ALTER TABLE "users" ADD "location" text;
```

The DROP command within the ALTER TABLE statement looks just like the ADD command, except that we need not specify the column's type—only its name is sufficient. Looking at the output of DESCRIBE again, we've now got the columns set up the way we'd like:

```
CREATE TABLE users (
  username text,
  email text,
  encrypted_password blob,
  location text,
  PRIMARY KEY (username)
) WITH
```

Before we proceed with table operations, let's change the `email` of user `alice` to maintain similarity. Remember, we changed the `email` earlier in `Chapter 2, The First Table`. We can do the same again:

```
INSERT INTO "users"
("username", "email")
VALUES ('alice', 'alice@gmail.com');
```

Now that we've got our expanded schema, we can take a look at the actual contents of the table:

```
SELECT * FROM "users";
```

The output now includes our new `location` column, as shown in the following image:

```
 username | email            | encrypted_password                                 | location
----------+------------------+----------------------------------------------------+----------
      bob |             null | 0x10920941a69549d33aaee6116ed1f47e19b8e713         |     null
     dave |   dave@gmail.com | 0x6d1d90d92bbab0012270536f286d243729690a5b         |     null
    carol |  carol@gmail.com | 0xed3d8299b191b59b7008759a104c10af3db6e63a         |     null
    alice |  alice@gmail.com | 0x8914977ed729792e403da53024c6069a9158b8c4         |     null

(4 rows)
```

Recall from `Chapter 2, The First Table`, that Cassandra does not have the concept of NULL values in the sense that SQL databases do; rather, the `null` displayed by `cqlsh` simply indicates that the rows do not have data in the `location` column.

> For a full account of the ALTER TABLE command, refer to the DataStax CQL documentation at `http://www.datastax.com/documentation/cql/3.3/cql/cql_reference/alter_table_r.html`.
>
> Similar to ALTER TABLE, you can modify materialized views as well. You can find the documentation for ALTER MATERIALIZED VIEW at `https://docs.datastax.com/en/cql/3.3/cql/cql_reference/cqlRefAlterMV.html`.

# Updating the existing rows

Now that we've got a new `location` column, we can add some data to it. Any new user records we create, of course, can have a `location` value, but perhaps some of our existing users would like to input their `location` value too. To do this, we need to be able to update existing rows. The process should, once again, look quite familiar to anyone who is familiar with SQL:

```
UPDATE "users"
SET "location" = 'New York, NY'
WHERE "username" = 'alice';
```

Like the `INSERT` and `DELETE` statements, the `UPDATE` statement does not give us any feedback on the operation. However, we can confirm whether it worked by reading from the `users` table again:

```
SELECT * FROM "users";
```

As we hoped, `alice` now has a location:

```
 username | email           | encrypted_password                                 | location
----------+-----------------+----------------------------------------------------+--------------
      bob |            null | 0x10920941a69549d33aaee6116ed1f47e19b8e713 |         null
     dave |  dave@gmail.com | 0x6d1d90d92bbab0012270536f286d243729690a5b |         null
    carol | carol@gmail.com | 0xed3d8299b191b59b7008759a104c10af3db6e63a |         null
    alice | alice@gmail.com | 0x8914977ed729792e403da53024c6069a9158b8c4 | New York, NY

(4 rows)
```

 A full reference for the `UPDATE` statement can be found in the DataStax CQL documentation at `http://www.datastax.com/documentation/cql /3.3/cql/cql_reference/update_r.html`.

# Updating multiple columns

As in the SQL `UPDATE` statement, we can specify multiple column-value pairs to be updated in a single statement. Let's say `dave` wants to change his e-mail address and also enter a location:

```
UPDATE "users"
SET "email" = 'dave@me.com', "location" = 'San Francisco, CA'
WHERE "username" = 'dave';
```

On checking the table again, we see that both columns have been updated in the `dave` row:

| username | email | encrypted_password | location |
|---|---|---|---|
| bob | null | 0x10920941a69549d33aaee6116ed1f47e19b8e713 | null |
| dave | dave@me.com | 0x6d1d90d92bbab0012270536f286d243729690a5b | San Francisco, CA |
| carol | carol@gmail.com | 0xed3d8299b191b59b7008759a104c10af3db6e63a | null |
| alice | alice@gmail.com | 0x8914977ed729792e403da53024c6069a9158b8c4 | New York, NY |

# Updating multiple rows

As it turns out, `bob` and `carol` both live in `St. Louis, MO`. We could update each of their records individually, but the `UPDATE` statement also supports the same `WHERE...IN` construct that we used previously in the `SELECT` statements, so we can update both of their records in a single query:

```
UPDATE "users"
SET "location" = 'St. Louis, MO'
WHERE "username" IN ('bob', 'carol');
```

Now, on checking the `users` table again, we'll see that the change was applied to both rows:

| username | email | encrypted_password | location |
|---|---|---|---|
| bob | null | 0x10920941a69549d33aaee6116ed1f47e19b8e713 | St. Louis, MO |
| dave | dave@me.com | 0x6d1d90d92bbab0012270536f286d243729690a5b | San Francisco, CA |
| carol | carol@gmail.com | 0xed3d8299b191b59b7008759a104c10af3db6e63a | St. Louis, MO |
| alice | alice@gmail.com | 0x8914977ed729792e403da53024c6069a9158b8c4 | New York, NY |

While the preceding `UPDATE` statement allows us to update rows in a single statement, these updates are not isolated; it is possible that while the update is in progress, another client may see a value in one of the rows but not the other. Writes to Cassandra are always isolated within a single partition, but there is no way to guarantee isolation across partitions.

# Removing a value from a column

Let's say `bob` decides he doesn't want his location on his profile. We'd like to get the `location` column back to the state it was in earlier, which appears as `null` in `cqlsh`, but simply means no data here.

## Missing columns in Cassandra

As we discussed previously, Cassandra doesn't have the concept of `NULL` columns in the SQL sense. Technically, the following statement is not possible in Cassandra:

```
SELECT * FROM "users" WHERE "location" IS NULL;
```

Relational databases typically store a separate bit in each column to indicate whether that column contains a `NULL` value. In Cassandra, on the other hand, all data columns are optional, and only the columns with a value are represented in storage. We can visualize Cassandra rows as maps of key-value pairs, with some keys possibly missing; relational database rows are more like fixed-size lists of columns, where some columns may have a `NULL` value. The following diagram shows how we might visualize the `dave` row in Cassandra and the equivalent row in a relational database:

| Cassandra | | |
|---|---|---|
| **username** | **email** | **encrypted_password** |
| dave | dave@gmail.com | 0x6d1d90d |

| Relational Database | | | |
|---|---|---|---|
| **username** | **email** | **encrypted_password** | **location** |
| dave | dave@gmail.com | 0x6d1d90d | NULL |

# Deleting specific columns

To remove data from a column in Cassandra rather than setting it to `NULL`, we'll want to simply delete it from the column. The syntax for CQL's `DELETE` statement allows us to do just this by specifying one or more specific columns that we want to delete from:

```
DELETE "location"
FROM "users"
WHERE "username" = 'bob';
```

We can now check the `users` table again to confirm that `bob` no longer has a location in his profile:

```
username | email            | encrypted_password                         | location
---------+------------------+--------------------------------------------+------------------
    bob  |             null | 0x10920941a69549d33aaee6116ed1f47e19b8e713 |             null
   dave  |       dave@me.com | 0x6d1d90d92bbab0012270536f286d243729690a5b | San Francisco, CA
  carol  | carol@gmail.com  | 0xed3d8299b191b59b7008759a104c10af3db6e63a |     St. Louis, MO
  alice  | alice@gmail.com  | 0x8914977ed729792e403da53024c6069a9158b8c4 |     New York, NY
```

# Syntactic sugar for deletion

Although Cassandra doesn't have real NULL columns, CQL does provide some syntactic sugar to provide a more familiar interface to remove data from columns. You can, in fact, write UPDATE statements that set values to `null`:

```
UPDATE "users"
SET "location" = NULL
WHERE "username" = 'alice';
```

Note that this is purely syntactic sugar; the preceding statement is precisely the same operation as the following one:

```
DELETE "location"
FROM "users"
WHERE "username" = 'alice';
```

The DELETE form of the statement is more expressive of what we are actually doing—removing a value from a column—but the UPDATE form is more familiar to anyone used to working with SQL. Another advantage of the UPDATE statement is that we can write a statement that simultaneously sets data in some columns and removes data from others:

```
UPDATE "users"
SET "email" = 'carol@hotmail.com', "location" = NULL
WHERE username = 'carol';
```

Checking up on the status of the `users` table, we can see that the `carol` row reflects our latest changes:

| username | email | encrypted_password | location |
|---|---|---|---|
| bob | null | 0x10920941a69549d33aaee6116ed1f47e19b8e713 | null |
| dave | dave@me.com | 0x6d1d90d92bbab0012270536f286d243729690a5b | San Francisco, CA |
| carol | carol@hotmail.com | 0xed3d8299b191b59b7008759a104c10af3db6e63a | null |
| alice | alice@gmail.com | 0x8914977ed729792e403da53024c6069a9158b8c4 | null |

# Deleting table data (TRUNCATE)

There might be situations where data within a table gets corrupted. In such situations, you might want to delete the entirety of the data within a table without deleting the schema and then restore from a previous backup. To perform this, CQL protocol provides the TRUNCATE command. To delete the data from a table, such as the users table, you will have to execute either of the following statements:

```
TRUNCATE "users";
```

You could also use the following:

```
TRUNCATE TABLE "users";
```

# Deleting table/keyspace with schema (DROP)

Suppose that you decided to scrap an entire application that uses a particular keyspace, or replace a particular table with a new table. You might want to delete an entire keyspace (along with the tables) or an entire table along with the schema respectively. To perform these operations, CQL protocol provides the DROP KEYSPACE and DROP TABLE functions:

```
DROP KEYSPACE "my_status";
DROP TABLE "users";
```

Dropping a keyspace schema will delete the data as well as the schema of all the tables within the keyspace.

 The effect of the TRUNCATE and DROP statements is not reversible. Data that has been deleted cannot be recovered. Also, data doesn't get deleted immediately. It gets removed during a compaction or repair process, which we take a look at in the later chapters.

# Inserts, updates, and upserts

So far, we've used the INSERT statements to add new rows to our tables and the UPDATE statements to update information in existing rows. As it turns out, both the INSERT and UPDATE statements can modify existing rows and can create new rows. We took a brief look at how INSERT statements can modify existing data as well in Chapter 2, *The First Table*. We will expand a bit more on this functionality of Cassandra in this section. At their core, we can most accurately think of the INSERT and UPDATE statements as providing different syntax for the same underlying operation, an upsert.

This is quite astonishing for those of us who are used to SQL, in which the INSERT and UPDATE statements are entirely distinct. While there are some situations in which the upsert behavior is quite handy, it can also be a stumbling block, especially for developers who are new to Cassandra. Fortunately, Cassandra offers us ways to ensure that our write operations behave the way we intend; we'll explore these techniques after taking a closer look at upserts.

# Inserts can overwrite existing data

Let's add a fifth user to our application, eve. We'll sign her up with a full complement of profile fields:

```
INSERT INTO "users"
("username", "email", "encrypted_password", "location")
VALUES
('eve', 'eve@gmail.com',
  0x85e36ed9f726295921a4a6f40d95c202c895180c,
  'Washington, D.C.');
```

On checking the users table, we can confirm that eve has the data we intended:

| username | email | encrypted_password | location |
|---------|-------|-------------------|----------|
| bob | null | 0x10920941a69549d33aaee6116ed1f47e19b8e713 | null |
| dave | dave@me.com | 0x6d1d90d92bbab0012270536f286d243729690a5b | San Francisco, CA |
| eve | eve@gmail.com | 0x85e36ed9f726295921a4a6f40d95c202c895180c | Washington, D.C. |
| carol | carol@hotmail.com | 0xed3d8299b191b59b7008759a104c10af3db6e63a | null |
| alice | alice@gmail.com | 0x8914977ed729792e403da53024c6069a9158b8c4 | null |

Now let's imagine that another user, also named eve, would like to use MyStatus. If we naively allow her to choose any username she wants, we will end up attempting to create her username like this:

```
INSERT INTO "users"
("username", "email", "encrypted_password")
VALUES
('eve', 'eve123@hotmail.com',
   0x411ebd49a24f8be2250c527160509264622d7883);
```

Intuitively, we would expect this statement to generate an error because we're trying to insert a row with the `primary` key `eve`, which is already assigned to an existing row. In fact, Cassandra will report no such error, and, much to our horror, we'll find that we've overwritten data from the first `eve`'s profile:

```
username | email              | encrypted_password                         | location
---------+--------------------+--------------------------------------------+-------------------
     bob |               null | 0x10920941a69549d33aaee6116ed1f47e19b8e713 |              null
    dave |        dave@me.com | 0x6d1d90d92bbab0012270536f286d243729690a5b | San Francisco, CA
     eve | eve123@hotmail.com | 0x411ebd49a24f8be2250c527160509264622d7883 | Washington, D.C.
   carol |   carol@hotmail.com | 0xed3d8299b191b59b7008759a104c10af3db6e63a |              null
   alice |    alice@gmail.com | 0x8914977ed729792e403da53024c6069a9158b8c4 |              null
```

Looking at the current state of the `users` table, we can see that the `email` and `encrypted_password` columns from the original `eve` account have been overwritten by the new `eve`. However, the `location` column is untouched; it still shows `Washington, D.C.`, the value from the first `eve` account.

This is because we did not specify a `location` column in the second `INSERT` statement. The `INSERT` statements only touch columns that are listed in the parenthesized list of columns that directly follows the table name. So we can think of our most recent query as saying, set the `email` and `encrypted_password` columns in the row with key `eve` to the specified values.

Clearly we've got a problem. The row at key `eve` now contains a mishmash of information from two different user profiles, and we've lost data from the first `eve`'s profile. How can we prevent this from happening?

# Checking before inserting isn't enough

Our first instinct might simply be to check the `users` table to make sure there isn't already a row with the requested `username` in the table. To keep things concise, we might do something like the following:

```
SELECT "username" FROM "users" WHERE "username" = 'eve' LIMIT 1;
```

This will return a single row containing only the `username` value if the `username` value is taken:

```
 username
----------
      eve

(1  rows)
```

If the username is available, rows eve 1 and eve 2 try to create an account with the username eve at the same time:

1. The character  eve 1 sends a request to our application to create an account.
2. The character  eve 2 sends a request to our application to create an account.
3. The process of creating eve 1's account checks for an existing row with the username eve. It finds that there is none.
4. The process of creating eve 2's account checks for an existing row with the username eve. It also finds that there is none.
5. The process of creating eve 1's account issues an INSERT statement to create a new row with the username eve.
6. The process of creating eve 2's account issues an INSERT statement to create a row with the username eve, overwriting the row created for eve 1.

For the problem to occur, step 4 must happen before step 5; it's important that both processes check the database for an existing row before either writes to the database. It's an improbable scenario in which two users would attempt to sign up with the exact same username at roughly the exact same time, but it's not an impossible one. As our service becomes more popular, we're more and more likely to run across such unlikely events, so we're much better off with a system that guarantees that no new user account will overwrite an existing one.

# Another advantage of UUIDs

As it turns out, the `users` table is the only table in the MyStatus `keyspace` that has this problem. All the other tables use UUIDs in their primary keys; since UUIDs are guaranteed to be globally unique, we simply don't have to worry about what might happen in the case of a primary key collision.

UUIDs are great in the case where the table doesn't have a natural key, as we discussed in `Chapter 2`, *The First Table*. However, using a `UUID` key in the `users` table won't solve the fundamental problem, since we still want to guarantee that usernames are unique. A username collision would be less catastrophic, since at least we wouldn't overwrite data. However, we'd have also forfeited the only structure Cassandra gives us for guaranteeing uniqueness, the primary key. Fortunately, there's a better way.

# Conditional inserts and lightweight transactions

Version 3.1 of CQL introduced new support for **lightweight transactions**, which allow us to modify data only if certain conditions are met. Unlike the application-level integrity checks we discussed earlier, lightweight transactions are safe in concurrent environments. If two processes attempt to conditionally create a row with the same key, lightweight transactions guarantee that only one will succeed.

To perform a conditional insert, we simply add the clause `IF NOT EXISTS` to the end of the `INSERT` statement. Let's start fresh with a new user account, `frank`:

```
INSERT INTO "users"
("username", "email", "encrypted_password", "location")
VALUES
('frank', 'frank@gmail.com',
  0xa71451665e16d8c6e6edfd444c60156efc861432,
  'Los Angeles, CA')
IF NOT EXISTS;
```

When we perform this insert, we'll immediately see something surprising—Cassandra has feedback on the operation:

```
[applied]
----------
    True
```

While normal write operations give no feedback on their outcome, lightweight transactions do give feedback. After all, a conditional insert would only be applied if the row did not exist prior to the write operation; we would like to know what the outcome was. To see how conditional inserts behave with a key collision, we can attempt to insert another user with the username `frank`:

```
INSERT INTO "users"
("username", "email", "encrypted_password")
VALUES
('frank', 'frank123@hotmail.com',
  0xed945334b49ea005967cd4c48ff0493e2d3ff8d3)
IF NOT EXISTS;
```

We'll expect this insert to *not* be applied, since we are performing a conditional `insert` and there is already a row with the username `frank`. Indeed, Cassandra's feedback for us is that the insert did not happen:

| [applied] | username | email | encrypted_password | location |
|---|---|---|---|---|
| False | frank | frank@gmail.com | 0xa71451665e16d8c6e6edfd444c60156efc861432 | Los Angeles, CA |

As with the feedback for a successful application, we see an `[applied]` column, which tells us the outcome of the lightweight transaction. In the case where a key collision prevented it from being applied, Cassandra also helpfully returns the data in the existing row with the key we were trying to write to.

For a detailed account of how lightweight transactions are implemented, refer to the DataStax Cassandra documentation page at `http://www.datas` `tax.com/documentation/cassandra/2.1/cassandra/dml/dml_ltwt_tra` `nsaction_c.html`.

Conditional inserts allow us to protect the data integrity of tables that use a natural primary key that is not globally unique. However, overwriting existing rows isn't the only way Cassandra's `upsert` behavior can get us into trouble.

# Updates can create new rows

The `INSERT` statements aren't the only write operations in CQL that can have unexpected effects. To see how `UPDATE` can take us by surprise, let's update the `gina` row to add a location:

```
UPDATE "users"
SET "location" = 'Houston, TX'
WHERE "username" = 'gina';
```

Wait a second—who's `gina`? So far, we haven't had a user with the username `gina` in our table. We might expect the preceding `UPDATE` statement to have no effect; after all, our `WHERE` statement specifies a row that does not exist.

The contents of the `users` table, however, tell a different story:

```
username | email             | encrypted_password                           | location
---------+-------------------+----------------------------------------------+------------------
     bob |              null | 0x10920941a69549d33aaee6116ed1f47e19b8e713 |              null
    dave |       dave@me.com | 0x6d1d90d92bbab0012270536f286d243729690a5b | San Francisco, CA
    gina |              null |                                            |       Houston, TX
     eve | eve123@hotmail.com | 0x411ebd49a24f8be2250c527160509264622d7883 |  Washington, D.C.
   carol |  carol@hotmail.com | 0xed3d8299b191b59b7008759a104c10af3db6e63a |              null
   frank |    frank@gmail.com | 0xa71451665e16d8c6e6edfd444c60156efc861432 |     Los Angeles, CA
   alice |    alice@gmail.com | 0x8914977ed729792e403da53024c6069a9158b8c4 |              null
```

There is now a row with the primary key `gina`. It turns out that an `UPDATE` statement, just like an `INSERT` statement, is, in fact, an `upsert` operation: If the specified row exists, it will update values in the row, but if it doesn't, a new row will be created.

As it turns out, in their basic forms, the INSERT and UPDATE queries are syntactic variants of the exact same underlying operation. For instance, the following two queries are functionally identical to one another:

```
INSERT INTO "users"
("username", "email", "encrypted_password")
VALUES
('alice', 'alice@gmail.com',
   0x8914977ed729792e403da53024c6069a9158b8c4);

UPDATE "users"
SET "email" = 'alice@gmail.com',
"encrypted_password" =  0x8914977ed729792e403da53024c6069a9158b8c4
WHERE "username" = 'alice';
```

In both cases, the query simply instructs Cassandra to set the email and encrypted_password columns to the given values in the row whose primary key is alice.

INSERT and UPDATE are not entirely redundant; however, each provides certain capabilities that the other does not. For instance, only INSERT supports the IF NOT EXISTS clause that we explored earlier. The UPDATE queries also have distinctive functionality, not the least of which is conditional updates.

# Optimistic locking with conditional updates

As the MyStatus service becomes more popular, we're likely to see organizations beginning to create accounts that are managed by multiple people. Once we have multiple people accessing the same resource at the same time, we need to think about what might go wrong when different people try to make conflicting changes to the same piece of data.

Let's create a new account on behalf of an organization called happycorp. We'll just start with some basic information:

```
INSERT INTO "users"
("username", "email", "encrypted_password")
VALUES
('happycorp', 'media@happycorp.com',
   0x368200fa910c16cc644f3512e63b541c85fa2a3c)
IF NOT EXISTS;
```

We use a conditional update, of course, to ensure that we're not overwriting another row with the same primary key.

Now let's imagine that two members of the happycorp social media team decide to update the location listed in the company's profile on MyStatus at the same time. One of them elects to enter New York, the location of happycorp corporate offices, and the other thinks it would make more sense to list Palo Alto, where the company's main R & D campus is located. Unfortunately, the two employees decide to make this update at the exact same time, so each one sees a blank location field, types a value in, and tries to save it without realizing that they are stomping on each other's work.

A popular solution to this sort of problem is known as **optimistic locking**, which uses a version column to ensure that two simultaneous updates will not conflict with each other. Each time a record is displayed to a user for the purpose of updating it, the application keeps track of what version was displayed (on the web, this might be done using a hidden form field). Changes are saved to the database using a **conditional update**, ensuring that they're only applied if the current version of the database is the same as the version that was initially displayed to the user. As part of the operation, we also update the version itself.

To see how this works, let's first add a version column to the users table. We could do this with a simple integer, incrementing it each time we update a row; however, given Cassandra's excellent support for UUIDs, we might as well use one and get the added advantage of knowing when a column was last updated:

```
ALTER TABLE "users" ADD "version" timeuuid;
```

Now we need to give each existing row a version. This can be done easily enough with a WHERE...IN update query:

```
UPDATE "users"
SET "version" = NOW()
WHERE "username" IN (
  'alice', 'bob', 'carol', 'dave', 'eve', 'frank', 'gina',
  'happycorp'
);
```

This will give every user profile the same initial version UUID, but that's fine; we just need to make sure version numbers are unique over time within a single row.

# Optimistic locking in action

Now it's time to implement actual optimistic locking. When we initially display the profile to the two `happycorp` employees for editing, we'll keep track of the version that we displayed. Then, when the first employee goes to save their update, we'll perform a conditional update to make sure that we're updating the same version that the user thinks we are:

```
UPDATE "users"
SET "location" = 'New York, NY', "version" = NOW()
WHERE "username" = 'happycorp'
IF "version" = ec0c1fb7-321f-11e4-8eeb-5f98e903bf02;
```

The `IF` clause at the end of the query makes this a conditional update, another type of lightweight transaction. You'll notice that, just like conditional inserts, conditional updates give us feedback on whether the update was applied:

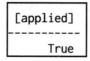

```
[applied]
-----------
       True
```

The key fact about this optimistically locked update is that we do two things with the `version` column. First, we use a conditional update to instruct Cassandra to only perform the update if the version is the same as it was when the user initiated the update. Second, in the same query, we change the `version` column to a new value. Taken together, these two interactions with the `version` column ensure that we cannot unwillingly overwrite changes made by another user to the same row.

On checking the relevant columns in the `users` table, we see that both the `location` and `version` columns have been updated:

```
username   | location     | version
-----------+--------------+------------------------------------
happycorp  | New York, NY | 8a810110-3220-11e4-8eeb-5f98e903bf02
```

Now let's see how our system behaves in the case of concurrent updates by different users. The situation we're most concerned about is the one in which a second user of the system also tries to update the `happycorp` location and initiates the process before the update we just performed is completed. From the perspective of this second updater, the `location` field is blank, and we know that the version we've read is the original version, `ec0c1fb1-321f-11e4-8eeb-5f98e903bf02`.

So, when the second updater tries to save their work, we'll once again make the update conditional on finding the version number we started with:

```
UPDATE "users"
SET "location" = 'Palo Alto, CA', "version" = NOW()
WHERE "username" = 'happycorp'
IF "version" = ec0c1fb7-321f-11e4-8eeb-5f98e903bf02;
```

From a bird's eye view of this process, we know that this update will not be applied, because the process that updated the `location` value to `New York` also changed the `version` column. However, the process that's trying to make the change to `Palo Alto` doesn't need to know this fact; it can simply ask Cassandra to make the update conditional on finding the right version, and Cassandra will do the right thing, no matter what. In this case, we see that the update is indeed not applied:

```
 [applied] | version
-----------+------------------------------------
    False | 8a810110-3220-11e4-8eeb-5f98e903bf02
```

Much like conditional inserts, conditional updates include relevant information from the row in question if the update is not applied. In this case, it tells us what the actual version in the row is—we see that it's the one that we set when we changed the location to New York.

## Optimistic locking and accidental updates

Our optimistic locking strategy also solves another problem: That of accidentally creating or recreating rows when we think we're updating existing rows. By only allowing the update to happen if the `version` column matches what we expect it to, we also implicitly ensure that the row exists. For instance, let's see what happens if we try to modify a nonexistent row with a conditional update:

```
UPDATE "users"
SET "location" = 'Denver, CO', "version" = NOW()
WHERE "username" = 'ivan'
IF "version" = ec0c1fb7-321f-11e4-8eeb-5f98e903bf02;
```

Fortunately, the update is not applied, so we don't unwillingly create a new row for the `ivan` character:

```
[applied]
-----------
    False
```

Since there's no row to take a `version` value, Cassandra omits that information from the feedback, simply telling us that the operation was not applied.

If you're not using optimistic locking, you can get the same effect by adding a `boolean` column that is set to `true` for every row in the table, and performing conditional updates based on the presence of `true` in that column.

# Lightweight transactions and their cost

Lightweight transactions allow us to maintain data integrity in the face of concurrent updates, but they don't do it for free. Because of Cassandra's distributed architecture, it actually goes to great lengths to guarantee that the data is in a certain state before modifying it, as all the machines that store that piece of data need to be in agreement.

Accordingly, there's a performance penalty in using lightweight transactions. As a result, you shouldn't use them in situations where you don't need to.

# When lightweight transactions aren't necessary

As we discussed earlier, concurrent insertions aren't a concern for any table that uses UUIDs that are generated by the application or by Cassandra at row-creation time. Simply using UUIDs guarantees that we'll never have a row key collision.

Another scenario in which we can skip conditional inserts is when we have a globally unique natural key. For instance, if you're building a **Rich Site Summary** (**RSS**) reader, you might identify individual posts by their canonical URL. There's no concern about overwriting one post with another post's data because each row has a key that acts as a global unique identifier. In that case, you may choose to periodically update a local copy of the feed by downloading the latest posts from the RSS server.

It truly doesn't matter whether or not any given post already exists in your local table since you'll only be overwriting data with the same data. This is a situation in which Cassandra's `upsert` behavior allows us to perform very efficient write-without-read updates.

# Summary

In this chapter, we added several new tools to our arsenal of Cassandra knowledge. You learned, among other things, that CQL's `INSERT` and `UPDATE` have behavior that's quite surprising to those who are accustomed to the equivalent operations in SQL, and that, in reality, both queries in CQL are performing an underlying `upsert` operation.

We explored situations in which `upserts` can produce undesirable behavior, particularly in situations where there is concurrent access to the same resource by multiple actors. Also, we introduced lightweight transactions in the form of conditional inserts and conditional updates as a way to mutate Cassandra data with some of the data integrity guarantees that we are used to having in relational databases.

In the next chapter, we will undertake an exploration of data structures within individual columns, exploring several different ways to store and manipulate multiple values within a single column.

# 8
# Collections, Tuples, and User-Defined Types

In the preceding chapters, we focused largely on the high-level structure of Cassandra tables, and particularly on the forms and uses of primary keys. We paid scant attention to data columns, generally defining our table schemas with one or two text columns at most. While this type of scalar data column is the workhorse of Cassandra schemas, they're not the only arrow in Cassandra's quiver. Cassandra offers three different structures that store multiple values in a single column. Collection columns can store an arbitrary number of values, all of the same type. Tuples and user-defined types store a fixed number of values but these values can be of different types. While the fields in a tuple are specified by position, user-defined types give a name to each field; when reading data from a user-defined type, it's possible to retrieve a subset of the fields within the column.

Collections come in three flavors:

- **Lists**: List columns store ordered collections of values and allow duplicates
- **Sets**: Set columns store unordered, unique collections of values
- **Maps**: Map columns store dictionaries of key-value pairs

The true power of collection columns comes from the ability to make discrete modifications to their contents without reading their value first. It is possible, for instance, to push a value on to the end of a list, without reading the list's current contents first. We will see many more such examples in this chapter.

Collection columns are particularly useful in scenarios with multiple processes concurrently writing data to the same target. However, collection columns have their limitations and are not appropriate for every scenario in which they could conceivably be used.

We'll discuss the upsides and downsides of collection columns in this chapter.

Tuples and user-defined types are useful when we want to store a single piece of data that has a complex structure. They are especially powerful when used in combination with other CQL features, particularly secondary indexes. We'll see how tuples and user-defined types can be used to work around one of the major limitations of secondary indexes in Cassandra: the restriction of indexes to a single column.

By the end of this chapter, you'll learn the following:

- How to declare a collection column
- The different types of collection columns
- How to add and remove values from a collection
- How to create secondary indexes on collections
- The limitations of collection columns
- How to declare a tuple column
- How to create a user-defined type
- How to declare a column with a user-defined type
- How tuples and user-defined types facilitate more powerful secondary indexes

# The problem with concurrent updates

Let's add a new feature to our MyStatus application: the user's ability to *star* their friend's status updates to indicate their approval. For each status update, we'll store a list of the users who have starred that status update so that we can display the usernames to the author of the update.

# Serializing the collection

One approach is to simply store the list of users in a text column in some serialized form. JSON is a versatile serialization format for such scenarios, so we'll use that. First, we'll add the column to the `user_status_updates` table, recalling the technique from the *Adding columns to tables* section in `Chapter 7`, *Expanding Your Data Model*:

```
ALTER TABLE "user_status_updates"
ADD "starred_by_users" text;
```

Simple enough. Now let's suppose that `bob` wants to star one of the status updates of `alice`. From the application's standpoint, this means appending `bob` to the list of users who have starred `alice`'s update. First, we'll read the existing list:

```
SELECT "starred_by_users"
FROM "user_status_updates"
WHERE "username" = 'alice'
AND "id" = 76e7a4d0-e796-11e3-90ce-5f98e903bf02;
```

We see that there's currently no value in the `starred_by_users` column, which we can just interpret as an empty list:

```
 starred_by_users
-------------------
              null

(1 rows)
```

Since the column was empty before, we know that the new value of the column should just be a one-element array containing `bob`. We can update the status update row accordingly:

```
UPDATE "user_status_updates"
SET "starred_by_users" = '["bob"]'
WHERE "username" = 'alice'
AND "id" = 76e7a4d0-e796-11e3-90ce-5f98e903bf02;
```

Note that the value in the preceding CQL is simply a string literal containing a JSON representation of the array `["bob"]`. From Cassandra's standpoint, it is simply text.

# Introducing concurrency

While this approach works fine in isolation, we'll run into a problem if more than one process needs to concurrently update the `starred_by_users` column in the same row. Concretely, if two users star a status update at roughly the same time, we'll run into a problem. Consider the following sequence of events:

1. Both `carol` and `dave` want to star `alice`'s status update.
2. Each of their requests is handled by a separate, concurrent process within the MyStatus application.
3. The process of the character `carol` receives the request and begins by reading the current value of the `starred_by_users` column, retrieving `["bob"]`.
4. The process of the character `dave` receives its request and also reads the current value of `starred_by_users`, which is still `["bob"]`.
5. The process of the character `carol` adds her name to the list and writes it back to the row, setting it to `["bob", "carol"]`.
6. The process of the character `dave` adds his name to the list that it read, oblivious to the fact that it has now changed in the database, writing `["bob", "dave"]` to the row.
7. The character `carol` has now lost the star of the status update.

This scenario is similar to the one we explored in `Chapter 7`, *Expanding Your Data Model*, with concurrent updates to the `users` table and, indeed, optimistic locking would be a viable solution. By introducing a version column to the `user_status_updates` table and performing conditional updates, we could ensure that the aforementioned scenario did not result in data loss. In particular, step 6 would result in a conditional update not applied. The process of the character `dave` could then reread the updated value of the `starred_by_users` list, append the username of `dave` to the list, and retry the update.

This solution works, but it's not completely satisfying. In particular, it requires at least one read operation from the database before the row can be updated; in the case of a version conflict, additional reads are required. As we discussed in the previous chapter, conditional writes do carry a performance cost. Finally, this approach adds additional complexity to our application: we need to have code that handles the case of a stale version and retries the operation.

# Collection columns and concurrent updates

Thankfully, Cassandra's collection columns allow us to bypass the entire read-mutate-write process, allowing us to express the exact operation we want to do in CQL without regard to the current value of the column.

## Defining collection columns

Given the limitations of the serialized approach, let's drop our `text` column and replace it with a `collection` column of the same name. Cassandra offers three flavors of collections: lists, sets, and maps. We'll explore all three in this chapter, starting with a set column, which is the most appropriate for our `starred_by_users` column:

```
ALTER TABLE "user_status_updates"
DROP "starred_by_users";

ALTER TABLE "user_status_updates"
ADD "starred_by_users" SET<text>;
```

The last line introduces a new syntax to define a collection column type. The new column that we have created is a collection column using the `SET` data structure; the values it contains have type `text`. Like normal scalar data columns, collection columns must define the type of their values, and any type is permitted.

As the name suggests, set columns contain collections of values with the following properties:

- Values are not in a defined order
- Values are unique within the collection

This is just what we want for our `starred_by_users` column: a user can only star a status update once, and we don't care about the order in which users star an update.

## Reading and writing sets

Before getting into the more powerful operations we can perform on sets, let's start with the basics. Rerunning the scenario we explored earlier, let's naïvely use the exact same approach as we did the first time to record `bob`'s status update. First, we'll read the value of the set:

```
SELECT "starred_by_users"
```

```
FROM "user_status_updates"
WHERE "username" = 'alice'
AND "id" = 76e7a4d0-e796-11e3-90ce-5f98e903bf02;
```

Once again, we see that the value of the set is currently `null`:

```
 starred_by_users
------------------
             null

(1 rows)
```

This means that we can write a one-element set containing the text value `bob` to the `starred_by_users` column in the status update:

```
UPDATE "user_status_updates"
SET "starred_by_users" = {'bob'}
WHERE "username" = 'alice'
AND "id" = 76e7a4d0-e796-11e3-90ce-5f98e903bf02;
```

This query introduces some new syntax, specifically the value we're writing to `starred_by_users`. The value we specify is a set literal, which is simply a comma-delimited list of values surrounded by curly braces. Each collection type has its own literal format.

Let's check the contents of the status update row to see the effect of our update:

```
 username | id                                   | starred_by_users
----------+--------------------------------------+------------------
    alice | 76e7a4d0-e796-11e3-90ce-5f98e903bf02 |          {'bob'}

(1 rows)
```

Observe that `cqlsh` outputs the value of a set column using the same set literal we encountered previously and that our update of the column worked as intended.

# Advanced set manipulation

This access pattern is quite familiar, and we can anticipate that it's just as vulnerable to data loss as the serialized approach we explored previously. The beauty of a collection column is that if we want to add a value to the set, we can write a CQL statement to do just that. Let's pick up our scenario with the addition of `carol`'s star to `alice`'s status update:

```
UPDATE "user_status_updates"
SET "starred_by_users" = "starred_by_users" + {'carol'}
WHERE "username" = 'alice'
AND "id" = 76e7a4d0-e796-11e3-90ce-5f98e903bf02;
```

Note that in the preceding statement, the previous value of the `starred_by_users` column does not appear; in fact, during the entire operation, there is no need for us to read data from the row at all. The `SET` clause in our `UPDATE` statement simply instructs Cassandra to set `starred_by_users` to the union of its current value and the one-element set containing `'carol'`, or, put more simply, to add `'carol'` to the existing set.

Let's check the value of the set after our update:

```
 username | id                                   | starred_by_users
----------+--------------------------------------+------------------
    alice | 76e7a4d0-e796-11e3-90ce-5f98e903bf02 | {'bob', 'carol'}

(1 rows)
```

As we instructed, the set now contains both `'bob'` and `'carol'`, putting it in the exact state we would expect. In a similar fashion, we can now add `'dave'` to the list:

```
UPDATE "user_status_updates"
SET "starred_by_users" = "starred_by_users" + {'dave'}
WHERE "username" = 'alice'
AND "id" = 76e7a4d0-e796-11e3-90ce-5f98e903bf02;
```

Again, on reading the row, we can confirm that the list contains all the usernames that we expected:

```
 username | id                                   | starred_by_users
----------+--------------------------------------+-------------------------
    alice | 76e7a4d0-e796-11e3-90ce-5f98e903bf02 | {'bob', 'carol', 'dave'}

(1 rows)
```

Crucially, this approach is entirely resilient to the concurrent update scenario we explored previously. The problem with concurrent updates in the naive approach was that one process read a value for `starred_by_users`, which subsequently became stale when a different process wrote an updated value to the column. This problem simply can't occur with our strategy of directly adding a new value to the set in CQL, for the simple reason that we never actually read a value that can become stale. The underlying structure of Cassandra sets guarantees that concurrent additions to the set will not result in data loss; the new value is added discretely to the set, not as part of a full overwrite of the set's values.

# Removing values from a set

Let's say that `dave` has second thoughts and no longer wishes to have starred `alice`'s status update. We can just as easily remove his name from the list:

```
UPDATE "user_status_updates"
SET "starred_by_users" = "starred_by_users" - {'dave'}
WHERE "username" = 'alice'
AND "id" = 76e7a4d0-e796-11e3-90ce-5f98e903bf02;
```

This is identical to our previous query, except that we use a – operator to indicate removal rather than a + operator to indicate addition.

# Sets and uniqueness

What happens if we try to add a value to a set that it already contains? Let's try adding `carol` to the list again:

```
UPDATE "user_status_updates"
SET "starred_by_users" = "starred_by_users" + {'carol'}
WHERE "username" = 'alice'
AND "id" = 76e7a4d0-e796-11e3-90ce-5f98e903bf02;
```

Now, let's read the row from the database to see our update's effects:

```
 username | id                                   | starred_by_users
----------+--------------------------------------+------------------
    alice | 76e7a4d0-e796-11e3-90ce-5f98e903bf02 | {'bob', 'carol'}

(1 rows)
```

As the definition of the SET data structure suggests, we see only one instance of `carol` in the set; the column itself guarantees the uniqueness of its values.

## Collections and upserts

In our previous example, we directly set the initial value of the `starred_by_users` column in the status update row, and only then did we perform discrete additions and removals. What happens if we try to add a value to a set that doesn't exist? Let's try it on a different status update, one that has no value in the `starred_by_users` column:

```
UPDATE "user_status_updates"
SET "starred_by_users" = "starred_by_users" + {'alice'}
WHERE username = 'bob'
AND id = 97719c50-e797-11e3-90ce-5f98e903bf02;
```

On running the query, we don't get any error message, which is a promising sign. Let's have a look at the contents of that row now:

```
 username | id                                   | starred_by_users
----------+--------------------------------------+------------------
      bob | 97719c50-e797-11e3-90ce-5f98e903bf02 |        {'alice'}

(1 rows)
```

As it turns out, we now have a one-element set containing the `alice` username. Adding data to a set is, in fact, an `upsert` operation: the collection will be created as part of the operation if it does not already exist. This observation generalizes to all operations on all collection column types; you never need to check for the existence of a collection before adding data to it.

# Using lists for ordered, non-unique values

Let's say that we'd like to allow users to share other user's status updates with their own followers. For each status update, we'll keep track of the shares so that we can display them to the author. Unlike starring a status update, the same user can share the same status update more than once, so we will track shares as discrete events, retaining the order in which they occurred.

A list column fits this task perfectly. Like sets, lists contain collections of values; but unlike sets, values in sets are non-unique and have a stable and defined order.

# Defining a list column

First, let's add a new list column to our `user_status_updates` table:

```
ALTER TABLE "user_status_updates"
ADD "shared_by" LIST<text>;
```

The syntax for defining a list column is identical to that for defining a set column; we simply swap in `LIST` for `SET`.

# Writing a list

As with sets, we can directly specify the entire contents of a list, overwriting the current contents:

```
UPDATE "user_status_updates"
SET "shared_by" = ['bob']
WHERE "username" = 'alice'
AND "id" = 76e7a4d0-e796-11e3-90ce-5f98e903bf02;
```

The literal for a list is just like that of a set, except that square brackets are used instead of curly braces. This, of course, is the syntax for array literals in a wide variety of programming languages.

# Discrete list manipulation

Lists, like sets, allow us to discretely add and remove elements without reading the existing contents or overwriting the entire collection. However, since elements in a list have a defined order, we have many more ways to specify what we'd like to add or remove, and where in the list we'd like it to go.

One of the simplest operations we can do is to append an element to the end of a list. This looks just like adding an element to a set, correcting for the different literal syntax:

```
UPDATE "user_status_updates"
SET "shared_by" = "shared_by" + ['carol']
WHERE "username" = 'alice'
AND "id" = 76e7a4d0-e796-11e3-90ce-5f98e903bf02;
```

This append operation specifically instructs Cassandra to put `carol` at the end of the list. If we want to add a value to the beginning of the list instead, we simply flip the order of the values on the right side of the assignment:

```
UPDATE "user_status_updates"
SET "shared_by" = ['dave'] + "shared_by"
WHERE "username" = 'alice'
AND "id" = 76e7a4d0-e796-11e3-90ce-5f98e903bf02;
```

Let's check the current contents of the list to see the effects of our operations:

```
 username | id                                   | shared_by
----------+--------------------------------------+--------------------------
    alice | 76e7a4d0-e796-11e3-90ce-5f98e903bf02 | ['dave', 'bob', 'carol']

(1 rows)
```

The order of the values of the list is exactly what we asked for: `dave` at the beginning; `carol` at the end, and `bob`, the initial sole occupant of the list, taking up the middle.

# Writing data at a specific index

What if we want to replace the data at a specific place in the list, rather than adding it to the beginning or the end? We can perform a direct assignment to the index we want as follows:

```
UPDATE "user_status_updates"
SET "shared_by"[1] = 'robert'
WHERE "username" = 'alice'
AND "id" = 76e7a4d0-e796-11e3-90ce-5f98e903bf02;
```

Like array indexes in most programming languages, the index for list element assignment is zero, meaning that in the preceding query, we are setting the second element of the list.

List element assignment must reference an index that is within the list's current size. For instance, if we try to assign the fourth element in our current three-element list:

```
UPDATE "user_status_updates"
SET "shared_by"[3] = 'maurice'
WHERE "username" = 'alice'
AND "id" = 76e7a4d0-e796-11e3-90ce-5f98e903bf02;
```

We'll get an out-of-bounds error:

```
Bad Request: List index 3 out of bound, list has size 3
```

 Replacing the value at a given index requires a scan of the list's contents internally, unlike prepending and appending, which can be performed without reading any data. This scan makes replacement more expensive than prepending or appending. However, since the actual write is still performed discretely, the operation is still resilient to concurrent updates.

# Removing elements from the list

Elements can be removed from a list, either by value or by index. Removal by value is identical to set removal, other than the literal format:

```
UPDATE "user_status_updates"
SET "shared_by" = "shared_by" - ['carol']
WHERE "username" = 'alice'
AND "id" = 76e7a4d0-e796-11e3-90ce-5f98e903bf02;
```

This will remove all instances of the 'carol' string from the list. To remove an element from the list by index, we use a special form of the DELETE statement:

```
DELETE "shared_by"[0]
FROM "user_status_updates"
WHERE "username" = 'alice'
AND "id" = 76e7a4d0-e796-11e3-90ce-5f98e903bf02;
```

Recall from the previous chapter that we can remove data from individual columns in a row by specifying the column names directly after the DELETE keyword; in a similar fashion, we can remove data from individual indexes in a list.

Let's check the contents of the list to see the effects of our deletions:

```
 username | id                                   | shared_by
----------+--------------------------------------+------------
    alice | 76e7a4d0-e796-11e3-90ce-5f98e903bf02 | ['robert']

(1 rows)
```

What we've got left is a one-element list. The first deletion, by value, removed `carol` as the last element; the second deletion, by index, removed `david` as the first element. Note that in both cases, the element in question was completely removed from the list, making the list one element shorter.

 Like writing an element at a specific index, both approaches to remove data from a list require a scan of the list's contents before updating them. Removal of elements from lists is thus slower than other collection manipulation operations and should be avoided in performance-sensitive code paths.

# Using maps to store key-value pairs

The third and final collection type offered by Cassandra is the map, which stores key-value pairs. Keys are unique and unordered, like the elements of a set.

Suppose we'd like to keep track of our users' identities on other social networks. We could create a column for each network, but that would require changing the schema each time we discovered a new network that we want to track, and would also potentially result in a large number of columns in the `users` table just to keep track of a given user's identity.

Instead, let's create a map column that maps the name of a social network to the numeric ID of the user on that network:

```
ALTER TABLE "users"
ADD social_identities MAP<text,bigint>;
```

This definition looks a bit different from the earlier ones in this chapter since we're now specifying a pair of types rather than just one. Maps do not require their keys and values to be of the same type, so each is specified individually. The first type given is the key type, and the second is the value type. So our keys—the names of social networks—are strings and our values—IDs on those networks—are long integers.

# Writing a map

Like sets and lists, maps have a literal syntax that allows you to directly set the entire contents of a column:

```
UPDATE "users"
SET "social_identities" = {'twitter': 353637}
WHERE "username" = 'alice';
```

The literal syntax for a map separates keys and values with a colon and optional whitespace, delimits key-value pairs with commas, and encloses the whole thing in curly braces. Both keys and values themselves are written in the literal format for their type.

# Updating discrete values in a map

When we allow a user to link up to a new social network, we'd like to be able to add their ID to the `social_identities` collection without any regard to its current contents. To do so, we use a syntax similar to that of element replacement in a list:

```
UPDATE "users"
SET "social_identities"['instagram'] = 9839025,
    "social_identities"['yo'] = 25
WHERE "username" = 'alice';
```

It's also perfectly valid to overwrite a value at an existing key; since keys are unique, the previous value will be replaced with the given one:

```
UPDATE "users"
SET "social_identities"['twitter'] = 2725634
WHERE "username" = 'alice';
```

Checking the value of the map in the `alice` row, we can confirm that the Twitter ID is the most recently written one, along with the Instagram and Yo values:

```
 username | social_identities
----------+----------------------------------------------------------
    alice | {'instagram': 9839025, 'twitter': 2725634, 'yo': 25}

(1 rows)
```

Note that though the syntax for a map update looks like list replacement, updating a key-value pair in a map does not carry the performance penalty that replacing a list item does.

# Removing values from maps

Continuing the parallels, we can remove a value from a map using the `DELETE` statement, in a way similar to removing items from a list by index:

```
DELETE "social_identities"['instagram']
FROM "users"
WHERE "username" = 'alice';
```

On checking the table again, we can see that the Instagram key-value pair has been removed:

```
username | social_identities
----------+---------------------------------
   alice | {'twitter': 2725634, 'yo': 25}

(1 rows)
```

> For further reference on the uses of CQL collections, refer to the DataStax CQL documentation at http://www.datastax.com/documentation/cql/3.1/cql/cql_using/use_collections_c.html.
> Collection manipulation operations are documented with the UPDATE statement at http://www.datastax.com/documentation/cql/3.3/cql/cql_reference/update_r.html and the DELETE statement at http://www.datastax.com/documentation/cql/3.3/cql/cql_reference/delete_r.html.
> Further information can be found in the official Apache CQL documentation at http://cassandra.apache.org/doc/old/CQL-3.0.html#collections.

# Collections in inserts

So far, all the examples we saw of collection manipulation have used the UPDATE and DELETE statements. It is possible to write the full value of a collection in an INSERT statement as well, by simply providing a literal representation of the collection's contents:

```
INSERT INTO "users" (
  "username", "email", "encrypted_password",
  "social_identities", "version"
) VALUES (
  'ivan',
  'ivan@gmail.com',
  0x48acb738ece5780f37b626a0cb64928b,
  {'twitter': 875958, 'instagram': 109550},
  NOW() qq
);
```

The INSERT statement does not, however, support discrete updates. As we explored in the previous chapter, INSERT and UPDATE are, at their core, different ways of expressing the same operation. However, in the context of collection manipulation, as with partial writes, the two statements have different capabilities.

# Collections and secondary indexes

Let's say we'd like to get a list of all of the status updates that alice has starred; we can display this as part of her user profile. In order to do this, we'd like to be able to look up all the rows in the user_status_updates table, where the starred_by_users column contains the value alice. This is similar to the use case for a secondary index that we explored in the *Using secondary indexes to avoid denormalization* section of Chapter 5, *Establishing Relationships*, except that in this case, we'd like to be able to perform a lookup based on a single value within a collection column.

Fortunately, it is entirely valid to put a secondary index on a collection column. The syntax for this is identical to putting an index on any other column:

```
CREATE INDEX ON "user_status_updates" ("starred_by_users");
```

So far so good.

Now, we'll introduce the CONTAINS operator, which can be used to look up rows by a value in a collection column:

```
SELECT * FROM "user_status_updates"
WHERE "starred_by_users" CONTAINS 'alice';
```

The WHERE...CONTAINS clause will restrict results to those rows whose starred_by_users set contains the exact value alice. In this case, we'll receive a single result:

```
 username | id                                   | body                    | shared_by | starred_by_users
----------+--------------------------------------+-------------------------+-----------+------------------
      bob | 97719c50-e797-11e3-90ce-5f98e903bf02 | Eating a tasty sandwich.|      null |        {'alice'}

(1 rows)
```

Creating secondary indexes on collections is a powerful tool for relating data; now we can model many-to-many relationships using a single, normalized data structure. In this case, the many-to-many relationship is between users and status updates: a user can star many status updates, and a status update can be starred by many users.

It's worth re-emphasizing the warning in the *Limitations of secondary indexes* section of `Chapter 5`, *Establishing Relationships*. In particular, lookup by a secondary index on a collection column has the same performance characteristics as lookup by a secondary index on a scalar column. As always, it's best to avoid using secondary index lookup for the core access patterns in our applications. In this case, our secondary index enables us to answer the question, *Which status updates has a given user starred?* Since this is not a core feature of the MyStatus application, it's a good use case for secondary indexes.

# Secondary indexes on map columns

We just created a secondary index on a set column, which allows us to retrieve rows that contain a given value in that set. Secondary indexes on list columns work in precisely the same way. However, map columns have both keys and values, so it's not immediately obvious what data populates the index.

By default, a secondary index on a map will index the values in the map; the `CONTAINS` keyword similarly filters for map values. However, it is possible to create an index on map keys as well and then select rows with a given key in a map column.

Let's say we'd like to look up users for whom we have an associated Twitter identity. Recall that in the `social_identities` column of the `users` table, the map keys are the names of social networks, and the map values are user IDs from those networks. So, we'll create an index on the keys of the `social_identities` map:

```
CREATE INDEX ON "users" (KEYS("social_identities"));
```

Note the use of the `KEYS` operator to indicate that we are creating an index on the map's keys; had we omitted this operator, we would have created an index on the map's values.

Now we can look up all users who have an associated Twitter identity, using the `CONTAINS KEY` operator:

```
SELECT "username", "social_identities"
FROM users
WHERE "social_identities" CONTAINS KEY 'twitter';
```

The WHERE...CONTAINS KEY clause works exactly the same as WHERE...CONTAINS, except that we are looking up rows that contain the given key in the specified map column. In this case, we get back the two rows with the twitter key in the social_identities map:

```
 username | social_identities
----------+-----------------------------------------
     ivan | {'instagram': 109550, 'twitter': 875958}
    alice |              {'twitter': 2725634, 'yo': 25}

(2 rows)
```

# The limitations of collections

As we saw, collection columns are a useful and versatile feature of CQL. In fact, we might suppose that collections would be a good way to model data we've modeled in other ways in previous chapters. For instance, why not model a user's status updates as a list of text values in the users table?

As it turns out, collection columns do have some limitations that circumscribe the cases in which they're the best solution. We'll explore the major limitations now.

# Reading discrete values from collections

The most powerful feature of CQL collections is the ability to write discrete values to a collection. It's possible to append a single value to a list, update a single key-value pair in a map, remove a specific value from a set, and so on.

At read time, however, there is no special support for reading discrete values. For instance, we might want to be able to do something like the following to read a specific element from a list column:

```
SELECT "shared_by"[2]
FROM "user_status_updates"
WHERE "username" = 'alice'
AND "id" = 76e7a4d0-e796-11e3-90ce-5f98e903bf02;
```

Or we might like to read the value at a specific key within a map column:

```
SELECT "social_identities"['twitter']
FROM "users"
WHERE "username" = 'alice';
```

However, both queries will result in an error; partial reads of collection columns are not possible in CQL. The only way to retrieve data from a collection is to read the collection in its entirety; for this reason, it's generally impractical to store large, unbounded datasets within a collection column. Were we to store status updates in a collection column in the users table, we would need to read all of a user's status updates whenever we wanted to display any status update.

## Collection size limit

Lack of support for partial reads is one reason to keep collections fairly small; another is that there is a built-in size limit for collections that Cassandra can store. In particular, any given collection can contain no more than 64 KB of data. Nothing will prevent you from inserting more than 64 KB of data into a collection, but when you try to read the collection back, the result will be truncated at 64 KB, resulting in data loss.

> Of course, a collection that large would be quite unwieldy to work with, so you should stick with collections that are far smaller than that threshold.

In general, data that can be expected to grow in an unbounded fashion is inappropriate for collection columns; stick with datasets that you expect to stay fairly small.

## Reading a collection column from multiple rows

Suppose we'd like to retrieve a handful of status updates from the database and display information about them, including who starred them. Naively, we might expect to be able to perform a query of this form:

```
SELECT * FROM "user_status_updates"
WHERE "username" = 'alice'
AND "id" IN (
  3f9b5f00-e8f7-11e3-9211-5f98e903bf02,
  3f9b5f00-e8f7-11e3-9211-5f98e903bf02
);
```

However, if we perform this query, we'll see an error:

```
InvalidRequest: code=2200 [Invalid query] message="Cannot restrict clustering columns by IN relations when a collection is selecte
d by the query"
```

One limitation of Cassandra collections is that you cannot read collections when selecting multiple rows using a `WHERE...IN` clause. Once you have collection columns in your table, you must explicitly select only non collection columns when using `WHERE...IN`. On the other hand, it's entirely legal to read collection columns when retrieving multiple rows via a range of clustering columns:

```
SELECT * FROM "user_status_updates"
WHERE "username" = 'alice'
ORDER BY "id" ASC
LIMIT 2;
```

This query completes successfully and displays the data from the collection columns:

```
 username | id                                   | body               | shared_by | starred_by_users
----------+--------------------------------------+--------------------+-----------+------------------
    alice | 76e7a4d0-e796-11e3-90ce-5f98e903bf02 | Learning Cassandra!| ['robert']| {'bob', 'carol'}
    alice | 3f9b5f00-e8f7-11e3-9211-5f98e903bf02 |     Alice Update 1 |      null |             null

(2 rows)
```

# Unable to reuse collection names

A limitation of using collections is that you cannot reuse the name used for a collection column with another collection type. Let's try to drop a collection column and recreate it with a different collection type (drop all depending indexes before dropping the column):

```
DROP INDEX user_social_identities_idx;
ALTER TABLE "users" DROP social_identities;

ALTER TABLE "users" ADD social_identities set<text>;
```

You will get an error:

```
InvalidRequest: code=2200 [Invalid query] message="Cannot add a collection with the name social_identities because a collection with the same n
ame and a different type (map<text, bigint>) has already been used in the past"
```

# Performance of collection operations

Most collection operations do not involve Cassandra reading data internally; they are purely write-without-reading, which, we recall, is the most efficient pattern for Cassandra data manipulation. Lists, however, are a partial exception to this rule, in three cases, as follows:

- Writing an element at a specific index
- Removing an element at a specific index
- Removing all occurrences of a given value

These three operations do require Cassandra to read the full list before manipulating it and are, therefore, slower than other collection manipulations. It's best to avoid these three operations in performance-sensitive code.

All other collection updates are entirely write-without-reading and can thus be performed very efficiently. In Appendix A, *Peeking under the Hood*, we will take a closer look at exactly how collections are stored and updated.

# Working with tuples

We saw that collections are a versatile tool for working with multiple values in a single column. One limitation of collections, however, is that all elements of a collection must be of the same type. If we want to store values of different types in the same collection, we can instead turn to tuples.

Unlike collections, which can store an arbitrary number of elements, a tuple column stores a fixed number of elements, each of which has a predefined type. So, while we gain the flexibility to store elements of different types in the same column, we give up flexibility in the number of elements stored.

## Creating a tuple column

Let's say we'd like to allow users to add some information about their education to their profile. In particular, users should be able to enter where they went to university and what year they graduated.

There are two distinct pieces of information here: school name and graduation year. However, the two are really two components of a single piece of information. It would make no sense, for instance, to store a graduation year but not a school name. For this reason, education is a good candidate for using a tuple type. The syntax for creating a tuple column is similar to that for creating a collection column: we specify both the fact that we would like to use a tuple type and the individual types of each component of the tuple:

```
ALTER TABLE "users"
ADD "education" frozen <tuple<text, int>>;
```

This statement introduces two new CQL keywords, `frozen` and `tuple`. Working from the inside out, the `tuple` keyword takes one or more type arguments, separated by commas; each type is applied to a component of the tuple. Order matters here: our `education` tuple has two components, the first of which contains `text`, and the second of which contains an `int`.

The `frozen` keyword means that the `education` column will be stored as a single, indivisible unit. Practically, this means that we cannot insert, change, or remove data in an individual component of the tuple; whenever we write to this column, we write all components together. This stands in contrast to the discrete element modifications we can perform on collection columns.

In earlier versions of Cassandra 2.1, tuple columns had to be declared frozen. Support for nonfrozen tuple columns that would allow discrete modification of individual tuple components was introduced starting Cassandra 2.2.

A tuple type declaration, such as `frozen <tuple<text, int>>`, can be used anywhere a primitive type such as ASCII or UUID is valid. You can create collections of tuples, nest tuples within tuples, or even use tuples as a primary-key column.

For more on tuples, refer to the DataStax CQL documentation at http://www.datastax.com/documentation/cql/3.3/cql/cql_reference/tupleType.html.

If you are using Cassandra 2.2 or later, you can remove the previously created tuple column with the frozen keyword and create a tuple without the frozen keyword:

```
ALTER TABLE "users"
DROP "education";

ALTER TABLE "users"
ADD "education" tuple<text, int>;
```

# Writing to tuples

To write data to a tuple column, we provide values for all of the tuple components, in order, separated by commas and grouped by parentheses:

```
UPDATE "users"
SET "education" = ('Big Data University', 2003)
WHERE "username" = 'alice';
```

When we read alice's user record back, cqlsh displays tuple data using the same format:

```
 username | education
----------+-------------------------------
    alice | ('Big Data University', 2003)

(1 rows)
```

If we wish to populate some of the components of a tuple but leave others empty, we can use the null keyword:

```
UPDATE "users"
SET "education" = ('Cassandra College', null)
WHERE "username" = 'bob';
```

As a shorthand, we can omit the last value or values when writing a tuple, as long as we specify at least the first value:

```
UPDATE "users"
SET "education" = ('BDU')
WHERE "username" = 'alice';
```

Note, however, that any components that we omit will be assigned `null` values. Let's take a look at the `alice` and `bob` rows now:

```
username | education
---------+--------------------------------
   alice |                  ('BDU', None)
     bob | ('Cassandra College', None)

(2 rows)
```

Even though we did not explicitly provide a value for the second component of `alice`'s education, the previous value of `2003` was overwritten with a `null` value by our last update. This observation serves to emphasize the `frozen` nature of tuples: any time we update any part of a tuple, we update the entire thing.

Before we move on, let's restore `alice`'s education column to its previous state:

```
UPDATE "users"
SET "education" = ('Big Data University', 2003)
WHERE "username" = 'alice';
```

# Indexing tuples

In the previous section, we observed that it would not make much sense for a user to have a graduation year without also naming an educational institution; this provided a rather abstract motivation for grouping those two pieces of information together in a single column. A more practical motivation is the fact that, like any other column, tuples can be indexed.

Let's put an index on our education column; the syntax is no different from creating an index on any other column:

```
CREATE INDEX ON "users" ("education");
```

Armed with this index, we can now perform efficient lookup of user records based on their educational institution and year of graduation:

```
SELECT "username", "education" FROM users
WHERE "education" = ('Big Data University', 2003);
```

As we would hope, the query produces `alice`'s record:

```
username | education
---------+----------------------------
   alice | ('Big Data University', 2003)

(1 rows)
```

The ability to index tuples provides an important workaround to a constraint we discussed in the section *Limitations of secondary indexes* of Chapter 5, *Establishing Relationships*. As you learned in that chapter, a secondary index can only be applied to a single column. If, for instance, we had separate `school_name` and `graduation_year` columns, it would be impossible to create an index that allowed us to efficiently look up records with a given combination of values in these two columns. Using a tuple, we can place both values in a single column and index that column, giving us much the same effect as a multicolumn index.

# User-defined types

Using a tuple column to group educational information into a single column has several advantages, but there's also something missing. The `education` column comprises two components: the first, a string, is the name of an educational institution, and the second, an integer, is a graduation year. As the developers of the MyStatus application, we know what the two components of the tuple represent; however, this knowledge is not made explicit anywhere in the database definition.

To solve this problem, we can instead use a user-defined type. User-defined types are very similar to tuples, except that each component has a name. This makes it easier for application developers to easily infer the intent of a user-defined type. As we'll see shortly, user-defined types offer a couple of other advantages over tuples.

# Creating a user-defined type

Whereas tuples are specified ad hoc when declaring the type for a column, user-defined types are defined separately and then referred to by name in column definitions. Let's make a user-defined type that we can use for our education column:

```
CREATE TYPE "education_information" (
  "school_name" text,
  "graduation_year" int
);
```

Just like the tuple, we declared for our education column, this user-defined type contains two fields: a string containing the name of an educational institution, and an integer containing a year of graduation. Unlike the tuple, the type is declared independently of any particular table or column; it is a first-class entity within the my_status keyspace. This is advantageous when we want to reuse a user-defined type across multiple columns in our keyspace.

> For reference on user-defined types, refer to the DataStax CQL documentation at http://www.datastax.com/documentation/cql/3.3/cql/cql_reference/cqlRefUDType.html.

# Assigning a user-defined type to a column

Since the education_information type is designed to play the same role as the tuple used in our existing education column, let's drop the tuple column and replace it with the more semantic user-defined type:

```
ALTER TABLE "users" DROP "education";
```

This query will initially fail with the following error:

```
InvalidRequest: code=2200 [Invalid query] message="Cannot drop column ColumnDefinition{name=education, type=org.apache.cassandra.d
b.marshal.TupleType(org.apache.cassandra.db.marshal.UTF8Type,org.apache.cassandra.db.marshal.Int32Type), kind=REGULAR, position=-1
} because it has dependent secondary indexes (users_education_idx)"
```

Since the column "education" has a secondary index on it, we would have to delete the index in order to delete the column itself:

```
DROP INDEX "users_education_idx";
```

After deleting the secondary index, try deleting the column again:

```
ALTER TABLE "users"
ADD "education" frozen <"education_information">;
```

Observe that we must use the `frozen` keyword when creating columns with user-defined types unlike tuples. This makes explicit the fact that an `education_information` value is unitary despite having an internal structure comprising multiple fields.

# Adding data to a user-defined column

The syntax for a user-defined type literal is similar to that of a map literal, except that the keys are identifiers rather than literal values. For instance, we can re-add `alice`'s education information into our new column as follows:

```
UPDATE "users"
SET "education" = {
  "school_name": 'Big Data University',
  "graduation_year": 2003
}
WHERE "username" = 'alice';
```

Now we can observe that the `education` information is present in `alice`'s profile:

```
username | education
---------+-------------------------------------------------------------
   alice | {school_name: 'Big Data University', graduation_year: 2003}

(1 rows)
```

# Indexing and querying user-defined types

Like tuple columns, columns with user-defined types can be indexed and queried. Let's add an index to our new education column:

```
CREATE INDEX ON "users" ("education");
```

Now we can query for a given value of `education` keeping in mind that just as with a tuple, we must specify the full value of the user-defined type, with all fields:

```
SELECT "username", "education" FROM "users"
WHERE "education" = {
```

```
    "school_name": 'Big Data University',
    "graduation_year": 2003
};
```

As expected, the result consists of the `alice` row, which contains the exact value we specified in her `education` column:

```
 username | education
----------+-----------------------------------------------------------
    alice | {school_name: 'Big Data University', graduation_year: 2003}

(1 rows)
```

# Partial selection of user-defined types

In some situations, we might only be interested in which school `alice` went to, but not her year of graduation. In this case, we would like to be able to perform a query that returns precisely the information we're interested in, without wasting network bandwidth on irrelevant data. Fortunately, user-defined types have this capability.

In order to do this, we simply use a dot operator to specify a single field within a user-defined type that we would like to return. For instance, to retrieve only the `school_name` field from the `alice education` field, we can perform the following query:

```
SELECT "username", "education"."school_name"
FROM "users"
WHERE "username" = 'alice';
```

Now, the school name is presented as its own column in the results:

```
 username | education.school_name
----------+-----------------------
    alice |    Big Data University

(1 rows)
```

Note that internally, a user-defined type is stored as a single, indivisible entity; in order to return a partial value for a user-defined type, Cassandra must, under the hood, deserialize the entire value and then extract the field we requested. The advantage here is merely that of avoiding the network bandwidth of transferring extraneous fields within the user-defined type.

# Choosing between tuples and user-defined types

As we saw, tuples and user-defined types have a lot in common. In both structures, a column contains a fixed, predefined set of fields, each of which can have its own type. Both structures are stored as `frozen`, meaning that Cassandra cannot perform discrete operations on their internal components. Both can be indexed and used in the `WHERE` clause of a query. So how do we decide which to use?

In most cases, a user-defined type is a better option. User-defined types give names to their fields, making it easier for application developers to reason about their usage. Also, user-defined types can be partially selected in queries, tuples cannot.

The only reason to use a tuple is convenience: a tuple does not need to be defined separately from its use in a column definition. So, for quick prototyping of schema structures, a tuple can be a better option. However, for a schema that's going into production, a user-defined type is nearly always going to be the right choice.

# Nested collections

Suppose that we wish store a set of phone numbers for a user each identified by a category of phone type, such as home phone or office phone. We can do this by using a map where the key is phone type and value can be a set of phone numbers, assuming there are multiple phone numbers of each type. This is an example of nested collection where we are using a set as value within a map. Let us try to create the collection:

```
ALTER TABLE "users"
ADD "telephone_numbers" map<text, set<text>>;
```

You will get an error saying non-frozen collections are not allowed inside collections:

```
InvalidRequest: code=2200 [Invalid query] message="Non-frozen collections are not allowed inside collections: map<text, set<text>>"
```

Cassandra lets us use nested collection types only if we use the `frozen` collections nested within the `frozen` or non-frozen collections. This means we cannot update individual values of the `frozen` collection. To create the preceding collection, use this:

```
ALTER TABLE "users"
ADD "telephone_numbers" map<text, frozen<set<text>>>;
```

Now let's add some `home` as well as office phone numbers to the user `alice`:

```
UPDATE "users"
SET "telephone_numbers"['home'] = {'123456789', '123789456'}
WHERE "username" = 'alice';

UPDATE "users"
SET "telephone_numbers"['office'] = {'123654789', '123987456'}
WHERE "username" = 'alice';
```

Let's take a look at `alice`'s row now; you will notice that the nested collection has been added:

```
 username | telephone_numbers
----------+-------------------------------------------------------------------
    alice | {'home': {'123456789', '123789456'}, 'office': {'123654789', '123987456'}}
```

# Nested tuples/UDTs

We have seen that we can use the `frozen` collections nested within other collections. Similarly, we can also use tuples nested within a tuple (no need to be frozen).

For example, `column_name` tuple `<int, tuple <int, text>>`.

We can also use tuples and UDTs within other generic collections such as set, list, and map albeit they have to be frozen. Suppose that we are trying to store the education history of users. We can do so by creating a set of the user-defined type `"education_information"`. We can create the set like this:

```
ALTER TABLE "users"
ADD "education_history" set<frozen<"education_information">>;
```

Let's try adding some education history for the user `'alice'`:

```
UPDATE "users"
SET "education_history" = {{
```

```
   "school_name": 'Big Data University',
   "graduation_year": 2003
},{
   "school_name": 'Cassandra College',
   "graduation_year": 2005
}}
WHERE "username" = 'alice';
```

Upon taking a look at the field of the row for user `'alice'`, you will see that nesting a UDT within a collection column works:

```
username | education_history
---------+------------------------------------------------------------------------------------------------------------------------
   alice | {{school_name: 'Big Data University', graduation_year: 2003}, {school_name: 'Cassandra College', graduation_year: 2005}}
```

# Comparing data structures

We've now seen five different data structures that allow us to store multiple values within a single field. Each data structure has certain advantages and disadvantages, and each is best suited to particular use cases. In the following table, we summarize the important features of each of the data structures from this chapter:

|  | Set | List | Map | Tuple | User-defined Type |
|---|---|---|---|---|---|
| **Size** | Flexible | Flexible | Flexible | Fixed | Fixed |
| **Discrete updates** | Yes | Yes | Yes | No | No |
| **Partial Selection** | No | No | No | No | Yes |
| **Name-value pairs** | No | No | Yes | No | Yes |
| **Multiple Types** | No | No | Keys and Values | Yes | Yes |
| **Index** | Individual elements | Individual elements | Individual elements | Entire value | Entire value |
| **Can be used as primary key** | No | No | No | Yes | Yes |

# Summary

Collection columns are a powerful feature of CQL that allow us to store multiple values in a single column. Most importantly, it's possible to discretely update single values in a collection without reading the collection's current contents or fully providing the new contents of the collection.

This capability is particularly useful when multiple processes might need to concurrently modify a collection. By avoiding the need to read and then fully overwrite a collection's contents, we avoid situations in which concurrent updates can lead to data loss and can support concurrent updates without resorting to optimistic locking.

Collections are best suited to datasets that are small and bounded. This is both because there is a hard upper limit on the amount of data a collection can hold, and because when a collection is read, it is always read in full. For larger data sets, it is usually most appropriate to create a separate table whose partition key reflects the full primary key of the parent row, as we covered in Chapter 3, *Organizing Related Data*.

Tuples and user-defined types are both data structures that store a fixed number of values in a column. Values can be of different types, but they must be of the exact number and types declared in the column definition. Tuples and user-defined types are particularly useful in the way that they can be indexed, providing a workaround for the rule that a secondary index can only apply to a single column. In most situations, user-defined types are a better choice than tuples because they offer the additional benefit of named fields and partial selection.

In the next chapter, we will explore another special type of column that allows us to increment and decrement counter information without reading first. Like collection columns, counter columns are useful primarily because we can perform discrete mutations on their values without knowing what the value is. Counter columns are particularly useful for time-series statistical aggregation; we'll explore data structures for this use case next.

# 9
# Aggregating Time-Series Data

In the preceding chapters, you learned how to use Cassandra as a primary data store for the MyStatus application, with a focus on modeling the data that drives the main user experience on the site. In this chapter, we'll shift focus to another popular use of Cassandra: aggregating data that we observe over time. In particular, we'll build a small analytics component into our schema, which will allow us to keep track of how many times a given status update was viewed on a given day.

In order to do this, we'll introduce a new type of column, the counter column, which is a special numeric column type that can be discretely incremented or decremented. Counter columns have a lot in common with collection columns, which we explored in the previous chapter: you can make discrete changes to them without reading their current value, and they're good for scenarios in which many threads or processes might need to update the same piece of data at the same time.

There are also big differences between counter columns and collection columns: most obviously, counter columns only hold a single scalar value, whereas collection columns hold multiple values. There are also more subtle differences and limitations, which we'll explore in this chapter.

Starting with Cassandra 2.2, we can create functions to perform some computation on data within a table and return the result as part of a SELECT query. These are called **user-defined functions**. Cassandra also provides certain standard functions, such as max, min, avg, and so on. We will take a look at using both UDFs as well as some aggregate functions.

To facilitate the usage of user-defined functions, we will have to make a configuration change and restart Cassandra. We will take a look at how to make configuration changes for different operating system environments.

By the time you're done with this chapter, you'll have learned the following:

- How to construct tables for time-series aggregation
- How to define a counter column
- How to increment and decrement a counter column
- Limitations of counter columns
- Make configuration changes
- How to create **user-defined functions** (**UDF**)
- How to use standard aggregate functions
- How to define **user-defined aggregate** (**UDA**) functions

# Recording discrete analytics observations

Let's say we want to keep very close track of how many times our user's status updates are viewed by someone else. Status updates may be viewed on the MyStatus website, or using our mobile app, or via a third-party app using our API. We'll want to track that, as well as which status update was viewed and when. To do this, let's create a table to store analytics observations:

```
CREATE TABLE "status_update_views" (
  "status_update_username" text,
  "status_update_id" timeuuid,
  "observed_at" timeuuid,
  "client_type" text,
  PRIMARY KEY (
    ("status_update_username", "status_update_id"),
    "observed_at"
  )
);
```

In this new table, we store a partition for each individual status update, with the full primary key of the status update serving as the partition key for our table. Each time someone views a status update, we'll store a new row in the table, generating a timestamp **UUID (Universally unique identifier)** for the row to populate the observed_at clustering column.

We'll also, for each observation, keep track of what type of client was used to view the status update: the website, our mobile app, or a third-party API client. We could, of course, keep track of many other bits of metadata about the observation, such as the IP address of the user, the exact browser or app version being used, and so on.

# Using discrete analytics observations

The `status_update_views` table gives us a complete and highly discrete view of the usage data we're collecting, but it is limited in terms of what questions it can answer. Of course, by analyzing the primary key structure, we know that the question it is best suited to answer is: *What do we know about each view of a given status update in a given time range?* We can answer this question using a range slice query of the following form:

```
SELECT "observed_at", "client_type"
FROM "status_update_views"
WHERE "status_update_username" = 'alice'
  AND "status_update_id" = 76e7a4d0-e796-11e3-90ce-5f98e903bf02
  AND "observed_at" >= MINTIMEUUID('2014-10-05 00:00:00+0000')
  AND "observed_at"  < MINTIMEUUID('2014-10-06 00:00:00+0000');
```

A range slice query is a query that fetches a certain portion of the partition based on the inequality constraints specified in the clustering columns. This query will give us information about all the observed status update views on October 5, 2014. We know that because we are asking for rows in a single partition and a specified range of clustering columns, Cassandra can perform the query very efficiently.

What about other questions we'd like to ask regarding the user behavior we've observed? One thing we can do is simply ask how many total status updates have been observed in a given time range:

```
SELECT COUNT(1)
FROM "status_update_views"
WHERE "status_update_username" = 'alice'
  AND "status_update_id" = 76e7a4d0-e796-11e3-90ce-5f98e903bf02
  AND "observed_at" >= MINTIMEUUID('2014-10-05 00:00:00+0000')
  AND "observed_at"  < MINTIMEUUID('2014-10-06 00:00:00+0000');
```

Compared with retrieving the data in each row and then counting the number of rows we get back, we do save some data transfer using a COUNT query. However, under the hood, Cassandra is doing roughly the same thing: reading all the rows in the table that match our criteria and then counting them.

What's worse, since CQL does not offer anything like the GROUP BY clause in SQL, is that we can only get *one* count back at a time. If we want to know how many views a given status update has received on each day in September, we either need to perform thirty COUNT queries, or we need to read all the observation rows for September and then calculate aggregate counts in our application.

# Slicing and dicing our data

There are many interesting questions we can ask about our analytics observations; most of them can't efficiently be answered by the `status_update_views` table. Here are a few:

- How many total views did status updates receive on each day of September?
- What percentage of status update views are via the Web, via our mobile app, and via third-party applications?
- Which hours of the day are most popular for viewing status updates?
- What is the average monthly growth of status update views this year?

In order to answer any of these questions efficiently, we will require a precomputed table that's structured with that question in mind. Instead of reading massive quantities of raw observations into memory and then computing aggregate information about it, we'll keep the aggregate information up to date as we make the discrete observations.

# Recording aggregate analytics observations

When we explore precomputed aggregate data storage, let's focus on the first question posed earlier: how many total views did status updates receive on each day of September?

More generally, we want to store the daily overall view counts in a structure that allows us to easily retrieve the counts for a given range of time. We don't need to store discrete information about every view event that happened; simply knowing how many views occurred per day is sufficient.

Let's create a new `daily_status_update_views` table that aggregates our analytics observations at just the right granularity:

```
CREATE TABLE "daily_status_update_views" (
  "year" int,
  "date" timestamp,
  "total_views" counter,
  "web_views" counter,
  "mobile_views" counter,
  "api_views" counter,
  PRIMARY KEY (("year"), "date")
);
```

Of course, the most striking thing about this table definition is the introduction of the `counter` column type; we'll dive into this a little later in this chapter. First, let's take a close look at the structure of the primary key and the data columns.

# Answering the right question

Recall that the job of this table is to be able to answer questions such as - *How many total status update views happened on each day of September?* In order to do so, we need to store view counts aggregated daily, and we need to be able to query for ranges of days.

By forming a primary key out of the year, month, and day on which the views were counted, we aggregate at the right granularity: there will be one row per day, containing the counts for that day. We use the year of the observation as the partition key, thus giving ourselves the ability to retrieve a series of daily counts for any range of days within the same year. In the event that we want to retrieve a series of daily counts for a range that spans multiple years, our application will need to make multiple queries, one for each year we're interested in, and then stitch together the results on the client side.

We use a `timestamp` column as the clustering column, storing the day we're counting views on. The information in the `year` partition key is redundant with the year component of the clustering column, so we'll never need to read it directly, but year-based partitions still allow us to keep the size of each partition reasonable and bounded.

For instance, if we want to retrieve total view counts for each day over the month of September, it's as simple as this:

```
SELECT "date", "total_views"
FROM "daily_status_update_views"
WHERE "year" = 2014
  AND "date" >= '2014-09-01'
  AND "date"  < '2014-09-30';
```

Another fact about the schema that's worth noting is the use of four data columns: a total count, and three columns for client-specific counts. Another way to model the same information would have been to add another clustering column called, say, `client_type`; then, for each day, we'd have four rows - one per client type. One approach is not obviously better than the other; in fact, as we'll see in `Appendix A`, *Peeking under the Hood*, the two schemas are more similar than we might imagine.

An advantage of the approach we took is that there's exactly one row per day, which is easier to reason about and more naturally fits our intuitions about the data. An advantage of the one-row-per-client-type approach is that we can introduce new client types without having to add additional columns to the schema. If we expect that new client types will be introduced regularly, storing the client type in a clustering column, rather than as part of the schema definition, becomes very appealing.

# Precomputation versus read-time aggregation

Now we have a table that's optimized to aggregate our analytics data in a specific way. The advantage of this approach is that we can now answer questions about daily views very efficiently; the downside is that we need to create and maintain a table just to aggregate the data in this one way. Each time we record a view, we need to update both the `status_update_views` and `daily_status_update_views` tables. We can easily imagine dozens of different ways in which we might want to aggregate analytics data, each requiring its own purpose-built table, each needing to be updated when an observation is made.

Cassandra is well-suited to this sort of **precomputed aggregation** because of properties that we explored in previous chapters. As we can horizontally scale our dataset by simply adding more machines to our cluster, storing many different aggregates of the same underlying observations isn't hugely expensive. As Cassandra is extremely efficient at writing data, it isn't a deal breaker to have to update several different tables when we make an observation. The trade-off is analogous to the one we considered in our exploration of data denormalization in Chapter 6, *Denormalizing Data for Maximum Performance*: by keeping multiple views of the same underlying data, we increase the complexity of writing data, but give ourselves very efficient structures from which to read that data.

An alternative to precomputation is aggregating data at read time. SQL databases give us a substantial toolset for performing ad hoc aggregation of data when reading it back, using aggregate functions, such as SUM, AVERAGE, MINIMUM, MAXIMUM, and so on, combined with a GROUP BY clause to perform the aggregations at the desired level of granularity. CQL does not offer built-in aggregation functionality; however, Cassandra is capable of integrating with the Hadoop MapReduce framework, which provides an efficient means of performing aggregate computations over massive datasets. DataStax Enterprise, a commercial package that bundles Cassandra, Hadoop, and the Solr search engine, is worth exploring if you need to aggregate data in an ad hoc way.

You can read up more on DataStax Enterprise here: `http://docs.datastax.com/en/lates t-dse/datastax_enterprise/aboutDSE.html`.

# The many possibilities for aggregation

Having satisfied ourselves that precomputed aggregation is worth adding some complexity to the process of recording an observation, let's explore some other ways in which we might want to aggregate data. Here are a few examples of questions we might want to answer and the type of table schema we might set up to efficiently store precomputed aggregates to answer these questions:

| Question | Partition Key | Clustering Column |
|---|---|---|
| How many total views did status updates receive in September? | `year` | `date` |
| What percentage of status update views are via the Web, via our mobile app, and via third-party applications? | `month` | `client_type` |
| Which hours of the day are most popular for viewing status updates? | `month` | `hour_of_day` |
| What is the average monthly growth of status update views this year? | `year` | `month` |

In each case, we choose a partition key that divides our observations into large chunks of time that we'll most likely want to query within, rather than across; then we choose a clustering column that aggregates data using the appropriate level of granularity.

## The role of discrete observations

One question that might come to concern us is the purpose of the first table we created in this chapter: `status_update_views`. As we observed, this table isn't very useful for answering any aggregate questions about our usage data, so why store it at all?

As it turns out, we probably won't interact directly with `status_update_views` when exploring our analytics observations on a day-to-day basis. However, `status_update_views` stores the raw material for all of the aggregate tables. If, in a few months, we decide that we'd like to aggregate data on a previously unforeseen dimension, we can backfill our aggregates using the raw observations in `status_update_views`. Keeping the raw data around gives us some flexibility when it comes to designing new aggregates down the road.

# Recording analytics observations

At this point, we've explored structuring both discrete and aggregate analytics data and looked at accessing that data. However, to have interesting data aggregates to access, we first need to record our observations.

# Updating a counter column

The `daily_status_update_views` table introduces a new type of column: the counter column. Counter columns store integer values, just like `int` and `bigint` columns; however, unlike a normal data column, counter columns are always incremented or decremented rather than having a value set directly.

We've currently got two tables to store usage data: `status_update_views` to store raw view observations, and `daily_status_update_views` to store views by day. We'd like to record that one of `alice`'s status updates was viewed on the Web on October 5, 2014 at 3:12 P.M. EDT:

```
INSERT INTO "status_update_views" (
  "status_update_username", "status_update_id",
  "observed_at", "client_type"
) VALUES (
  'alice', 76e7a4d0-e796-11e3-90ce-5f98e903bf02,
  85a53d10-4cc3-11e4-a7ff-5f98e903bf02,
  'web'
);

UPDATE "daily_status_update_views"
SET "total_views" = "total_views" + 1,
    "web_views" = "web_views" + 1
WHERE "year" = 2014
  AND "date" = '2014-10-05 00:00:00+0000';
```

The first `INSERT` statement should look familiar: we're adding a new row whose partition key columns contain the full primary key of the status update that was viewed, and whose clustering column is a timestamp UUID encoding the exact time at which the status update was viewed. We also record what kind of client was used to view the status update; in this case, a web browser.

The second statement, `UPDATE`, introduces the manipulation of counter columns. Syntactically, we've seen this before; specifically, when adding an item to a list or set column, we used the same syntax of *column_name = column_name + incremental_value*. In this case, however, the incremental value is an integer rather than one or more items we want to add.

The overall effect is the same: the values of the `total_views` and `web_views` columns are incremented by one each. As with the discrete modification of collection columns, at no point did we need to read the current value of the column into memory; for this reason, we don't need to worry about the sort of race condition we explored in the previous chapter.

Let's take a look at the contents of the `daily_status_update_views` table:

```
SELECT * FROM "daily_status_update_views";
```

As we can see, our observation has been recorded for the day in question:

```
 year | date                    | api_views | mobile_views | total_views | web_views
------+-------------------------+-----------+--------------+-------------+-----------
 2014 | 2014-10-05 00:00:00+0000 |      null |         null |           1 |         1

(1 rows)
```

You'll notice that the date column contains not just a date, but also a time. CQL does not offer a built-in date type, but it does allow us to specify `timestamp` literals using only a date; it will interpret this as midnight on that day in the system time zone of the machine on which Cassandra is running.

# Counters and upserts

We'll also note that our earlier UPDATE statement attempted to increment a column in a row that did not yet exist. As we saw in Chapter 7, *Expanding Your Data Model*, this is an upsert operation; the UPDATE statement actually creates the row and increments the values accordingly. Not surprisingly, if we attempt to increment a counter column that doesn't yet have a value, its initial value is considered zero.

# Setting and resetting counter columns

In certain situations, we might want to set a counter column directly; for instance, if we are backfilling our `daily_status_update_views` table from historical information in `status_update_views`, one approach would be to calculate the view counts for each day in our application and then write the counts directly to `daily_status_ update_views`.

The natural way to do this would be to issue an INSERT statement to put the known total view count in the row for a given day:

```
INSERT INTO "daily_status_update_views"
("year", "date", "total_views")
VALUES (2014, '2014-02-01 00:00:00+0000', 500);
```

However, if we try to perform this operation, we'll see an error:

```
Bad Request: INSERT statement are not allowed on counter tables, use UPDATE instead
```

As it turns out, the *only* way to mutate a counter column value is to increment or decrement it; the value cannot be set directly. For the backfill use case, our best bet is just to issue an increment statement for each of the raw views we have stored. If we know that the `daily_status_update_views` table has no information stored for the day in question prior to the backfill, we can also simply perform a single increment, since adding our computed aggregate to the current value of zero will effectively insert the computed aggregate:

```
UPDATE "daily_status_update_views"
SET "total_views" = "total_views" + 500
WHERE "year" = 2014
   AND "date" = '2014-02-01 00:00:00+0000';
```

On checking our daily aggregates table again, we'll see our upsert has had the intended effect:

| year | date | api_views | mobile_views | total_views | web_views |
|------|------|-----------|--------------|-------------|-----------|
| 2014 | 2014-02-01 00:00:00+0000 | null | null | 500 | null |
| 2014 | 2014-10-05 00:00:00+0000 | null | null | 1 | 1 |

(2 rows)

## Counter columns and deletion

Just as the INSERT statements are not a useful operation on counter columns, neither are DELETE statements. It is possible to delete a row containing counter columns:

```
DELETE FROM "daily_status_update_views"
WHERE "year" = 2014
   AND "date" = '2014-02-01 00:00:00+0000';
```

Upon reading the table, you will notice that the deleted row is missing, just as expected:

| year | date | api_views | mobile_views | total_views | web_views |
|------|------|-----------|--------------|-------------|-----------|
| 2014 | 2014-10-05 00:00:00+0000 | null | null | 1 | 1 |

(1 rows)

Let's try re-adding some data to the row for February 1:

```
UPDATE "daily_status_update_views"
SET "total_views" = "total_views" + 100
WHERE "year" = 2014
  AND "date" = '2014-02-01 00:00:00+0000';
```

On reading the data in the table, we'll see something surprising:

```
year | date                        | api_views | mobile_views | total_views | web_views
------+-----------------------------+-----------+--------------+-------------+----------
2014 | 2014-02-01 00:00:00+0000 |      null |         null |         600 |      null
2014 | 2014-10-05 00:00:00+0000 |      null |         null |           1 |         1

(2 rows)
```

The data we've just inserted has been added to the previous counter column value, which we had already deleted.

Because of the way counter columns handle deletions, it's inadvisable to ever issue a DELETE statement against a counter column. Counters are great for aggregating values that you will never need to reset or remove; as long as you only need to modify counters via increments and decrements, they perform admirably. Aggregating user behavior is one use case that precisely fits within this domain.

# Counter columns need their own table

Another surprising fact about counter columns is that they cannot coexist with regular data columns in the same table. For instance, let's imagine that along with view counts, we'd like to record the timestamp of the last view of a status update on a given day. We might think we can add a timestamp column to our daily_status_update_views table:

```
ALTER TABLE "daily_status_update_views"
ADD "last_view_time" timestamp;
```

However, if we attempt to perform this schema modification, we'll see an error:

```
Bad Request: Cannot add a non counter column (last_view_time) in a counter column family
```

Cassandra requires that counter columns live in their own table; they cannot coexist with regular data columns or collection columns. Of course, counter tables still have primary key columns with the full range of data types; in fact, primary key columns cannot have the counter type, since using a primary key that cannot be directly set would not make sense.

# Cassandra configuration

So far, we have been running Cassandra without modifying the default configuration. The default configuration is suited to a minimalistic Cassandra cluster with a single node and no security. Often, it is required to modify a few configuration files to get a multinode production cluster up and running. Here, we will take a look at the location where these configuration files are persisted and modify one of those files to facilitate the usage of the user-defined functions.

# Configuration location

Depending on the operating system and the installation method you might have chosen at the beginning, the configuration files might exist in different locations.

The configuration files are usually located in one of the  following directories based on your installation type:

- Cassandra package installations (`apt-get` or `yum` installation): `/etc/cassandra`
- Cassandra Tarball installation: `install_location/conf`
- Cassandra Windows installations: `C:Program/FilesDataStax/Community/apache-cassandra/conf`

If you go to the location where your configuration files are located and take a look at the list of files persisting there, it should look like this:

```
README.txt
cassandra-env.ps1
cassandra-env.sh
cassandra.yaml
commitlog_archiving.properties
cqlshrc.sample
hotspot_compiler
jvm.options
logback-tools.xml
logback.xml
metrics-reporter-config-sample.yaml
triggers
```

Your list might vary depending on the Cassandra version and the installation type.

Ideally, you would need to modify only two or three files for a stable multinode Cassandra environment. We will take a look at the most important configuration files and what purpose each one of them serves:

- `cassandra-env.sh`: This file contains Cassandra **Java Virtual Machine** (**JVM**)-related configuration options. You can adjust the JVM heap size, as well as adding certain JVM startup options. Whatever changes you make to the JVM options could drastically change Cassandra's performance.

 Tuning JVM parameters has a huge impact on memory consumption/garbage collection, which, in turn, might impact Cassandra's performance drastically. You can find recommended JVM settings here: `https://docs.datastax.com/en/cassandra/3.0/cassandra/operations/opsTuneJVM.html`.

- `cassandra.yaml`: This file contains most of the configuration parameters that would need to be changed to run a production cluster. It includes various properties, such as the cluster name, data directories, other commonly used options, performance tuning options, and security options.

 You can take a look at all the configuration options within this file along with a brief explanation here: `https://docs.datastax.com/en/cassandra/3.0/cassandra/configuration/configCassandra_yaml.html`.

- `logback.xml`: This file is used to configure logging properties of Cassandra, such as the log level and location of log files.
- `metrics-reporter-config-sample.yaml`: This file is used to configure the metrics reporting properties, such as the metrics reporting interval and output location.

Depending on the Cassandra cluster and the functionality required, you might need to modify other configuration files as well. Here is a full list of configuration options: `https://docs.datastax.com/en/cassandra/3.0/cassandra/configuration/configTOC.html`.

# Modifying configuration

To work with user-defined functions, we need to add a configuration option to the `cassandra.yaml` file. Add the following line to the end of the `cassandra.yaml` file if the parameter `enable_user_defined_functions` is not present:

```
enable_user_defined_functions: true
```

If the parameter is present, change the false value to true. The line is pretty self-explanatory. This enables user-defined functions. For the change in configuration to take effect, you will need to restart Cassandra. This is applicable to any configuration change within any configuration file.

# Restarting Cassandra

The final step required to start using user-defined functions is to restart Cassandra. For most installations, you can stop and start Cassandra, as mentioned in Chapter 1, *Getting up and Running with Cassandra*.

- For Package installations, you can run the following command, which will restart Cassandra:

  ```
  $ sudo service cassandra restart
  ```

- On some Linux distributions, you can also run the following command to restart Cassandra:

  ```
  $ sudo /etc/init.d/cassandra restart
  ```

- For Tarball installations, you can either close the program by pressing *Ctrl+C* if you started Cassandra in the foregroundor, if you started Cassandra in the background, you can fetch the process ID of the Cassandra process by entering `ps -ef | grep cassandra`. You should get a result similar to this:

```
    0 21747 21118    0  6:47PM ttys001    0:00.02 sudo ./bin/cassandra -f
    0 21748 21747    0  6:47PM ttys001    0:12.00 /usr/bin/java -Xloggc:./bin/../logs/gc.log -XX:+UseParNewGC -XX:+UseConcMarkSweep
GC -XX:+CMSParallelRemarkEnabled -XX:SurvivorRatio=8 -XX:MaxTenuringThreshold=1 -XX:CMSInitiatingOccupancyFraction=75 -XX:+UseCMSI
nitiatingOccupancyOnly -XX:CMSWaitDuration=10000 -XX:+CMSParallelInitialMarkEnabled -XX:+CMSEdenChunksRecordAlways -XX:+CMSClassUn
loadingEnabled -XX:+PrintGCDetails -XX:+PrintGCDateStamps -XX:+PrintHeapAtGC -XX:+PrintTenuringDistribution -XX:+PrintGCApplicatio
nStoppedTime -XX:+PrintPromotionFailure -XX:+UseGCLogFileRotation -XX:NumberOfGCLogFiles=10 -XX:GCLogFileSize=10M -Xms4096M -Xmx40
96M -Xmn800M -XX:+UseCondCardMark -ea -Xss256k -XX:+AlwaysPreTouch -XX:-UseBiasedLocking -XX:StringTableSize=1000003 -XX:+UseTLAB
-XX:+ResizeTLAB -XX:+PerfDisableSharedMem -XX:CompileCommandFile=./bin/../conf/hotspot_compiler -javaagent:./bin/../lib/jamm-0.3.0
.jar -XX:+UseThreadPriorities -XX:ThreadPriorityPolicy=42 -XX:+HeapDumpOnOutOfMemoryError -Djava.net.preferIPv4Stack=true -Dcassan
dra.jmx.local.port=7199 -XX:+DisableExplicitGC -Djava.library.path=./bin/../lib/sigar-bin -Dlogback.configurationFile=logback.xml
-Dcassandra.logdir=./bin/../logs -Dcassandra.storagedir=./bin/../data -Dcassandra-foreground=yes -cp ./bin/../conf:./bin/../build/
classes/main:./bin/../build/classes/thrift:./bin/../lib/ST4-4.0.8.jar:./bin/../lib/airline-0.6.jar:./bin/../lib/antlr-runtime-3.5.
2.jar:./bin/../lib/apache-cassandra-3.0.7.jar:./bin/../lib/apache-cassandra-clientutil-3.0.7.jar:./bin/../lib/apache-cassandra-thr
ift-3.0.7.jar:./bin/../lib/asm-5.0.4.jar:./bin/../lib/cassandra-driver-core-3.0.1-shaded.jar:./bin/../lib/commons-cli-1.1.jar:./bi
n/../lib/commons-codec-1.2.jar:./bin/../lib/commons-lang3-3.1.jar:./bin/../lib/commons-math3-3.2.jar:./bin/../lib/compress-lzf-0.8
.4.jar:./bin/../lib/concurrentlinkedhashmap-lru-1.4.jar:./bin/../lib/disruptor-3.0.1.jar:./bin/../lib/ecj-4.4.2.jar:./bin/../lib/g
uava-18.0.jar:./bin/../lib/high-scale-lib-1.0.6.jar:./bin/../lib/jackson-core-asl-1.9.2.jar:./bin/../lib/jackson-mapper-asl-1.9.2.
jar:./bin/../lib/jamm-0.3.0.jar:./bin/../lib/javax.inject.jar:./bin/../lib/jbcrypt-0.3m.jar:./bin/../lib/jcl-over-slf4j-1.7.7.jar:
./bin/../lib/jna-4.0.0.jar:./bin/../lib/joda-time-2.4.jar:./bin/../lib/json-simple-1.1.jar:./bin/../lib/libthrift-0.9.2.jar:./bin/
../lib/log4j-over-slf4j-1.7.7.jar:./bin/../lib/logback-classic-1.1.3.jar:./bin/../lib/logback-core-1.1.3.jar:./bin/../lib/lz4-1.3.
0.jar:./bin/../lib/metrics-core-3.1.0.jar:./bin/../lib/metrics-logback-3.1.0.jar:./bin/../lib/metrics-statsd-common-4.1.2.jar:./bi
n/../lib/metrics3-statsd-4.1.2.jar:./bin/../lib/netty-all-4.0.23.Final.jar:./bin/../lib/ohc-core-0.4.3.jar:./bin/../lib/ohc-core-j
8-0.4.3.jar:./bin/../lib/reporter-config-base-3.0.2-595b3c23.jar:./bin/../lib/reporter-config3-3.0.2-595b3c23.jar:./bin/../lib/see
dprovider-1.0.5.jar:./bin/../lib/sigar-1.6.4.jar:./bin/../lib/slf4j-api-1.7.7.jar:./bin/../lib/snakeyaml-1.11.jar:./bin/../lib/sna
ppy-java-1.1.1.7.jar:./bin/../lib/stream-2.5.2.jar:./bin/../lib/thrift-server-0.3.7.jar:./bin/../lib/jsr223/*/*.jar org.apache.cas
sandra.service.CassandraDaemon
```

In this case, the pid is `21748`. You can kill the process by entering the following:

```
$ sudo kill -9 21748
```

Once you have killed the Cassandra process, you can start it again, similar to how you did in `Chapter 1`, *Getting up and Running with Cassandra*.

# User-defined functions

So far, we have only done simple `SELECT` operations that are inherently permitted by Cassandra. In the case of complex queries, where we could not fetch results based on just the primary key indexes, we built secondary indexes and materialized views. What if there arises a situation where you are required to perform some custom computations? Fortunately, Cassandra provides custom user-defined functions to perform some simple computations on the data present in Cassandra.

UDFs allow the execution of user code on the server side. The coordinator node takes care of the computation. In Cassandra 3.0 and later, UDFs are executed in a sandbox. You can also use custom security managers to prevent UDFs from accessing the filesystem or to prevent the execution of harmful code. Java and JavaScript are supported by default.

 Cassandra UDFs can be written in any language with JSR223 support. The list of languages includes Java, JavaScript, Ruby, and Python, among others. Though using some of these might require adding additional libraries. You can find more info at `https://docs.datastax.com/en/cql /3.3/cql/cql_using/useCreateUDF.html`.

For our users table, the location stored is a combination of the city as well as the state.

Out-of-the-box, Cassandra doesn't support splitting up a column value into multiple components and fetching a certain part of the value. But you can define a simple UDF to do this job for you. Before we proceed with constructing the UDF, let's fetch the location results of the users table just for reference purposes. This will help us in developing a function that takes into account null values and other unexpected values:

```
 username  |  location
-----------+--------------------
       bob |               null
 happycorp |       New York, NY
      dave | San Francisco, CA
      gina |       Houston, TX
       eve |  Washington, D.C.
     carol |               null
     frank |    Los Angeles, CA
      ivan |               null
     alice |               null
```

Looking at the location values, we notice that a comma separates the city and state values. In order to fetch just the city value, we need to split location by comma and fetch the first component. Now that we have a clear route on how to achieve our goal, let's implement it as a UDF and test it out. The UDF can be created as follows:

```
CREATE OR REPLACE FUNCTION selectCity(location text)
CALLED ON NULL INPUT
RETURNS text
LANGUAGE java
AS '
if (location == null)
return null;
 else
    return location.split(",")[0];
';
```

- The CQL syntax to create a user-defined function begins with the CREATE OR REPLACE FUNCTION statement. This creates a UDF in the current keyspace. You can use just CREATE FUNCTION as well. selectCity is the UDF name that will be used in our SELECT statements.
- The UDF takes a single argument, which is the location column. The arguments in a UDF have to be valid CQL types.

- The `CALLED ON NULL INPUT` construct makes sure the code is executed at all times (even for null input). This is often replaced with `RETURNS NULL ON NULL INPUT`, which ensures the function will return null value when any of the input values is null.
- The `RETURNS` construct tells us that the output value is of the CQL type text.
- The `LANGUAGE` construct is used to specify the programming language we are going to use for our user-defined function.
- `AS` defines the meat of the UDF, which is the function itself.

The function itself is pretty simple. It returns a null value when the input location is null. If the input is not null, we split the string by the delimiter , into an array and fetch the element at index '0', which is the first element of the array. To use the UDF within a `SELECT` statement, let's execute the following code:

```
SELECT username, selectCity(location) FROM "users";
```

We get the result as expected:

```
 username    | my_status.selectcity(location)
-------------+-------------------------------
         bob |                           null
   happycorp |                       New York
        dave |                  San Francisco
        gina |                        Houston
         eve |                     Washington
       carol |                           null
       frank |                    Los Angeles
        ivan |                           null
       alice |                           null

(9 rows)
```

 Since we didn't use any double quotes around the function name when declaring the function, we notice that the function name is case insensitive. This applies to keyspace, table, and column names. Any name defined without double quotes is case insensitive.

The same function could have been defined as follows:

```
CREATE OR REPLACE FUNCTION selectCity(location text)
RETURNS NULL ON NULL INPUT
RETURNS text
LANGUAGE java
AS '
```

```
    return location.split(",")[0];
';
```

This would still return the same result as the first function we created. We moved the processing of null input values from the function definition to the `RETURNS NULL ON NULL INPUT` construct.

Here are certain things to keep in mind when defining a UDF:

- The function can be used in `SELECT` clauses
- The function can take any number of columns as arguments
- The function input and output have to be valid CQL types
- The function has to be stateless

# User-defined aggregate functions

Earlier, we created a `status_update_views` table to keep track of the views on status updates. We also keep track of the origin of these status-update views. They could have originated from a web site, mobile app, or other apps using our API. But to keep track of the count of each type of view, we had to create a separate table with counter columns partitioned by year and clustered by date.

We can also do the same without actually creating a separate table. This can be done using Cassandra's user-defined aggregate functions. You can create custom aggregate functions, which can be applied to data persisting within Cassandra and returned as part of the query result. The coordinator performs aggregation.

Before we proceed with the aggregation, let's populate the `status_update_views` table with raw data:

```
    INSERT INTO "status_update_views" ("status_update_username",
"status_update_id", "observed_at", "client_type") VALUES ('alice',
76e7a4d0-e796-11e3-90ce-5f98e903bf02, NOW(), 'web');
    INSERT INTO "status_update_views" ("status_update_username",
"status_update_id", "observed_at", "client_type") VALUES ('alice',
76e7a4d0-e796-11e3-90ce-5f98e903bf02, NOW(), 'web');
    INSERT INTO "status_update_views" ("status_update_username",
"status_update_id", "observed_at", "client_type") VALUES ('alice',
76e7a4d0-e796-11e3-90ce-5f98e903bf02, NOW(), 'mobile');
    INSERT INTO "status_update_views" ("status_update_username",
"status_update_id", "observed_at", "client_type") VALUES ('alice',
76e7a4d0-e796-11e3-90ce-5f98e903bf02, NOW(), 'mobile');
    INSERT INTO "status_update_views" ("status_update_username",
```

```
"status_update_id", "observed_at", "client_type") VALUES ('alice',
76e7a4d0-e796-11e3-90ce-5f98e903bf02, NOW(), 'api');
```

On fetching the results, we notice that there are three web views, two mobile views, and one API view for the status update made by the user `alice` with status ID `76e7a4d0-e796-11e3-90ce-5f98e903bf02`:

```
status_update_username | status_update_id                       | system.totimestamp(observed_at) | client_type
-----------------------+----------------------------------------+---------------------------------+------------
                 alice | 76e7a4d0-e796-11e3-90ce-5f98e903bf02   | 2014-10-05 19:12:17+0000        |         web
                 alice | 76e7a4d0-e796-11e3-90ce-5f98e903bf02   | 2016-12-21 07:42:00+0000        |         web
                 alice | 76e7a4d0-e796-11e3-90ce-5f98e903bf02   | 2016-12-21 07:42:00+0000        |         web
                 alice | 76e7a4d0-e796-11e3-90ce-5f98e903bf02   | 2016-12-21 07:42:00+0000        |      mobile
                 alice | 76e7a4d0-e796-11e3-90ce-5f98e903bf02   | 2016-12-21 07:42:00+0000        |      mobile
                 alice | 76e7a4d0-e796-11e3-90ce-5f98e903bf02   | 2016-12-21 07:42:00+0000        |         api
```

Now that we have populated the `status_update_views` table, we can go ahead with creating the aggregate function. Creating a UDA requires us to create a function, which is called from the aggregate. The function consists of a state, which can be any CQL type along with other parameters. User-defined aggregates call the function you defined on every row that is returned by the `SELECT` query. The first value of the function is state, and it is passed between rows. For the following scenario, the UDA can be created as follows:

```
CREATE OR REPLACE FUNCTION state_group_and_count (state map<text,
int>, client_type text)
CALLED ON NULL INPUT
RETURNS map<text, int>
LANGUAGE java AS '
Integer count = (Integer) state.get(client_type);
if (count == null)
        count = 1;
else
        count++;
state.put(client_type, count);
return state;
';

CREATE OR REPLACE AGGREGATE group_and_count (text)
SFUNC state_group_and_count
STYPE map<text, int>
INITCOND {};
```

The function we created is similar to the one we created in the UDF section of this chapter. Only the logic has changed. For every row returned, we check the count that corresponds to the client type and update it accordingly. This is depicted in the following figure:

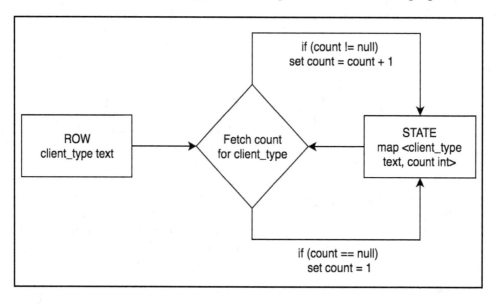

Let's look at the semantics for creating a user-defined aggregate:

- The CREATE OR REPLACE AGGREGATE construct is used to define the aggregate. Here, the aggregate name is group_and_count, and it takes just one parameter, which is a text value.
- SFUNC represents the state function to be used or called for every row.
- STYPE represents the state type used within the function, which has to be a valid CQL type.
- INITCOND initializes the state passed to the first state function call. If not set, it takes a default value of null.

Let's try to fetch the count for different views on a status update for the user alice with status ID 76e7a4d0-e796-11e3-90ce-5f98e903bf02:

```
SELECT status_update_username, status_update_id,
group_and_count(client_type)
FROM status_update_views
WHERE status_update_username='alice' AND status_update_id=76e7a4d0-
e796-11e3-90ce-5f98e903bf02;
```

This gives us the expected result in the form of a map:

```
status_update_username | status_update_id                       | my_status.group_and_count(client_type)
-----------------------+----------------------------------------+---------------------------------------
                 alice | 76e7a4d0-e796-11e3-90ce-5f98e903bf02 |        {'api': 1, 'mobile': 2, 'web': 3}
```

Suppose you want to fetch the view count for a particular day; you can execute the following query:

```
    SELECT status_update_username, status_update_id,
group_and_count(client_type)
    FROM status_update_views
    WHERE status_update_username='alice' AND status_update_id=76e7a4d0-
e796-11e3-90ce-5f98e903bf02
    AND "observed_at" >= MINTIMEUUID('2016-12-21 00:00:00+0000')
    AND "observed_at" < MINTIMEUUID('2016-12-22 00:00:00+0000');
```

This gives us the following result:

```
status_update_username | status_update_id                       | my_status.group_and_count(client_type)
-----------------------+----------------------------------------+---------------------------------------
                 alice | 76e7a4d0-e796-11e3-90ce-5f98e903bf02 |        {'api': 1, 'mobile': 2, 'web': 2}
```

While user-defined aggregates seem useful for analytics, they might perform poorly if you are performing aggregation on huge datasets. The query might take a while before returning the result. UDAs also put a lot of pressure on the coordinator node. Also, you cannot return non-partition key columns when you use UDAs within a SELECT query.

# Standard aggregate functions

On top of creating custom aggregate functions, Cassandra provides certain standard aggregate functions by default. These include max, min, avg, count, and sum. You can read more about these functions at https://docs.datastax.com/en/cql/3.3/cql/cql_using/useQueryStdAggregate.html.

# Summary

In this chapter, we explored strategies for aggregating observed time-series data (in this case, user behavior in viewing status updates in our application). While user behavior analytics are a fantastic and common use case for Cassandra, we could also take the same approach to aggregate scientific data, economic data, or anything else where we'd like to roll up discrete observations into high-level aggregate values.

Our structure for recording time-series data used a table containing discrete observations as the raw material and acting as the data record in case we want to introduce new aggregate dimensions down the line. We also used a table that precomputed aggregate observations by day; by keeping the aggregate up to date at write time, we built a structure that allows us to very efficiently retrieve aggregates over a given time period, without any expensive computation at read time. We can easily imagine constructing dozens of such tables, one for each level of granularity at which we would like to analyze aggregate information.

We explored using counter columns to effortlessly maintain the precomputed aggregates. Each time we made an observation, we simply issued an upsert to increment the relevant counter columns; this allowed us to record observations simply by issuing a series of UPDATE statements, without having to read the current aggregate values from Cassandra first.

We saw that while counter columns are a useful tool for precomputed data aggregation, they also have their downsides. Counter columns do not allow us to directly set values; we can only increment or decrement them. Because deletion of a counter column value is not permanent and the previous value gets updated, this operation is of little use in a counter column table. We saw that counter columns can coexist in a table only with other counter columns; they can't be in the same table as other data columns or collection columns.

We also saw that using user-defined functions and aggregates required us to make a configuration change. We looked at the location of the configuration files and various configuration changes that can be made in Cassandra.

We defined new functions to retrieve data from Cassandra columns that wouldn't have been possible with in-built functions. We also created custom aggregates that could be used in place of counter columns, albeit that their efficiency and performance are questionable.

In the next chapter, we will look more deeply into how Cassandra stores and retrieves data, with particular focus on how data is distributed among multiple machines in a multinode cluster, the typical configuration of a production Cassandra deployment. You'll learn how Cassandra handles conflicting updates to the same piece of data using timestamps, and you'll see how we can override those timestamps to an interesting effect. You'll also learn more about what happens when data is deleted from Cassandra and use that knowledge to avoid common pitfalls with data deletion.

# 10
## How Cassandra Distributes Data

Much of Cassandra's power lies in the fact that it is a **distributed database**: rather than storing all of your data on a single machine, it is designed to distribute data across multiple machines. A distributed architecture is hugely beneficial for scalability, since you're not bound by the hardware capacity of a single machine; if you need more storage or more processing power, you can simply add more nodes to your Cassandra cluster. It's also a boon for availability: by storing multiple copies of your data on multiple machines, Cassandra is resilient to the failure of a particular node.

The beauty of a distributed database such as Cassandra is that, as application developers, we rarely need to think about the fact that we're working with data that's spread across multiple servers. We've spent the last nine chapters exploring a wide range of Cassandra's functionality, and the interfaces we've worked with never require us to explicitly account for the fact that data is distributed. From the application's perspective, we simply write data to Cassandra and then read it back; the database takes care of figuring out which machine or machines the data is written to or read from.

Cassandra internally uses gossip protocol for communication to maintain the entire cluster view. Gossip is also used to identify any status changes to Cassandra nodes. Also, the responsibility of safely putting data onto the correct machine is attributed to the partitioner. We will take a look at the several partitioners that are available.

That said, when developing applications using Cassandra as a persistence layer, it's important to understand how data is distributed and replicated. One topic of keen interest to application developers is **consistency**: if multiple copies of a piece of data exist on different machines in the cluster, how do I know that I'm reading the most up-to-date version of the data? In distributed data stores, there is always a trade-off between consistency and availability; Cassandra provides tunable consistency, which allows us to decide which is more important in any given scenario.

Another important consideration in a distributed data store is conflict resolution: if two clients attempt to write different data to the same location at the same time, which write wins? Under the hood, every piece of data written to Cassandra has a timestamp attached to it; conflicts are resolved with a simple last-write-wins strategy. Application developers have the ability to override the default timestamp attached to a write operation, sometimes to interesting effect.

We will briefly look at the different options available when creating a keyspace and a table. This will let us explore some of Cassandra's niche features, such as caching, hints, compaction, multidata center replication, and so on.

Finally, a fault-tolerant distributed database needs to take special care when deleting data. In particular, a deletion does not result in Cassandra immediately forgetting that a value ever existed; doing so might lead to the data unexpectedly reappearing in certain scenarios, which we will explore later in the chapter. Instead, Cassandra creates a **tombstone**, which encodes the knowledge that a certain value was deleted at a certain time. Understanding tombstones is crucial to avoiding certain performance-killing Cassandra anti-patterns.

With a solid understanding of how Cassandra distributes data and a keen eye on how those mechanisms affect our work as application developers, you'll be fully prepared to build highly scalable, efficient, and fault-tolerant applications using Cassandra. In this chapter, you will study the following:

- How Cassandra distributes data in a multinode cluster
- How Cassandra replicates data
- Multidata center cluster
- Keyspace replication options
- The difference between immediate consistency and eventual consistency
- The trade-off between consistency and availability
- How and when to tune consistency
- How Cassandra resolves conflicting writes
- How to provide your own timestamp when writing data
- Table configuration properties

- How and why Cassandra uses tombstones for data deletion
- Writing expiring data using TTLs

**A word about examples**:
In the preceding chapters, we've consistently used hands-on examples in the MyStatus application to demonstrate the features of Cassandra under discussion. In this chapter, we will be covering concepts whose effects are largely transparent to an application under normal circumstances. For that reason, much of the material in this chapter will consider specific scenarios - usually adverse ones - in a multinode cluster, which can't be easily demonstrated using the single-node development cluster you set up in Chapter 1, *Getting Up and Running with Cassandra*. The material in this chapter isn't entirely hands-off: you'll get a chance to play with timestamps and TTLs and observe their effects in the cqlsh console. But most of this chapter is devoted to developing a mental model of how your data behaves in a production environment, so you'll need to use your imagination a bit, amply aided by diagrams and illustrations. In the next chapter, you will set up a Cassandra multinode cluster and take a look at the more operational aspects of Cassandra. In Chapter 11, *Cassandra Multi-Node Cluster*, you will take a more hands-on approach to the theoretical aspects you're about to learn in this chapter.

# Data distribution in Cassandra

In a traditional relational database such as MySQL or PostgreSQL, the entire contents of the database reside on a single machine. At a certain scale, the hardware capacity of the server running the database becomes a constraint: simply migrating to more powerful hardware will lead to diminishing returns.

Let's imagine ourselves in this scenario, where we have an application running on a single-machine database that has reached the limits of its capacity to vertically scale. In that case, we'll want to split the data between multiple machines, a process known as **sharding** or **federation**. Assuming we want to stick with the same underlying tool, we'll end up with multiple database instances, each of which holds a subset of our total data. Crucially, in this scenario, the different database instances have no knowledge of each other; as far as each instance is concerned, it's simply a standalone database containing a standalone dataset.

It's up to our application to manage the distribution of data among our various database instances. Specifically, for any given piece of data, we'll need to know which instance it belongs to; when we're writing data, we need to write to the right instance, and when we're reading data, we need to read it back from that same place.

Assuming we are using integer primary keys - the standard practice in relational databases - one simple strategy is to use the modulus of the primary key. If we have four database instances, our primary key layout would look somewhat like this:

| Instance | Primary Keys |
|----------|--------------|
| Instance 1 | 1, 5, 9, 13, ... |
| Instance 2 | 2, 6, 10, 14, ... |
| Instance 3 | 3, 7, 11, 15, ... |
| Instance 4 | 4, 8, 12, 16, ... |

Of course, this strategy would likely result in great difficulty performing relational operations; it's quite likely that a foreign key stored on one instance would refer to a primary key stored on a different instance. For this reason, in a real application, we would likely design a more sophisticated partitioning strategy. Regardless of what we choose, the critical feature of any partitioning strategy is that we know which database instance a given piece of data belongs to, being given only the information we have before actually communicating with a database instance.

# Cassandra's partitioning strategy - partition key tokens

As application developers working with Cassandra, we never need to go through the earlier calculus: when we write or read data, we can perform the query on any node in the cluster and Cassandra will figure out where the data resides. The federation process is entirely transparent to the application.

As it turns out, Cassandra uses a strategy analogous to the naïve primary key modulus approach described earlier. Recall from Chapter 2, *The First Table*, that Cassandra has a TOKEN function that generates an integer value for any partition key; when we retrieve results over multiple partition keys, the rows are ordered by this token.

# Distributing partition tokens

When Cassandra distributes data, it assigns each node a range of tokens; a row is stored on the node within whose token range its partition key token falls. Since tokens are generated using a hashing function, token values are distributed evenly across the entire range of possible values. So, as long as the number of partition keys is much bigger than the number of nodes in the cluster, partition keys will be balanced evenly between the different nodes if each node is responsible for an equally sized portion of the token range.

Let's take a look at a few rows in our `users` table and examine how they would be distributed in a three-node cluster:

```
SELECT "username", TOKEN("username")
FROM "users"
WHERE "username" IN ('alice', 'bob', 'ivan');
```

We'll see that these three rows have primary key tokens that are pretty evenly distributed across the 64-bit space of possible tokens:

```
 username | token(username)
----------+---------------------
    alice |   5699955792253506986
      bob |  -5396685590450884643
     ivan |    962209788683003613
```

Now let's consider how data will be distributed across our three-node cluster. Cassandra tokens are signed 64-bit integers, so the minimum possible hash is $-2^{63}$ or -9223372036854775808, and the maximum possible hash is $2^{63}-1$ or 9223372036854775807. So, our nodes will be assigned to token ranges as follows:

| Node | Lowest Token | Highest Token |
|------|--------------|---------------|
| Node 1 | -9223372036854775808 | -3074457345618258604 |
| Node 2 | -3074457345618258603 | 3074457345618258601 |
| Node 3 | 3074457345618258602 | 9223372036854775807 |

It's common to visualize a topology as a ring, with each range in the token space corresponding to a portion of the circumference of the ring, much like degrees in an arc. We can apply that visualization to our three-node cluster like this:

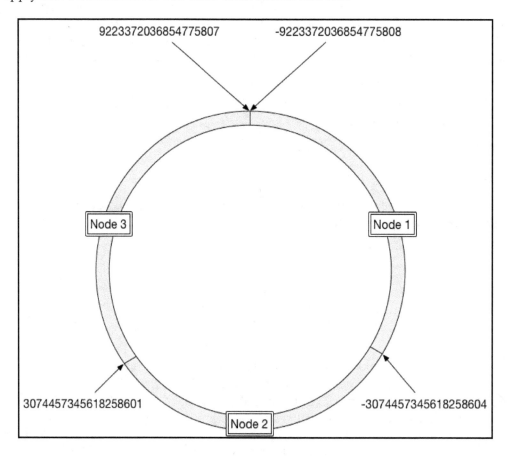

Now let's consider the location of each of the three rows we looked at previously. As it turns out, each row falls in a different range in the token space: alice lives on **Node 1**, ivan lives on **Node 2**, and bob lives on **Node 3**. Using our ring diagram, we can visualize how each row is assigned to a node:

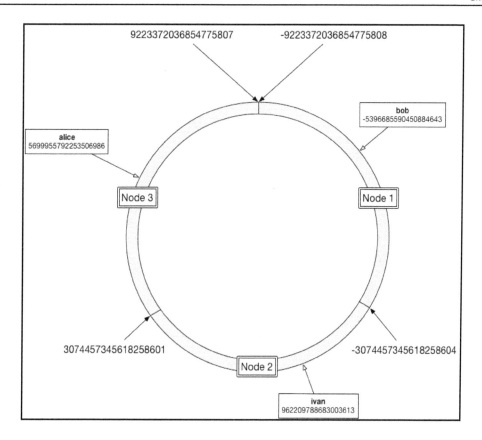

# Partitioners

So, we know that each Cassandra node is assigned a certain token range and is responsible for a subset of all the data. The component that is responsible for generating the partition key hash is called the **partitioner**. So, a partitioner is nothing but a hash function, which is used to calculate the hash for a given partition key and determines which node the data should reside on. Cassandra comes with three partitioners:

- Murmur3Partitioner: This is the default partitioner in Cassandra 1.2 or higher. This partitioner uniformly distributes data across the cluster by calculating Murmur hash values. The hash values range from -263 to 263-1. Murmur3Partitioner is preferred since it has a faster hashing algorithm and has better performance than other partitioners.

- `RandomPartitioner`: `RandomPartitioner` uniformly distributes data by calculating MD5 hash values of the partition key. This was the default partitioner in the earliest versions of Cassandra. The hash values are in the range of 0 to $2^{127}$-1.
- `ByteOrderedPartitioner`: This partitioner keeps an ordered distribution of data lexically by key bytes. This has been deprecated in the newer versions of Cassandra and is kept for legacy reasons. Using this partitioner is not recommended because it can generally cause hotspots and uneven load balancing.

Both `Murmur3Partitioner` and `RandomPartitioner` generate tokens in such a way that a roughly equal amount of data is distributed among the nodes. The number of tables within a keyspace and the variety of partition key types amongst the tables doesn't affect the hashing and equal data distribution in any way.

You cannot change the partitioner type within a live cluster. It is recommended to stick to the default value of `Murmur3Partitioner`. The property name is **partitioner**; it is present within the `cassandra.yaml` file and has a default value of `org.apache.cassandra.dht.Murmur3Partitioner`.

# Partition keys group data on the same node

In `Chapter 3`, *Organizing Related Data*, you learned that tables with compound primary keys store all rows sharing the same partition key in contiguous physical storage. This leads to the observation that querying for ranges of clustering column values within a single partition key is highly efficient. To perform this sort of lookup, Cassandra needs to only locate the beginning of the range on disk and can then read all the results beginning at that location. Conversely, querying for rows spanning multiple partition keys requires an inefficient random disk scan for each partition key being queried.

You new understanding of data partitioning expands this observation: you now know that querying for multiple partition keys not only requires Cassandra to make multiple disk scans, but most likely also requires retrieving data from multiple nodes and collating the results. Cassandra is entirely capable of performing this operation - the process of reading from multiple nodes and collating the results is performed by a **coordinator node** and is entirely transparent to the application. But it's important to remember that the process of reading data from multiple partitions, and thus possibly multiple nodes, is expensive and best avoided for performance-sensitive operations.

# Virtual nodes

The model of data distribution we have developed thus far is, in fact, a simplification of how a modern Cassandra cluster works. While versions of Cassandra prior to 1.2 did directly map ranges of tokens onto physical nodes, Cassandra 1.2 introduced **virtual nodes**, which act as an intermediary in the mapping process.

Virtual nodes replace physical nodes in the partitioned ring; each virtual node owns a portion of the token space. Virtual nodes themselves are then owned by physical nodes, but a physical node does not own a contiguous range of virtual nodes; rather, virtual nodes are distributed randomly among physical nodes. Crucially, there are many more virtual nodes than physical nodes; each physical machine is responsible for many virtual nodes.

Looking back at our three-node data cluster, let's examine how data is distributed using virtual nodes. For simplicity, we'll say there are twelve virtual nodes in the cluster, four per physical node; although in a real cluster, that number would be much higher. The makers of Cassandra recommend 256 virtual nodes in a production cluster.

Here's how our ring now looks, divided up into twelve virtual nodes:

 Each physical machine is no longer responsible for a contiguous range of tokens; instead, each machine is responsible for four virtual nodes, each of which covers a different token range.

## Virtual nodes facilitate redistribution

The main advantage of virtual nodes is their behavior when the cluster changes. Consider the simple example of adding a fourth node to our three-node cluster. Without virtual nodes, all three pre-existing physical nodes have their token range changed to make space for the fourth node. To accommodate the fourth machine, Cassandra must recalculate the target node for each individual row based on the mapping from its token to the new token range assignments of the four nodes. This is a process known as **rebalancing** and it's rendered unnecessary by virtual nodes.

When a new node joins the cluster, it's simply assigned a handful of virtual nodes that previously belonged to other machines. Rather than directly recalculating the physical location of each individual row, Cassandra can simply assign the correct number of virtual nodes to the new machine (in this case, three) and move their contents over wholesale. Unlike in a rebalancing scenario, where every physical machine is both losing and gaining data, redistributing virtual nodes only requires data to be moved from the original three machines to its new home on the fourth machine. Using vnodes also reduces the chances of hotspots and makes way for better load balancing. Here's how the ring will now look:

 While a treatment of virtual nodes is important to cultivate a complete understanding of how Cassandra data distribution works, it's worth emphasizing that the process of accommodating changes to cluster topology, such as adding, removing, or replacing nodes is entirely transparent to the application. Nodes can be added to, or removed from, a live Cassandra cluster with no degradation of functionality from the application's standpoint. The same is true for unexpected changes to the cluster, such as the failure of a node, thanks to Cassandra replication, which we'll cover next.

# Data replication in Cassandra

So far, we've developed a model of distribution in which the total data set is distributed among multiple machines, but any given piece of data lives on only one machine. This model carries a big advantage over a single-node configuration, which is that it's horizontally scalable. By distributing data over multiple machines, we can accommodate ever-larger data sets simply by adding more machines to our cluster.

But our current model doesn't solve the problem of fault tolerance. No hardware is perfect; any production deployment must acknowledge the fact that a machine might fail. Our current model isn't resilient to such failures: for instance, if **Node 1** in our original three-node cluster were to suddenly catch fire, we would lose all the data on that node, including the row containing the `alice` user record.

To solve this problem, Cassandra provides replication; in fact, no serious Cassandra deployment would store only one copy of a given piece of data. The number of copies of data stored is called the **replication factor**, and it's configured on a per-keyspace level. Recall the query that we used to create our `my_status` keyspace in Chapter 1, *Getting Up and Running with Cassandra*:

```
CREATE KEYSPACE "my_status"
WITH REPLICATION = {
  'class': 'SimpleStrategy',
  'replication_factor': 1
};
```

For our development environment, we chose a replication factor of 1; there is little reason to store multiple copies of the data since we're only using a single node for development. In a production deployment, however, we would choose a higher number; 3 is a good value.

# Masterless replication

If you've worked with a relational database in production, it's likely you have experience with replication. Relational databases typically provide **master-follower replication**, in which all data is written to a single master instance; then, behind the scenes, the writes are replicated to follower instances. The application can read data from any of the followers.

Note that master-follower databases are not distributed: every machine has a full copy of the dataset. Master-follower replication is great for scaling up the processing power available for handling read requests, but does nothing to accommodate arbitrarily large datasets. Master-follower replication also provides some resilience against machine failure: in particular, failure of a machine will not result in data loss, since other machines have a full copy of the same dataset.

However, a master-follower architecture cannot guarantee full availability in the case of hardware failure. In particular, if the master instance fails, the application will be unable to write any data until the master is restored, or one of the followers is promoted to become the new master. The process of promoting a new master can be automated using built-in database features or third-party tools, but there will still be some downtime during which the application cannot write data.

## Replication without a master

Cassandra solves this problem by simply removing the master instance from the picture. In Cassandra, when a piece of data is written, the write is sent to all of the nodes that should hold a copy of that data; no single node is authoritative. This neatly solves the availability problem: with no master instance, there is no single point of failure. If a node becomes unavailable, the data intended for it is still written to the other nodes that should store it; the application need not halt the writing of the data.

> In fact, Cassandra is even more robust when a node is unavailable to receive a write. Through a process called **hinted handoff**, other nodes in the cluster will store information about the write request and then replay that request to the missing node when it becomes available again.

Returning to our model of Cassandra replication from the previous section, we can now expand it to account for replication. In particular, each virtual node is in fact stored on multiple physical nodes. Let's pick up our four-node cluster, taking a look at how data would be distributed with a replication factor of three:

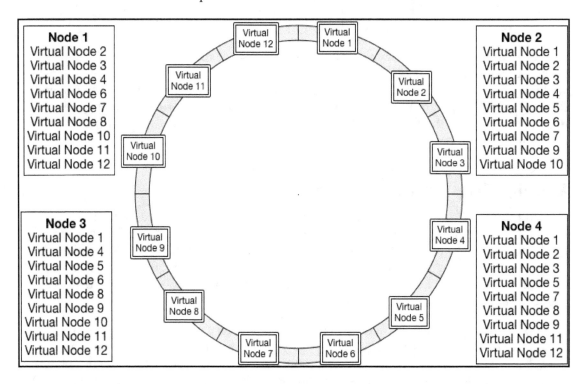

Each physical machine now claims responsibility for nine virtual nodes; each virtual node lives on three machines. If one machine fails, Cassandra can continue serving read and write requests since copies of each of the failed machine's virtual nodes also live on two other machines. Even better, since virtual nodes are assigned randomly, none of the three healthy machines has to bear the entire burden of handling the failed machine's requests:

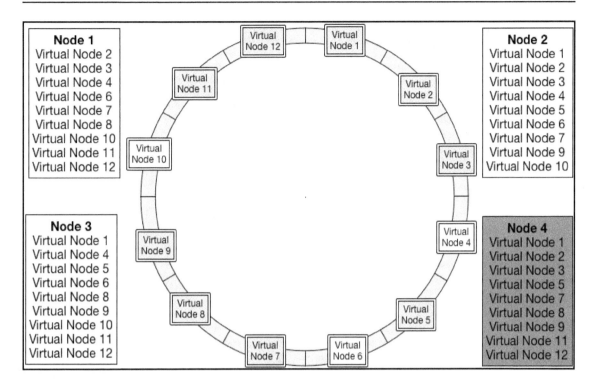

If the failed machine is permanently out of commission, it can be replaced by a new physical node; Cassandra will take care of populating the replacement machine with the data in the virtual nodes covered by the failed machine.

Further readings on Cassandra's data distribution and replication can be found in the DataStax Cassandra documentation at http://www.datastax.com/documentation/cassandra/2.1/cassandra/ar chitecture/architectureDataDistributeAbout_c.html.

# Gossip protocol

In past sections, we have dwelt on how Cassandra distributes data using partitioners and how Cassandra replicates data for high availability. For the earlier said features to work, every node within the cluster should have information about every other node. Cassandra nodes should get the information when a new node is added so they can rearrange the token ranges. They should know whenever a node is down so they can store hints. So, there has to be some sort of communication between the nodes so each node can maintain the entire cluster view up to date at all times. Cassandra uses a gossip protocol for internode communication.

Gossip protocol is mainly used to relay information about the location and state of other nodes in the cluster. Each node sends information about itself and other nodes they gossip with to up to three other nodes every second. This way, the entire cluster view is propagated to every node. Nodes also learn about topology changes quickly. Cassandra also uses gossip as part of failure detection to determine whether nodes are up/down for routing purposes.

Whenever a new node joins a cluster, it contacts a list of nodes knows as the seed nodes. This list is configurable and set in the `cassandra.yaml` configuration file. Seed nodes should be relatively stable and are specifically used for bootstrapping new nodes. The new node communicates with the seed nodes via gossip protocol to get information about the rest of the cluster.

# Multidata center cluster

One of the nice features of Cassandra that makes it a popular NoSQL database in the industry is its native support for multidata center clusters. There are no manual steps required to clone data from one data center to another. Once the cluster is properly configured with two data centers, all the requests (read or write) are forwarded to both data centers. For this setup to work, a few configuration changes, as well as schema changes, are required.

Here is an illustration of a multidata center cluster:

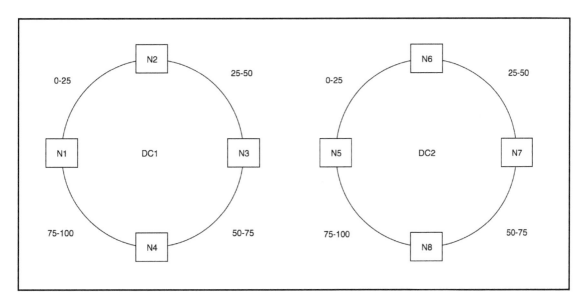

Here, we have two datacenters named **DC1** and **DC2,** each with four nodes. For simplicity purposes, I am assuming a token range of 0-100. We will notice that the entire token range is split into four ranges on both the data centers rather than eight ranges. This means the same data is written to both the data centers. Even though they are part of the same cluster, both of them are considered separate entities when it comes to topology. Also, there has to be connectivity between all the nodes in the cluster irrespective of the data center.

The main components of a multidata center cluster are:

- Snitch
- Replication Strategy
- Keyspace

# Snitch

A snitch determines the data center and rack configuration for the cluster. Every node can be configured to use a certain type of snitch. This configuration is available as `endpoint_snitch` within the `cassandra.yaml` file.

For single data center setups, it is common to leave the snitch to a default value of SimpleSnitch. For multi-data center setups, there are a bunch of snitches to select from depending on the networking setup and other factors.

PropertyFileSnitch reads the network configuration from the cassandra-topology.properties file. This file contains the list of nodes within the cluster and information about which data center and rack each node belongs to. The file might look like this:

```
# Datacenter One

127.0.0.1=DC1:RAC1
127.0.0.2=DC1:RAC1

127.0.0.3=DC1:RAC2

# Datacenter Two

127.0.0.4=DC2:RAC1

127.0.0.5=DC2:RAC2
127.0.0.6=DC2:RAC2

# Default (Nodes with IP address not present in this file will be assigned this DC and RACK)

default=DC1:RAC1
```

From this file, we can ascertain that **DC1** will contain three nodes, and **DC2** will contain three nodes. You can also specify different racks within a data center. Racks are used for replica placement. Cassandra will try to write replicas to different racks. But having multiple racks is not recommended, since it becomes hard to maintain consistency when you have an odd number of nodes within a data center. Any topology changes, such as adding/removing nodes, will require you to make changes to this file on all the nodes.

Both data center and racks are logical in this case. You can have multiple logical data centers even though all the nodes might exist on the same physical data center.

Another important snitch is GossipingPropertyFileSnitch. In this snitch, you will have to specify the data center and rack value of that particular node within the cassandra-rackdc.properties file. The file ideally contains two properties:

*dc=DC1*

*rack=RAC1*

This snitch uses the data center and rack information present in this file and propagates it to other nodes using gossip protocol. This snitch is recommended for production usage, since no file changes are required on nodes when you increase the cluster size.

Cassandra provides a host of other snitches for different scenarios. In the case of running a Cassandra cluster on Amazon Web Service, you can use the Ec2Snitch. You can find a full list of snitches, along with the explanation here at `http://docs.datastax.com/en/cassandra/3.x/cassandra/architecture/archSnitchesAbout.html?hl=snitch`.

# Replication strategy

Replication strategy determines how data is written to and read from Cassandra. This is set at the keyspace level. Together with replication factor, this guides the entire replication process of a keyspace.

- `SimpleStrategy`: So far, we have created keyspace with this replication strategy. This strategy places replicas on any node within cluster, irrespective of the snitch or data center. It treats the entire cluster as a single data center.
- `NetworkTopologyStrategy`: This replication strategy is used to specify data centers and the number of replicas to place within each data center. Together with the snitch, this ensures that Cassandra is aware of data centers and replica placement is immaculate. Suppose you have two data centers with the names `DC1` and `DC2`; you can create a keyspace with this replication strategy, as follows:

```
CREATE KEYSPACE "my_status"
WITH REPLICATION = {
  'class': 'NetworkTopologyStrategy',
  'DC1': 3, 'DC2': 3
};
```

This will ensure that three replicas are written to both the `DC1` and `DC2` data centers.

# Durable writes

Another keyspace option, which is often not required to tamper with, is `durable_writes`. By default, durable writes is set to true.

When a write request is received, the node first writes a copy of the data to an on-disk append-only structure called **commitlog**. Then, it writes the data to an in-memory structure called **memtable**. When the memtable is full or reaches a certain size, it is flushed to an on-disk immutable structure called **SSTable**. Setting durable writes to true ensures data is written to the commitlog. In case the node restarts, the memtables are gone since they reside in memory. However, memtables can be reconstructed by replaying the commitlog, as the disk structure won't get wiped out even with node restarts.

The following figure illustrates the Cassandra write path with durable writes turned on/off:

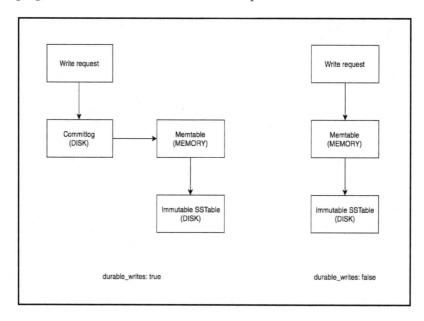

# Consistency

Masterless replication offers huge advantages in maintaining full availability in the face of hardware failure, but it also creates a thorny, if subtle, problem: how can we be sure that the data we're reading is the most recent version of that data?

Let's first consider the master-follower architecture we discussed earlier. When our application issues a write request to the master instance, that request only returns a successful response once the data has been successfully written to the master instance. A successful response does not, however, guarantee that the data has been replicated to all of the followers: any master-follower system will involve some delay before writes are replicated to the followers.

Still, in this system, there is a simple way to guarantee that, when we read a piece of data, we're reading the most up-to-date version of it: simply read from the master. Of course, if we only ever read from the master, the followers don't do much for us other than providing a hot standby in case the master fails. But if we identify specific situations in which it's critical to have a guarantee that we're reading the most up-to-date data, we can read data from the master in only those situations and make use of the followers in other scenarios.

# Immediate and eventual consistency

In the master-follower scenario, we can say that reads from the master provide **immediate consistency**. Immediate consistency is simply a guarantee that as soon as a piece of data is written successfully, it will be available to clients who are reading that data. There is no delay between writing data and being able to read it.

On the other hand, reads from the followers provide **eventual consistency**. Eventual consistency means that once the data is successfully written, it will, at some point in the future, become available for reads. There is no guarantee of how soon it will become available; the only guarantee is that the time will eventually come. Of course, in a healthy production deployment, the delay between write and read availability is typically in the order of milliseconds, but we have no guarantee that it won't be much longer.

# Consistency in Cassandra

As application developers using Cassandra, we also have a choice between immediate and eventual consistency. However, we don't implement this decision by selecting a particular machine to read from: when interacting with Cassandra, the particular node we're communicating with is irrelevant because requests are always forwarded to the node or nodes that should handle them.

Instead, Cassandra has a built-in notion of **tunable consistency**, which allows us to make a decision for each query about what consistency characteristics we want. Specifically, we tune consistency by telling Cassandra what constitutes a successful request.

# The anatomy of a successful request

From the application's standpoint, when we issue a query to Cassandra, we simply send some CQL over the wire and, at some later point, receive a response. Hopefully, the response will return successfully; if not, we will receive an error.

One requisite for a successful response is that our query is well formed: if we misspell the name of a column, for instance, we will certainly see an error. But this condition for success is of little concern to us, since an invalid query will always generate an error, regardless of external factors.

More interesting from the perspective of consistency is the other condition of a successful request: that Cassandra is internally able to fulfill it. For a write request, this means durably storing the data being written; for a read request, it means retrieving the data from storage and returning it.

The crux of the question is this: *how many nodes must be involved in the fulfillment of a request for it to be considered successful?* For instance, if we are writing data to a row, we might consider the write successful as soon as the data is written to a single replica of that row; or we might require that the data be written to all of the replicas it belongs on before we consider it a success.

When reading data, the same logic applies: we may want Cassandra to just read one copy of the data and return it to us; or we may want it to read all copies of the data, compare their timestamps, and return to us the most recent version.

# Tuning consistency

Cassandra's tunable consistency allows us to specify for each query how many replicas must be involved for the request to be considered a success. Consistency is not directly specified as part of the CQL query; instead, it is provided as an additional parameter given to the driver when performing a query. Different language drivers handle this differently, but any CQL driver should provide an interface for specifying the consistency for a given query.

Cassandra defines eleven different consistency levels, but many of them are for fairly specialized scenarios. We will explore the three most important and useful consistency levels: ONE, ALL, and QUORUM.

# Eventual consistency with ONE

For the remainder of our discussion of consistency, let's assume we're using a replication factor of three. That means, regardless of the total number of nodes we have in our cluster, any given piece of data will live on three different nodes.

Let's say we update the `alice` row in the `users` table, changing her e-mail address using the ONE consistency level. This means that the write should be considered a success as soon as one copy of the data is written durably. When the request is completed, we know that `alice`'s new e-mail address has definitely been written to one node, but we don't know whether the change has propagated to the other two replicas.

If, immediately after writing the `alice` row, we attempt to read it back, also using the ONE consistency, we're telling Cassandra that it can read any one of the three copies of the user row in the cluster and return that copy to us. For the sake of illustration, suppose that at the exact moment we try to read the row, the replicas are in the following states:

- Replica 1 is the replica that acknowledged the write request. By definition, it has the up-to-date e-mail address.
- Replica 2 has also written the updated e-mail address durably.
- Replica 3 has not yet received the updated e-mail address.

By reading with the ONE consistency, we're saying that we're fine receiving any of the three replicas' copies of the user row. If the copy we get back happens to come from Replica 1 or Replica 2, we'll get back `alice`'s record with her up-to-date e-mail address. If it comes from Replica 3, however, we'll get an outdated record with her old address.

This is a temporary state of affairs: eventually, Replica 3 will also get the update, and at that point, we will get the latest copy of the data, regardless of which replica serves the request. But we don't know when that will be: when we read and write data using consistency level ONE, we are in a scenario of eventual consistency.

On the other hand, using consistency level ONE, we're very resilient to failure. Even if two of the three machines that hold copies of `alice`'s user record are unavailable, Cassandra can still successfully fulfill requests at this consistency level using the one healthy machine. As long as we're willing to give up immediate consistency, we can sleep very soundly knowing that our application will continue working even in the case of a multinode hardware failure.

Eventual consistency is also beneficial for performance. When reading or writing data at the ONE consistency, Cassandra doesn't only send the request to one replica; instead, it sends the request to all the interested replicas and then fulfills the request as soon as the first one responds successfully. So, the time it takes to service a request at ONE consistency is bounded by the fastest node to respond.

## Immediate consistency with ALL

In many scenarios, however, eventual consistency is unacceptable. alice may be using the MyStatus web interface to update her e-mail address. After submitting the form with her updated information, the alice browser is redirected to a page where she can view her profile. At this point, the web application will need to read the profile data from Cassandra; if it happens to read from an out-of-data replica, it will appear to alice that her e-mail address was not actually updated.

At the other end of the consistency spectrum from ONE lies the ALL consistency level. At this level, all interested replicas must respond successfully in order for the request to be considered a success. If we update alice's e-mail address with the ALL consistency, our UPDATE query won't be completed successfully until the new e-mail address has been written durably to all three replicas. As soon as the request is complete, we know that all copies are up to date.

Similarly, if we read the row back with the ALL consistency, Cassandra will read all three replicas' copies of her user record and compare their timestamps. If the data is different on different replicas, Cassandra will return the copy with the most recent timestamp, ensuring that we are getting the most recently written copy of the row.

Using the ALL consistency for both reading and writing, however, is an overkill in virtually all cases. If we write the data at the ALL consistency, we can subsequently read it with the ONE consistency because we know that all of the replicas have the most recent copy of the data. Conversely, if we are reading with the ALL consistency, we will have immediate consistency, even if the profile was updated with the ONE consistency. At least one of the replicas has the most recent version of the data, and since we're reading all the copies, we're guaranteed to get the latest version back in one of them.

The downside of the ALL consistency is that when we use it, we have no tolerance for failure. If any one of the machines that should store alice's user profile is unavailable, the request at the ALL consistency will fail. Queries at the ALL consistency also have unpleasant performance characteristics. Since Cassandra must wait for all interested replicas to respond, the overall performance of the request is bounded by the response time of the slowest replica.

Fortunately, there is a middle ground that allows us to have immediate consistency without completely sacrificing performance and resilience to failure.

# Fault-tolerant immediate consistency with QUORUM

If we consider a request successful once it's been fulfilled by a single replica, we're very resilient to node failure, but we have to be willing to accept eventual consistency. If we require that every replica responds to a request before that request is complete, we have immediate consistency at the cost of making every replica a single point of failure. But we can achieve both immediate consistency and failure tolerance by defining a successful request as one that's fulfilled by just enough replicas.

This is the QUORUM consistency level, and just enough is precisely defined as the strict majority of replicas. For our replication factor of three, QUORUM requires that two nodes fulfill the request. Let's explore how the QUORUM consistency gives us the best of both worlds.

Returning to our e-mail update scenario, let's send the query to change alice's e-mail using the QUORUM consistency. Immediately after the UPDATE query completes, the worst-case scenario is as follows:

- Replica 1 is one of the replicas that acknowledged the write request, and by definition, it has the up-to-date e-mail address
- Replica 2 is the other replica that acknowledged the write request, so it also has the up-to-date e-mail address
- Replica 3 has not yet received the updated e-mail address

By the contract of the QUORUM consistency level, we are assured that at least two of the three replicas have persisted alice's new email address. If we then read the alice user profile, also at QUORUM consistency, Cassandra will wait to receive at least two copies of the profile from two replicas. In the previous scenario, at least one of the copies must come from Replica 1 or Replica 2; we're guaranteed that Cassandra will see the most recent version of the user profile before returning it to us.

This observation generalizes to quorums at any replication factor: as long as data is written to a strict majority of nodes and read from a strict majority of nodes, we know that there is some replica that was involved in both the write and the subsequent read. So, we're guaranteed immediate consistency.

Note that we are only guaranteed immediate consistency if data is written and read at the QUORUM consistency. This is in contrast to the ALL consistency, which guarantees immediate consistency if it's used for either writing or reading.

The QUORUM consistency is also resilient to failure: if one of the three nodes holding a copy of alice's user profile is unavailable, Cassandra can still successfully fulfill requests using the other two nodes. However, QUORUM is not an entirely free lunch; operations at the ONE consistency level can handle a failure of any two nodes, whereas the QUORUM consistency can only handle a single node failure.

The QUORUM performance is also a middle ground between ONE and ALL: the QUORUM operations are bounded by the median response time of the interested replicas. This is a big advantage over the ALL consistency if one replica happens to be under especially heavy load; but it is not as speedy as ONE, which will be as responsive as the fastest node.

## Local consistency levels

With multidata centers, requests can go to any data center. Often, when using the QUORUM consistency, requests go to both data centers before returning a successful result. This introduces cross-data center latency and is detrimental in situations where latency has to be minimal. To avoid this, Cassandra provides the LOCAL consistency levels. The alternatives for the ONE and QUORUM consistency levels in a multidata center scenario are the LOCAL_ONE and LOCAL_QUORUM consistency levels.

In the case of the LOCAL_ONE consistency, the request is successful as soon as one of the replica writes/reads on the local data center returns acknowledgement. By local data center, we mean the data center where the coordinator node for the request resides or the node where the request was sent. In the case of the LOCAL_QUORUM, a QUORUM of replicas in the local data center should return acknowledgement of successful read/write.

Cassandra also provides another consistency level, which isn't particularly useful and is known as EACH_QUORUM. As the name suggests, EACH_QUORUM requires that quorum be achieved in each of the data centers. To explain the difference between EACH_QUORUM and QUORUM, let's consider a cluster with two data centers, DC1 and DC2. Suppose we set the replication factor of our keyspace my_status to DC1: 3 and DC2: 3.

- In the case of EACH_QUORUM, two out of three replicas on DC1 and two out of three replicas on DC2 need to return acknowledgment in order for a request to be successful.

- In the case of QUORUM, four out of six replicas on DC1 + DC2 combined need to return acknowledgment in order for a request to be successful. It could be possible that three from DC1 and one from DC2 return acknowledgements, or vice-versa.

# Comparing consistency levels

Having explored the three most useful consistency levels Cassandra provides, let's compare their important characteristics:

| Level | Consistency behavior | Replicas required | Failure tolerance | Performance |
|---|---|---|---|---|
| ONE | Eventual | 1 | Tolerates failure of all but one replica | Fastest node |
| ALL | Immediate | All | None | Slowest node |
| QUORUM | Immediate, if used for both writes and reads | Strict majority | Tolerates failure of a minority of replicas | Median performing node |

Cassandra supports other consistency levels as well; their uses are more esoteric and many deal specifically with deployments where a cluster is spread across multiple data centers. For a full reference, take a look at `http://docs.datastax.com/en/cassandra/3.x/cassandra/dml/dmlConfigConsistency.html`.

# Choosing the right consistency level

We've explored how the process of updating `alice`'s e-mail address would work at the consistency levels ONE, ALL, and QUORUM. But what consistency levels should the MyStatus application actually use?

We recognized earlier that in the case where `alice` updates her own user profile and then views the results, eventual consistency is undesirable: if she sees an outdated copy of her profile, it may appear that her e-mail address update did not work at all. So, we will want to ensure that from `alice`'s standpoint, changes to her profile are immediately consistent.

We've seen that of the two levels that ensure immediate consistency, QUORUM has considerably more appeal from the perspective of fault tolerance and performance. We also know that in order to get immediate consistency from QUORUM, we'll need to both write and read at the QUORUM level.

So, when `alice` updates her e-mail address, we'll write that column to Cassandra at `QUORUM`. When `alice` views her own profile, we'll also read her profile data from the users table at the `QUORUM` consistency. By always using `QUORUM` when `alice` is interacting with her own profile, we guarantee that she'll see the effects of all the changes she has made. When other users are viewing `alice`'s profile, however, we have no strong need for immediate consistency. Here, `bob` will not know or care if the data he's seeing on `alice`'s profile is a few milliseconds out of date. So, eventual consistency is perfectly acceptable for the case of viewing another user's profile.

So, when displaying one user's profile to a different user, we'll use the more permissive `ONE` consistency. These requests will be more resilient to node failures, perform better, and impose less load on the cluster since they won't require coordinating reads across multiple replicas.

 For a deeper dive into consistency in Cassandra, see the DataStax Cassandra documentation at `http://docs.datastax.com/en/cassandra/3.x/cassandra/dml/dmlDataConsistencyTOC.html?hl=consistency`.

# The CAP theorem

Through tunable consistency, Cassandra allows us to choose where in the trade-off between consistency and failure-tolerance we are most comfortable. But the trade-off is there nonetheless; this is an unavoidable fact not just about Cassandra, but about all distributed systems. The trade-off between consistency and availability is formalized by the **CAP theorem**.

The CAP Theorem concerns the following three properties of a distributed system, from which it derives its name:

- Consistency in the CAP theorem refers to immediate consistency - the effects of a successful write operation must be immediately available to any client who wishes to read the data
- Availability refers to the ability of the system to give every request a response about whether it succeeded or failed
- Partition tolerance is resilience to a particular kind of hardware failure - the arbitrary loss of data in inter-node communication

The CAP theorem states simply that it is impossible for a distributed system to provide all three of the earlier properties, but that it is possible to provide any two of them. The CAP theorem is best treated as a framework from which to think about the properties of distributed systems, rather than a rigorous description of real-world databases. That said, we can briefly explore where Cassandra lies within the CAP framework.

When using the ONE consistency, Cassandra is clearly an AP system; we don't get immediate consistency, but the cluster can tolerate a complete partition between nodes. If the node that receives a request is able to communicate with one of the interested replicas, it will give a successful response; otherwise, it will fail. Note that returning a failed response does not violate availability as defined in CAP; the only requirement is that the request terminate with information about whether it succeeded.

When using the QUORUM or ALL consistency, Cassandra becomes a CA system. Immediate consistency is guaranteed, but only when all nodes in the cluster are able to communicate with one another. In the event of a partition of the cluster, any request that requires responses from nodes on both sides of the partition will fail.

The slides for the presentation that introduced the CAP conjecture (later the CAP theorem) can be found at
`http://www.cs.berkeley.edu/~brewer/cs262b-2004/PODC-keynote.pdf`.

# Handling conflicting data

As we explored earlier, Cassandra's masterless replication can lead to situations in which multiple versions of the same record exist on different nodes. Since there is no master node containing the canonical copy of a record, Cassandra must use other means to determine which version of the data is correct.

This situation comes into play when reading data at any consistency level other than ONE. When our application requests a row from Cassandra, we will receive a response with that row's data; each column will contain one value. However, if we're reading at a consistency level such as QUORUM or ALL, Cassandra internally will fetch the copies of the data from multiple nodes; it's possible that the different copies will contain conflicting data. It's up to Cassandra to figure out exactly what to return to us.

The problem is most acute when different clients are writing the same piece of data concurrently. Let's return to a scenario we explored in `Chapter 7`, *Expanding Your Data Model*: two employees of HappyCorp, Heather and Charles, are simultaneously attempting to update the `location` field in the user record of HappyCorp's shared account. Let's suppose that we are writing data at consistency level `ONE`. This concurrent operation could be carried out via the following sequence of events:

- Heather updates the location to New York; the update is acknowledged by Replica 1
- Charles updates the location to Palo Alto; the update is acknowledged by Replica 2

Just after Heather and Charles's concurrent updates, the Replica 1 copy of the HappyCorp user record will contain New York in its `location` field, and the Replica 2 copy will contain Palo Alto. Now, before the updates have a chance to propagate to any nodes except the ones that respectively acknowledged them, let's read the data back at the `ALL` consistency.

When Cassandra receives the read request, it will fetch HappyCorp's user record from Replicas 1, 2, and 3. Each replica will contain a different version of the record: Replica 1's copy has New York in the `location` field, Replica 2's copy has Palo Alto, and Replica 3's copy does not contain anything in that field. So, what location will Cassandra actually return to us?

# Last-write-wins conflict resolution

Under the hood, every time a piece of data is written to Cassandra, a timestamp is attached. Then, when Cassandra has to deal with conflicting data as in the scenario mentioned earlier, it simply chooses the data with the most recent timestamp. Even though the sequence of writes we discussed earlier was concurrent from the perspective of the distributed database, it's vanishingly unlikely that Cassandra received them at the exact same microsecond. So, one of them will have the more recent timestamp, and that's the one that Cassandra will return when we read the data back with the `ALL` consistency.

It's important to emphasize that each column has its own timestamp value; if we issue a query that only updates the location field in HappyCorp's user record, the location field will carry the timestamp of that operation, but the other fields in HappyCorp's record will still carry the timestamps of whenever they were last updated.

The ability to discretely update individual columns in a row and have the timestamp of the last write associated with the column rather than the whole row is why Cassandra is able to use the relatively simplistic last-write-wins strategy for conflict resolution. If, in the previous scenario, Heather had updated HappyCorp's location, but Charles had updated the e-mail address, Cassandra would simply take the most recent version of each column, synthesizing an up-to-date view of the row that does not yet exist on any individual replica.

 For an illuminating comparison of Cassandra's conflict resolution with strategies used by other distributed databases, see the blog post *Why Cassandra doesn't need vector clocks* at http://www.datastax.com/dev/blog/why-cassandra-doesnt-need-vecto r-clocks.

# Introspecting write timestamps

As it turns out, CQL gives us a mechanism for finding out when a particular column was last written. This is done using the WRITETIME function. Let's say we're interested in the write timestamps for the e-mail and the location fields in the happycorp user record:

```
SELECT "email", WRITETIME("email"),
  "location", WRITETIME("location")
FROM "users"
WHERE "username" = 'happycorp';
```

We'll see that Cassandra gives us the write times of each column formatted as microseconds since the UNIX epoch:

| email | writetime(email) | location | writetime(location) |
|---|---|---|---|
| media@happycorp.com | 1481711196093000 | New York, NY | 1481711604804000 |

Note that the timestamps are different; we initially wrote the email address when we created the happycorp record and later updated the row to have a location.

For more information on timestamp introspection in Cassandra, see the DataStax CQL documentation at
`http://www.datastax.com/documentation/cql/3.1/cql/cql_using/use_`
`writetime.html`.

# Overriding write timestamps

Typically, write timestamps are assigned to data automatically by Cassandra, reflecting the time at which the cluster initially receives the request. However, CQL gives us a mechanism to override the default timestamp and instead choose our own.

To demonstrate, let's say we want to add a `location` value to the `bob` user record at a specific timestamp: December 14, 2016 at 10.33.24 UTC. In order to do this, we can use the `USING TIMESTAMP` clause in our `UPDATE` query:

```
UPDATE "users"
USING TIMESTAMP 1481711604904000
SET "location" = 'Austin, TX'
WHERE "username" = 'bob';
```

Reading `bob`'s user record back, we can see that it now has the location we specified:

```
 username | location
----------+------------
      bob | Austin, TX

(1 rows)
```

Now let's issue another update to `bob`'s location using a `TIMESTAMP` one microsecond before the one we provided previously:

```
UPDATE "users"
USING TIMESTAMP 1481711604903999
SET "location" = 'Tulsa, OK'
WHERE "username" = 'bob';
```

Now let's check the state of the bob row:

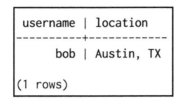

Notably, the location is still Austin. This leads to an important observation about write timestamps: in addition to giving Cassandra information about resolving conflicts at read time, they're also used to determine at write time whether a given value is more up to date than the value Cassandra currently has stored. This is true even in a single-replica, single-node configuration, such as the one we have set up for development.

Since the timestamp of our second update was earlier than the timestamp of our first update, Cassandra recognizes that the original value is actually a more recent version of the data, and thus, it discards the second update altogether.

# Distributed deletion

When we want to delete data from storage, we might assume that Cassandra simply removes the data from disk and forgets that it ever existed. In a non-distributed environment, this approach to deletion would be entirely sufficient, but deletion is a bit more complex in a distributed database such as Cassandra. To find out why, let's return to and modify our previous scenario with Heather and Charles making concurrent modifications to happycorp's user record.

In our modified scenario, Heather will still be updating the location column to contain New York, but Charles will be attempting to delete the contents of that column altogether. As with the original scenario, they'll be making their respective changes at roughly the same time, and our application will issue the UPDATE and DELETE queries at the ONE consistency level. Consider the following sequence of events:

1. Heather issues a request to update the location value to New York; this is acknowledged by Replica 1.

2. Charles issues a request to delete the contents of the `location` column; this is acknowledged by Replica 2.

Given that Charles's request to delete the location happened just after Heather's request to update it, the correct state of the `location` column is to contain no data. But with a naïve approach to deletion, that won't be the outcome. Let's consider what will happen if we read the `happycorp` user record at the `ALL` consistency just after Charles and Heather's requests completes, but before the requests have propagated to replicas other than the ones that respectively acknowledge them.

When the coordinator reads all copies of the `happycorp` user record, it will see one version with a `location` field containing `New York`, one version with no data in the `location` column, and one version with the old location prior to either of their updates. Observing that the version with the most recent timestamp contains `New York`, it will determine that this is the up-to-date value of the `location` field. This is a violation of immediate consistency; however, since the last change to the `location` column was the deletion, the `ALL` consistency read should reflect that fact.

To deal with scenarios like this, Cassandra does not completely forget that a value ever existed when it is deleted. Instead, it stores a tombstone in place of the deleted value; that tombstone is simply a marker that data was deleted from that column. Tombstones, like normal column values, carry a timestamp indicating when the deletion happened.

Armed with a tombstone, Cassandra can correctly serve our request to read `happycorp`'s user record just after the concurrent update and deletion. The node coordinating the read will now see a version of the row with `New York` in the `location` field, a version of the row with the old location, and a version of the row with the tombstone in the `location` column. Since the tombstone will have the most recent write timestamp of the three, the coordinator will correctly determine that there should be no data returned for the `location` field.

 For more on deletion and tombstones, see the DataStax Cassandra documentation at `http://docs.datastax.com/en/cassandra/3.x/cassandra/dml/dmlAboutDeletes.html?hl=deletes`.

# Stumbling on tombstones

We've seen that tombstones are critical to ensuring that Cassandra can correctly identify that a piece of data has been deleted in a distributed environment, but tombstones also have a downside. Since tombstones are stored in place of the deleted values, they continue to occupy space in the range of clustering columns in a given partition. In some situations, this can lead to unexpected performance degradation and even errors.

To use a somewhat artificial illustration, let's say that `alice` is now a long-time MyStatus user and has created tens of thousands of status updates. Let's also assume that `alice` decides one day that she wants to delete 1,000 recent status updates she's created. Once she's done with that process, we have stored a thousand tombstones, each of which is stored at the ID of the deleted status update in the table's data structure.

The next time someone wants to read `alice`'s user timeline, we're going to run into a slight problem. If we ask for 20 most recent status updates in her timeline, Cassandra will dutifully scan the 20 most recent IDs in the `alice` partition. But it will find that these are all tombstones! Luckily, Cassandra is smart enough to keep looking; it won't simply return an empty result set. But it will have to scan a thousand tombstones before it finds any non-deleted data. This scan carries a substantial performance overhead when compared to the same operation with no tombstones getting in the way.

For that reason, it's best to avoid situations in which your application will need to scan over-clustering column ranges containing lots of tombstones.

Tombstones do not live forever. Instead, they are automatically cleared by Cassandra's compaction process after a configured amount of time has elapsed. By default, that duration is ten days. This means that a node may rejoin the cluster after up to ten days of downtime without a risk of deleted records springing back to life. From our perspective as application developers, the relatively long life of tombstones means that we are best off thinking of them as permanent and strenuously avoiding situations where many tombstone records must be scanned in order to service a query.

# Expiring columns with TTL

We first encountered the CQL DELETE command, which allows us to remove the value of a column or an entire row, in Chapter 5, *Establishing Relationships*. Another way to remove data from Cassandra is to give it a **time-to-live** (TTL). This is equivalent to deleting data in the future: when we write data with a TTL, it is marked as deleted after the amount of time we specify has elapsed.

CQL allows us to attach a TTL to any INSERT or UPDATE statement. Let's experiment with setting an expiring location value:

```
UPDATE "users"
USING TTL 30
SET "location" = 'Vancouver'
WHERE "username" = 'bob';
```

TTL values are given in seconds, so what we've done here is tell Cassandra that bob's location should be Vancouver for the next thirty seconds, after which it should be deleted. CQL also allows us to introspect the TTL attached to any data column using the TTL function:

```
SELECT "username", "location", TTL("location")
FROM "users"
WHERE "username" = 'bob';
```

We'll see that the TTL column in the result tells us how many seconds remain until the location field expires:

```
username | location  | ttl(location)
----------+-----------+---------------
     bob | Vancouver |            17

(1 rows)
```

If we now wait the full thirty seconds and then check the bob user record again, we'll see that the location value has disappeared.

Expiring columns can be useful in situations where we don't want data to stick around forever. For instance, we may want to generate a password reset link using a random token that is e-mailed to a user. We might want that token to only work for 24 hours to reduce the risk of being used by someone else besides the user requesting the password reset. Expiring columns give us a seamless way to accomplish this.

# Table configuration options

So far, we have looked at a few configuration options, especially to enable certain functionalities in Cassandra or configure Cassandra as you would in a production cluster. We have looked at keyspace replication options, such as replication strategy and replication factor. Similarly, you can set certain configuration parameters for a table as well. Let's look at the schema of our table users:

```
CREATE TABLE my_status.users (
    username text PRIMARY KEY,
    education frozen<education_information>,
    education_history set<frozen<education_information>>,
    email text,
    encrypted_password blob,
    location text,
    telephone_numbers map<text, frozen<set<text>>>,
    version timeuuid
) WITH bloom_filter_fp_chance = 0.01
    AND caching = {'keys': 'ALL', 'rows_per_partition': 'NONE'}
    AND comment = ''
    AND compaction = {'class': 'org.apache.cassandra.db.compaction.SizeTieredCompactionStrategy', 'max_threshold': '32', 'min_threshold': '4'}
    AND compression = {'chunk_length_in_kb': '64', 'class': 'org.apache.cassandra.io.compress.LZ4Compressor'}
    AND crc_check_chance = 1.0
    AND dclocal_read_repair_chance = 0.1
    AND default_time_to_live = 0
    AND gc_grace_seconds = 864000
    AND max_index_interval = 2048
    AND memtable_flush_period_in_ms = 0
    AND min_index_interval = 128
    AND read_repair_chance = 0.0
    AND speculative_retry = '99PERCENTILE';
CREATE INDEX users_education_idx ON my_status.users (education);
```

Here, you will notice a bunch of configurations being mentioned after the `WITH` keyword. Even though we didn't mention them when creating the table, Cassandra automatically sets the default values. Let's take a look at some of these options:

- **Caching**: Cassandra provides two caching mechanisms to store data that is read frequently in memory so it can be fetched faster during later requests. Key cache is used to store partition keys and their locations on disk in memory. Row cache is used to store entire partitions in memory along with the actual rows.
- **Compaction**: Compaction is an internal mechanism used to get rid of excess data within Cassandra and merge multiple copies of the same partition (or row). As we discussed before, Cassandra updates are upserts. So, compaction is necessary to get rid of multiple copies of data as well as deleted data.
- **Compression**: Data is compressed when it is written to the disk to reduce disk usage. This increases the CPU usage as well as read latency.
- **Default_time_to_live**: This sets the TTL for the entire table. This can be overridden if you specify TTL while inserting a row into the table.
- **Gc_grace_seconds**: This is the amount of time in seconds Cassandra waits before actually deleting tombstoned data.

We will look at the other options in the next chapter, where we will dive into the internal aspects of Cassandra to a certain extent.

# Summary

In this chapter, we confronted and explored the major issues that stem from Cassandra's masterless, distributed, and replicated architecture. Interacting with Cassandra often feels indistinguishable from working with a single-node data store, but when working with any distributed database, we need to think about the trade-off between consistency and availability. In some situations, we might be willing to read slightly out-of-date data for the sake of performance and failure tolerance; in others, we will tolerate a higher probability of a request failing in order to ensure that the data we're reading is fully up-to-date.

You learned that the partition key for a row determines not only its physical location in storage but also which nodes within the cluster store copies of the row. This further motivates the practice of designing our table schemas such that most queries are looking for data grouped under a single partition key.

You discovered how in a distributed database, deletion is not as simple as removing a value from storage and forgetting it ever existed. We saw that maintaining tombstones for deleted data allows Cassandra to guarantee that deletions are always reflected when reading a row with strong consistency. We also saw that tombstones can lead to performance degradation in scenarios where we're trying to scan clustering column ranges that contain many deleted rows.

In the next chapter, we will set up a multinode Cassandra cluster and examine how the dynamic changes when you have more than one node. You will also see consistency level changes in action and how Cassandra handles node failures. We will also take a look at the caching mechanisms and some of the data structures used by Cassandra internally. Finally, we will focus on the repair mechanism provided by Cassandra to ensure data integrity in the cases of node failures or network outages.

# 11
# Cassandra Multi-Node Cluster

So far, we have been running a single Cassandra node to store all our data. This isn't how it is ideally supposed to run. This defeats the purpose of Cassandra being a distributed database. As you saw in the previous chapter, every Cassandra node stores a subset of data, which is based on the token range assigned to that node. Multiple nodes will have overlapping token ranges in case the replication factor is higher than 1. In our case, the entire token range resides on the single node that we have been running. To demonstrate the distributed nature of Cassandra and take an in-depth look at whatever concepts we learnt in the previous chapter, we will set up a **3-node cluster** and perform various operations.

Setting up a multinode cluster is slightly different from setting up the single-node cluster that we have been using so far. For a single-node cluster, leaving all the configuration options is usually sufficient. The same doesn't apply to a 3-node cluster. Since each instance has its own IP address, we will have to make some configuration changes for gossip protocol to work correctly. We will be looking at these options and what values to use under various circumstances.

We also learned about consistency levels and replication factor in the previous chapter. Cassandra has tunable consistency, where high consistency can be achieved at the cost of availability. We can tune consistency for each query. We will see how consistency and replication are interrelated. We will see how Cassandra cluster interruptions coupled with various consistency levels will impact queries.

So far, we have seen read and writes from the perspective of a developer. In this chapter, we will take an in-depth look at Cassandra's read and write paths. We will take a look at various data structures used by Cassandra to ensure data persistence and fast lookups.

Since Cassandra is eventually a consistent database, there will be cases where data is inconsistent because of various failures, including downed nodes and network failures, among others. We will take a look at different repair mechanisms used by Cassandra to keep the data consistent. Some of these are triggered automatically, while others need to be triggered manually.

Cassandra can be further tuned to speed up writes and reads. Enabling caching in certain scenarios can speed up the read queries substantially. Also, certain table properties will help keep the data consistent. We will look at some of these finer performance tuning configuration options at the end. We won't get to explore the effect of tuning some of these options on our local setup (laptop or desktop), but you can always play around if you have sufficient resources at your disposal.

In this chapter, you will study the following:

- How to set up a multinode cluster
- Cluster configuration options
- Impact of consistency level
- Cassandra write path
- Cassandra read path
- Cassandra repair mechanisms
- How to enable caching
- Fetching cluster information via nodetool

# 3 - node cluster

So far, through our journey across using Cassandra, we have been working with a single instance to create tables and test all the cool features provided by Cassandra. We haven't taken advantage of the distributed nature of Cassandra. With a single-node cluster, most operations don't require any sort of tweaking or performance tuning. Even the configuration operations can be left as default for the most part. But with a multi-node cluster, quite a few changes are required in order to get a balance between throughput and availability as well as getting gossip and other internal Cassandra operations to work properly. In this section, we will set up a 3-node cluster.

# Prerequisites

You can set up a single-node cluster on your personal laptop without making any network configuration changes since a single node requires a unique IP, and you can either use localhost or the public/private IP for gossip protocol and client communication. To run a multinode cluster, you would need to set up multiple unique IP addresses to be used by different instances of Cassandra. This should be straightforward if you had access to several physical servers or if you run Cassandra within virtual machines or docker containers. In our case, we will be setting up multiple loopback addresses apart from 127.0.0.1. Once we have multiple unique IP addresses, we will have to set up a unique directory space for each Cassandra instance to host data files, configurations files, and all the binaries. This part can be tricky if you're using a package manager for any of the operating systems. Thus, we will be downloading the binary tarball and extracting it to separate directories. After this step, we will have to change some configuration options, and we should be set to start a 3-node cluster.

Most of the aforementioned steps are common for various distributions on Linux, Mac, and Windows. Windows is a bit different when it comes to setting up multiple loopback addresses. To summarize, these are the prerequisites to run a multinode cluster:

- Multiple loopback addresses
- Cassandra binary tarball
- Multiple directories to store data and Cassandra binary files

# Tuning configuration options setting up a 3-node cluster

As discussed before, the first step would be to set up multiple loopback addresses. This step is not required on Linux machines as all the loopback IP addresses will respond by default. On a Mac, you can use the Terminal to create loopback addresses as follows:

```
$ ifconfig lo0 alias 127.0.0.2
$ ifconfig lo0 alias 127.0.0.3
```

Now to check whether these were created, you can simply run the following command on the Terminal:

```
$ ifconfig | grep 127.0.0
```

You should see three loopback addresses in the output, which are ready to be used:

```
inet 127.0.0.1 netmask 0xff000000
inet 127.0.0.2 netmask 0xff000000
inet 127.0.0.3 netmask 0xff000000
```

Once you have the three loopback addresses up and running, you will need to download the binary tarball and extract it to multiple directories with different names. This method was explained in `Chapter 1`, *Getting up and Running with Cassandra*, but let's quickly recap this.

Download the Cassandra binary tarball from here: `http://www.apache.org/dyn/closer.l ua/cassandra/3.9/apache-cassandra-3.9-bin.tar.gz`.

Make sure you keep track of the directory where you download the tarball as well as the directories to which you extract. Use the following commands to extract or untar the Cassandra package:

```
$ tar -xzf apache-cassandra-3.9-bin.tar.gz cassandra1
$ tar -xzf apache-cassandra-3.9-bin.tar.gz cassandra2
$ tar -xzf apache-cassandra-3.9-bin.tar.gz cassandra3
```

Running the sequence of the preceding shell commands will extract the contents of `apache-cassandra-3.9-bin.tar.gz` to three separate directories. Let's call them `CASSANDRA_DIR1`, `CASSANDRA_DIR2`, and `CASSANDRA_DIR3`. Each of these directories will have a `conf` directory containing all the configuration files, a `bin` directory, which contains all the binaries, utilities, and startup scripts, and a `data` directory, which contains commit logs and data files.

On Linux machines, the `tar` commands might not work and might require you to create the directories in advance depending on the OS and OS version. Take a look at the tar manpage for your respective operating systems.

Now that we have set up multiple loopback addresses and data directories, all that's left is to change configuration and run Cassandra.

For a Windows machine, I would recommend launching a Linux virtual machine and following the preceding steps. You can find several tutorials on the Internet on how to launch Ubuntu/CentOS or other Linux virtual machines on Windows using Virtualbox or VMWare. Here is a link to one such tutorial: `http://www.psychocats.net/ubuntu/virtua lbox`.

# Tuning configuration

This is the most important step in order to run a multinode Cassandra cluster without any issues. If the configuration options are left as default, gossip protocol will not work, and you will also face issues with client connections and JMX connections.

Ideally, you would need to change only two files (`cassandra.yaml` and `cassandra-env.sh`) to successfully run a multinode single data center cluster. To run a multi-data center cluster, you would have to modify some other files depending on the snitch used and the data center/rack names.

The following are some of the configuration options based on the two files that you will modify to run a 3-node cluster.

## Cassandra.yaml

This is the main configuration file of Cassandra. Almost every parameter, whether it is related to performance, security, or other features, is present within this file. JVM configuration options are not included within this file:

1. `listen_address`: This is the IP address that Cassandra binds to for internode communication (gossip). The default value is localhost (`127.0.0.1`). In our case, we will have to set this value to the relevant loopback address based on the instance number. Set these values as follows:
   - CASSANDRA_DIR1/conf/cassandra.yaml - 127.0.0.1
   - CASSANDRA_DIR2/conf/cassandra.yaml - 127.0.0.2
   - CASSANDRA_DIR3/conf/cassandra.yaml - 127.0.0.3

2. `rpc_address`: This is the IP address that Cassandra binds to for client connections. You should set these values similar to the `listen_address`.

3. `seeds`: This is a comma-delimited list of IP addresses that is used to bootstrap new nodes to the cluster. Whenever a node starts, it checks the seed nodes to start gossiping with nodes that are already up. It is recommended to have three nodes as part of the seed nodes. Since we are running a 3-node cluster, we will add all the IP addresses to seeds. Set the value of seeds to `127.0.0.1,127.0.0.2,127.0.0.3` on all three instances.

# Cassandra-env.sh

Any configuration related to JVM tuning is present within this file. Only one parameter needs to be changed within this file to get us running.

Cassandra exposes other statistics and management operations via **Java Management Extensions (JMX)**. Cassandra uses the JMX port for JMX connection. The `nodetool` utility is a JMX compliant tool.

You can set the JMX port by editing the `cassandra-env.sh` configuration file and adding the following line:

```
JMX_PORT="7199"
```

Set the value of the JMX port on the three instances as follows:

```
CASSANDRA_DIR1/conf/cassandra-en.sh - 7199
CASSANDRA_DIR2/conf/cassandra-env.sh - 7200
CASSANDRA_DIR3/conf/cassandra-env.sh - 7201
```

# Starting the 3-node cluster

Now that we have laid the groundwork to set up a 3-node cluster, we are ready to start the cluster. To start the cluster, you need to start one node at a time. Let's start the first node by running the following command:

```
$ CASSANDRA_DIR1/bin/cassandra -f
```

To figure out whether the first node has started or not, you can use the `nodetool` utility. We will take a look at `nodetool` in depth later, but for now, run the following command:

```
$ CASSANDRA_DIR1/bin/nodetool status
```

You should see a single node up and running within the cluster. The UN indicates the status is UP and the state is NORMAL:

```
Datacenter: datacenter1
=======================
Status=Up/Down
|/ State=Normal/Leaving/Joining/Moving
--  Address    Load       Tokens      Owns (effective)  Host ID                               Rack
UN  127.0.0.1  102.79 KB  256         100.0%            40d6e0b5-489a-4df1-a823-e218b6dd7baf  rack1
```

After the first node has started, you can proceed to start the second and third node, one after the other, as follows:

```
$ CASSANDRA_DIR2/bin/cassandra -f
$ CASSANDRA_DIR3/bin/cassandra -f
```

After starting all three nodes, running a `nodetool` status will show all three nodes as UN with the loopback addresses that we created as part of the cluster:

```
Datacenter: datacenter1
=======================
Status=Up/Down
|/ State=Normal/Leaving/Joining/Moving
--  Address    Load       Tokens   Owns (effective)  Host ID                               Rack
UN  127.0.0.1  104.21 KB  256      60.4%             40d6e0b5-489a-4df1-a823-e218b6dd7baf  rack1
UN  127.0.0.2  86.54 KB   256      68.8%             aed8cd4d-ca52-4cab-b0cc-97348ff36d17  rack1
UN  127.0.0.3  106.59 KB  256      70.8%             1375c591-6007-404f-b801-1b3b2b256bde  rack1
```

# Consistency in action

For a single-node cluster, consistency and replication factor didn't matter since you had only one copy of the data residing on the lone instance, and the instance had to be up all the time for the writes/reads to succeed regardless of the consistency level used. However, the dynamics change significantly for a multinode cluster as witnessed in the previous chapter. We will create two keyspaces; one with replication factor 2 and the other with replication factor 3. We will then stop a running instance and try out read/write operations with different consistency levels.

# Write consistency

Let's create the keyspaces with replication factors 2 and 3 as discussed in the preceding section. To distinguish both the keyspaces, we will include the replication factor within the name. Create keyspaces as follows:

```
CREATE KEYSPACE "keyspace2"
WITH REPLICATION = {
    'class': 'SimpleStrategy',
    'replication_factor': 2
};
CREATE KEYSPACE "keyspace3"
WITH REPLICATION = {
    'class': 'SimpleStrategy',
    'replication_factor': 3
};
```

Here, `keyspace2` has a replication factor of 2, and `keyspace3` has a replication factor of 3. After creating the keyspaces, let's recreate our users table within both the keyspaces with the default settings:

```
CREATE TABLE "keyspace2"."users" (
    "username" text PRIMARY KEY,
    "email" text,
    "encrypted_password" blob
);
CREATE TABLE "keyspace3"."users" (
    "username" text PRIMARY KEY,
    "email" text,
    "encrypted_password" blob
);
```

By default, the consistency is set to ONE when you run queries using `cqlsh`. To confirm this, you can enter CONSISTENCY in `cqlsh`:

```
cqlsh> CONSISTENCY
Current consistency level is ONE.
```

To get a better understanding of the effect of consistency, let's enable query tracing. Enabling tracing displays information about the coordinator node, the replicas to which the requests are forwarded along with the timestamps for various operations, as well as the confirmation of request completion. You can enable query tracing by entering the following in `cqlsh`:

```
TRACING ON;
```

Let's insert some data into the `keyspace` with the replication factor and leave the consistency set to the default value of ONE:

```
INSERT INTO "keyspace3"."users"
("username", "email", "encrypted_password")
VALUES (
    'alice',
    'alice@gmail.com',
    0x8914977ed729792e403da53024c6069a9158b8c4
);
```

You will get a query trace that looks similar to a Cassandra table. As a matter of fact, query traces are stored within a Cassandra table `events` under the keyspace `system_traces`. Also, the summary of every query is stored within the table `sessions` under the `system_traces` keyspace. The tracing information consists of multiple columns, which includes the activity, the timestamp at which the activity occurred, the source of the activity, as well as the time elapsed since the start of the request. You will find the request complete confirmation at the end along with the time taken to complete:

```
Tracing session: 4056e720-e62e-11e6-bb67-b126be40f4ae

 activity                                                      | timestamp                  | source    | source_elapsed
---------------------------------------------------------------+----------------------------+-----------+----------------

                                     Execute CQL3 query | 2017-01-29 06:21:40.370000 | 127.0.0.1 |              0
Parsing INSERT INTO "keyspace3"."users" ("username", "email", "encrypted_password") VALUES (   'alice',   'alice@yahoo.com',   0x8914977ed7297
92e403da53024c6069a9158b8c4 ); [SharedPool-Worker-1] | 2017-01-29 06:21:40.374000 | 127.0.0.1 |           3532

                          Preparing statement [SharedPool-Worker-1] | 2017-01-29 06:21:40.376000 | 127.0.0.1 |           6301
                                                                                                          MUTATION message received fr
om /127.0.0.1 [MessagingService-Incoming-/127.0.0.1] | 2017-01-29 06:21:40.377000 | 127.0.0.2 |             18
                                                                                                          MUTATION message received fr
om /127.0.0.1 [MessagingService-Incoming-/127.0.0.1] | 2017-01-29 06:21:40.377000 | 127.0.0.3 |             24
                                                                                                                                  Det
erming replicas for mutation [SharedPool-Worker-1] | 2017-01-29 06:21:40.377000 | 127.0.0.1 |           6777
              Appending to commitlog [SharedPool-Worker-1] | 2017-01-29 06:21:40.377000 | 127.0.0.2 |            206
                                                                                                        Sending MUTATION message
to /127.0.0.2 [MessagingService-Outgoing-/127.0.0.2] | 2017-01-29 06:21:40.377000 | 127.0.0.1 |           7036
                                                                                                        Sending MUTATION message
to /127.0.0.3 [MessagingService-Outgoing-/127.0.0.3] | 2017-01-29 06:21:40.377000 | 127.0.0.1 |           7039
              Appending to commitlog [SharedPool-Worker-2] | 2017-01-29 06:21:40.377000 | 127.0.0.1 |           7063
            Adding to users memtable [SharedPool-Worker-2] | 2017-01-29 06:21:40.377000 | 127.0.0.1 |           7203
            Adding to users memtable [SharedPool-Worker-1] | 2017-01-29 06:21:40.378000 | 127.0.0.2 |            386
```

Also, one thing to note is that the `source_elapsed` column is the elapsed time in microseconds before the event occurred on the source node. Try executing similar queries by either changing the e-mail or the `encrypted_password` along with changing the consistency level values to TWO, QUORUM, and ALL. You can change the consistency level within `cqlsh` as follows:

**CONSISTENCY QUORUM;**

When you run queries after changing the consistency levels, you will notice a slight difference in the time taken for request completion. The `source_elapsed` for request completion will be the highest for consistency level ALL and lowest for consistency level ONE. This is to be expected since ALL requires all the replicas to send a confirmation before sending a request complete confirmation to the client. The difference in requests response times might not be much in our case since we are running three instances on a single server. You will notice a much higher disparity when you're working with hundreds of instances in a production cluster.

# Consistency QUORUM

As discussed earlier, consistency QUORUM means that a majority of replicas need to acknowledge a write for the write request to succeed. In the case of keyspace3 with replication factor 3, this majority turns out to be two replicas. However, in case of keyspace2 with replication factor 2, this majority still turns out to be replicas.

To better understand how consistency works, let's bring a node down within the cluster. Go to the Terminal where you started Cassandra 3 (Cassandra with listen address 127.0.0.3), and simply press *Ctrl + C* on the keyboard in case you started Cassandra in the foreground mode with option -f. If you started Cassandra in the background mode, get the process ID of Cassandra, and simply kill it.

To get the process ID, enter the following:

```
$ ps -ef | grep Cassandra
```

To kill the process, enter the following:

```
$ kill -9 <pid>
```

After you have done this, the nodetool status will show the status of cassandra3 as DN (Down and Normal):

```
Datacenter: datacenter1
========================
Status=Up/Down
|/ State=Normal/Leaving/Joining/Moving
--  Address    Load      Tokens   Owns   Host ID                                Rack
UN  127.0.0.1  201.05 KB  256      ?      40d6e0b5-489a-4df1-a823-e218b6dd7baf   rack1
UN  127.0.0.2  248.78 KB  256      ?      aed8cd4d-ca52-4cab-b0cc-97348ff36d17   rack1
DN  127.0.0.3  244.59 KB  256      ?      1375c591-6007-404f-b801-1b3b2b256bde   rack1
```

After the node is down, let's try inserting some data into the 3-node cluster with two nodes UP and one node DOWN:

```
INSERT INTO "keyspace3"."users"
("username", "email")
VALUES (
  'alice',
  'alice@yahoo.com'
);
INSERT INTO "keyspace2"."users"
("username", "email", "encrypted_password")
VALUES (
  'alice',
  'alice@gmail.com',
```

```
        0x8914977ed729792e403da53024c6069a9158b8c4
);
INSERT INTO "keyspace2"."users"
("username", "email", "encrypted_password")
VALUES (
    'bob',
    'bob@gmail.com',
    0x10920941a69549d33aaee6116ed1f47e19b8e713
);
```

The first two queries execute successfully, whereas the third query fails with the following error:

```
Traceback (most recent call last):
  File "/Users/yarabsa/cassandra1/bin/cqlsh.py", line 1314, in perform_simple_statement
    result = future.result()
  File "/Users/yarabsa/cassandra1/bin/../lib/cassandra-driver-internal-only-3.0.0-6af642d.zip/cassandra-driver-3.0.0-6af642d/cassandra/cluster.py", line 3122, in result
    raise self._final_exception
Unavailable: code=1000 [Unavailable exception] message="Cannot achieve consistency level QUORUM" info={'required_replicas': 2, 'alive_replicas': 1, 'consistency': 'QUORUM'}
```

The third query fails because the write request requires two replicas to acknowledge the write, whereas in this case, one of the replica nodes is down. You must be wondering why the second query executed without throwing an error. The reason is that the second and third queries have different partition keys. Hence, the replica nodes for both the queries will be different too. The partition key for the second query belongs to the nodes with IP addresses `127.0.0.1` and `127.0.0.2`, which are both up. The partition key for the third query has a replica, which belongs to `127.0.0.3` that is down, which is why the query failed.

# Consistency ANY

Cassandra provides a write consistency, which is unique and almost never used in any situation. This consistency level is ANY. In this case, the write request is successful even if all the replica nodes are down for that partition key. To check this consistency level in action, let's bring down another node.

Before bringing down a second node, change the consistency to ONE, and execute the third query from the preceding section. You will see that it executed successfully, and a SELECT query will return the latest results:

```
username | email            | encrypted_password
---------+------------------+-------------------------------------------
     bob |   bob@gmail.com  | 0x10920941a69549d33aaee6116ed1f47e19b8e713
   alice | alice@gmail.com  | 0x8914977ed729792e403da53024c6069a9158b8c4
```

Now that you set the consistency level to ONE, every request requires only one replica node to acknowledge the read/write for the request to be successful.

After this, you will need to bring down the first node (node with listen address 127.0.0.1) similar to how you brought down the first node. You can then execute the nodetool status query from CASSANDRA_DIR2 as follows:

```
$ CASSANDRA_DIR2/bin/nodetool status
```

```
Datacenter: datacenter1
=======================
Status=Up/Down
|/ State=Normal/Leaving/Joining/Moving
--  Address    Load       Tokens  Owns   Host ID                               Rack
DN  127.0.0.1  234.38 KB  256     ?      40d6e0b5-489a-4df1-a823-e218b6dd7baf  rack1
UN  127.0.0.2  248.51 KB  256     ?      aed8cd4d-ca52-4cab-b0cc-97348ff36d17  rack1
DN  127.0.0.3  244.59 KB  256     ?      1375c591-6007-404f-b801-1b3b2b256bde  rack1
```

To start cqlsh, you will have to change the IP address to 127.0.0.2 in the command-line options:

```
$ CASSANDRA_DIR2/bin/cqlsh 127.0.0.2 9042
```

Let's execute the following query now with consistency set to ONE:

```
INSERT INTO "keyspace2"."users"
("username", "email")
VALUES (
 'bob',
 'bob@yahoo.com'
);
```

The query will fail complaining that it required one replica node to be alive for the query to be successful, but there were zero available replica nodes.

Now execute the same query by setting the consistency level to ANY. The query executes successfully. Even if the replica nodes for the partition are down, Cassandra uses the hints mechanism to store the data on the coordinator node. These hints are then replayed to the replica nodes when they come back up. Bring the other two nodes back up and run a Select query to see whether the data was written to the keyspace2.users table after the hints got replayed. The Select query will fail because the consistency level ANY is supported only for writes:

```
InvalidRequest: code=2200 [Invalid query] message="ANY ConsistencyLevel is only supported for writes"
```

Go ahead and set the consistency level to QUORUM and run the SELECT query again. The email has been updated for the user bob according to the preceding write query:

```
 username | email            | encrypted_password
----------+------------------+---------------------------------------------------
      bob |   bob@yahoo.com  | 0x10920941a69549d33aaee6116ed1f47e19b8e713
    alice | alice@gmail.com  | 0x8914977ed729792e403da53024c6069a9158b8c4
```

Read consistency levels have been skipped since they are similar to write consistency levels with the exception of the ANY consistency level not supported by reads.

# Cassandra internals

In this section, we will take a look at some of the internals of Cassandra including read and write paths along with some of the mechanisms used to optimize both read and write operations. The write path is fairly straightforward which appends records to a log structure providing really high throughput. The read path consists of several data structures which are used to reduce the amount of disk seeks and optimize reads.

# The write path

When Cassandra initially came out, it was widely considered a write-optimized database. Whenever a client makes a write request, a coordinator node receives it. The coordinator node forwards the request to the relevant nodes based on the partition key and replication factor. The reason local writes are fast in Cassandra is because all the writes are appended to an append-only commitlog and to an in-memory structure called **memtable**. This doesn't require any disk seeks unlike local reads. We will take a more in-depth look at the write path in this section as well as the different operations involved to get rid of unnecessary data and keep data consistent across nodes.

The write path consists of four steps:

1. Append data to the commitlog.
2. Write data to the memtable.
3. Flush data from the memtable.
4. Write data to immutable SSTables.

The write path on a high level looks like this:

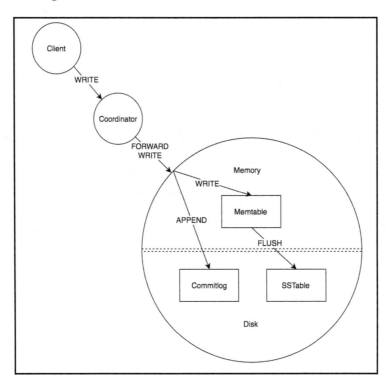

The first component in Cassandra's write path is the **commitlog**. This is an append-only log structure to which writes get appended. Commitlog consists of various segment files, which are preallocated with a certain size. When a segment file is full, the writes are written to the next segment. When all the writes within a segment get flushed from their respective memtables, the segment gets renamed and recycled. The recycled segment is ready to be used again. In case of system restarts, all the memtables are wiped out. The commitlog segments are replayed, and then the memtables are flushed to disk. After this, the commitlog segments are recycled for reuse. This provides durability in the face of system failures. Commitlog can be disabled (not recommended) by setting durable writes to false when creating a keyspace.

Apart from appending data to the commitlog, Cassandra writes data to an in-memory structure called memtable. When the memtable reaches a certain threshold size, it is flushed to disk. There are several memtable-related configuration parameters that you can tune. You can specify the memtable allocation type to either use heap or off-heap memory. You can specify the amount of heap or off-heap memory to be allocated for memtables. Memtable flushes happen based on this value and a cleanup threshold. You can also specify the commitlog size as a configuration parameter. Memtable flushes happen based on the commitlog size as well. By default, flush occurs automatically based on certain configurable thresholds as discussed. But you can also trigger a manual flush using the nodetool utility.

On reaching the flush threshold, memtables are flushed to immutable files on disk called **SSTables** (**Sorted String Tables**). Memtables are sorted by the token value and are sequentially written to disk. Since SSTables are immutable, a record might be spread across multiple SSTables if there are updates with the same partition key. Cassandra creates a few other structures, namely partition index, partition summary, and bloom filters when flushing to SSTables. These structures help speed up the reads and reduce disk seeks.

Cassandra provides a utility to view the contents of an SSTable. This utility is called `sstabledump`. To use this utility in order to view the contents of SSTables, switch the directory to CASSANDRA_DIR1, and run the following command:

```
$ ./tools/bin/sstabledump data/data/keyspace3/users-<table-id>/*-Data.db
```

The second part of the preceding command indicates the `Data.db` files present within the data directory for the `keyspace3.users` table. Run the earlier command for every `Data.db` directory present. You will get the results in a JSON format similar to this:

```json
{
  "partition" : {
    "key" : [ "alice" ],
    "position" : 0
  },
  "rows" : [
    {
      "type" : "row",
      "position" : 19,
      "liveness_info" : { "tstamp" : "2017-01-29T14:35:36.726114Z" },
      "cells" : [
        { "name" : "email", "value" : "alice@gmail.com" },
        { "name" : "encrypted_password", "value" : "8914977ed729792e403da53024c6069a9158b8c4" }
      ]
    }
  ]
}
```

```json
{
  "partition" : {
    "key" : [ "alice" ],
    "position" : 0
  },
  "rows" : [
    {
      "type" : "row",
      "position" : 19,
      "liveness_info" : { "tstamp" : "2017-02-08T03:47:45.731382Z" },
      "cells" : [
        { "name" : "email", "value" : "alice@yahoo.com" }
      ]
    }
  ]
}
```

# Compaction

As noted earlier, a Cassandra instance could have multiple copies of the same data residing on multiple SSTables. If you do a lot of updates to records over time, there is a chance that you will run out of disk space because of redundant data. To prevent this, Cassandra performs compaction, which merges multiple SSTables and gets rid of extra data. One other caveat of performing compaction is that the read will speed up. Consider the scenario where there is no compaction and a record is spread across multiple SSTables on disk. A read will require multiple seeks to fetch the data from all the SSTables and combine them. With compaction, a single row will exist on a single SSTable, and thus, it requires only one disk seek.

Cassandra provides multiple types of compaction strategies. You can configure compaction strategy when you create a table depending on the requirement and the type of load. Here are the three compaction strategy types built within Cassandra by default:

- **Size-tiered compaction strategy (STCS)**: Size-tiered compaction is triggered when a certain number of SSTables (defaults to four) of the same size exist for a single column family. This will merge data and remove expired tombstones. This process repeats itself, and the size of SSTables keeps growing over time. Whenever this compaction is triggered, both the old and new SSTables exist on disk until the entire process is complete. Hence, the disk space should be twice the amount of data you expect to exist on a node. This type of compaction doesn't ensure improvement in read performance since a row can still be spread across multiple SSTables after compaction.

- **Leveled compaction strategy (LCS)**: Leveled compaction creates SSTables of fixed sizes (relatively smaller compared to size-tiered compaction strategy) that are grouped into levels called L0, L1, L2, and so on. New SSTables are placed in L0 and immediately compacted with SSTables in L1. When L1 fills up, extra SSTables created in L1 are promoted to L2. Furthermore, SSTables created in L1 are compacted with SSTables in L2, and so on. Each level is 10 times the size of the previous level; so L1 is 10 times the size of L0, and L2 is 10 times the size of L1. This compaction ensures that a row can exist only on a single SSTable within a level. There can be multiple copies of a row on multiple levels. Leveled compaction guarantees that 90% of the reads are satisfied from a single SSTable and only 10% extra space is wasted on obsolete rows. Leveled compaction also uses considerably more I/O and is recommended to be used with SSDs.

- **Date-tiered compaction strategy (DTCS)**: Date-tiered compaction was introduced to be used with time series data. This compaction groups tables based on a certain time window and compacts those SSTables. If a table is created with a default TTL or all the data is inserted with a fixed TTL, all data within a time window will expire approximately at the same time. So entire SSTables can be deleted during compaction. DTCS is optimized for time series data with TTL.

You can read about configuring compaction and different compaction strategies here: `http://docs.datastax.com/en/archived/cassandra/3.x/cassandra/operations/opsConfigureCompaction.html`.

# The read path

Cassandra write path is fairly straightforward: writes are appended to commitlog on disk and written to memtables in memory. The memtables are flushed to disk once they are full. The read path is more complex and utilizes a bunch of data structures (both in memory and on disk) to optimize reads and reduce disk seeks. Cassandra has to combine the data in memtables along with data on disk (potentially multiple SSTables) before returning the data.

These are the different components used by Cassandra to process a read query:

- Memtable
- Row cache
- Bloom filters
- Key cache
- Partition summary
- Partition index
- Compression offset map
- SSTables
- **Memtable**: This is the first stage in the read process. Cassandra initially checks whether the queried partition is present within memtable. If it exists, Cassandra combines the data from memtable with data from SSTables and returns the result. Reading data from SSTables consists of several stages as listed next. Traditionally, memtables have always been on heap. While most data structures were moved from JVM heap to native memory, memtables and key cache were still a part of heap memory. Starting Cassandra 2.1, you have the option of moving memtables off heap to keep up with increasing data size. Memtables are not entirely off heap, but you can choose two options to reduce the heap memory footprint:
    - `offheap_buffers` moves the name and value of cell to `DirectBuffer` objects. This has the lowest impact on read performance and reduces the heap usage significantly only if you're storing large strings or blobs.
    - `offheap_objects` moves the entire cell to off heap, leaving only a pointer (to the cell) on heap. This is useful when you're storing small values such as ints or UUIDs. The data still has to be copied to heap memory before reading from it.

- **Row cache**: The row cache, if enabled, stores a subset of the data on SSTables in memory. Since it is faster to read data from memory than on disk, row cache can increase the read performance substantially. This is particularly useful for read-heavy workloads. While the operating system page cache can provide improved performance, there are certain optimizations in row cache, which make it ideal for certain read-heavy workloads. Row cache is stored fully off heap, and thus, it reduces the garbage collection pressure on the Cassandra JVM. The row cache size is configurable, and it uses LRU eviction to free up memory when it gets filled up.

  The row cache can be configured to be written to disk periodically. This ensures the row cache is populated from the data on disk in case of restart. By default, Cassandra loads an entire partition into row cache even if you read only a certain part of the partition. This fills up the cache pretty fast. To avoid this, you can configure the number of rows within a partition to be stored in row cache. This makes queries, which include reading only a certain part of the data (such as last 10 entries) considerably fast while reducing the memory footprint.

  If row cache is enabled, desired partition data is read from the row cache, potentially saving two seeks to disk for the data. The rows stored in row cache are frequently accessed rows that are merged and saved to the row cache from the SSTables as they are accessed. After storage, the data is available to later queries. The row cache is not write-through. If a write comes in for the row, the cache for that row is invalidated and is not cached again until the row is read. Similarly, if a partition is updated, the entire partition is evicted from the cache. When the desired partition data is not found in the row cache, then the bloom filter is checked.

- **Bloom filter**: After checking the memtables and the row cache, Cassandra checks the bloom filter to get all the SSTables where the partition might exist. The bloom filter is present off heap, and each SSTable has a bloom filter associated with it. A bloom filter is a probabilistic data structure that is used to figure out if a partition key exists on the SSTable or not. Since it is probabilistic, there are chances of getting false positives. But the partition will not exist on an SSTable if the bloom filter returns negative. The chances of returning a false positive depend on bloom filter configuration, which, in turn, affects the memory used by it. The bloom filter narrows down the process of partition key lookup. The bloom filter occupies 1-2 GB of memory per billion partitions. The bloom filter is tunable if you want to trade memory for performance. If the bloom filter determines a partition to exist on an SSTable, Cassandra then checks the key cache.

A bloom filter is a data structure that is used to determine whether an element exists within a set of elements. Bloom filters have strong space advantage over sets, hash tables, or binary search trees. You can read more about bloom filters here: `http://prakhar.me/articles/bloom-filters-for-dummies/`.

- **Key cache**: Key cache is an off-heap memory structure that stores the partition index. If a partition key is present within the key cache, the read process skips partition summary and partition index and goes directly to the compression offset map. The key cache size is configurable, and similar to row cache, it can be configured to be copied to disk periodically. The key cache hits save a disk seek during reads. The number of partition keys stored within the cache can also be configured.

  To get statistics related to caching, such as the number of cache hits, capacity, and partition key entries within a cache, you can run `nodetool info`:

```
ID                          : 40d6e0b5-489a-4df1-a823-e218b6dd7baf
Gossip active               : true
Thrift active               : false
Native Transport active: true
Load                        : 167.76 KB
Generation No               : 1486528624
Uptime (seconds)            : 1650
Heap Memory (MB)            : 124.92 / 4016.00
Off Heap Memory (MB)        : 0.00
Data Center                 : datacenter1
Rack                        : rack1
Exceptions                  : 0
Key Cache                   : entries 24, size 1.92 KB, capacity 100 MB, 66 hits, 90 requests, 0.733 recent hit rate, 14400 save period in seconds
Row Cache                   : entries 0, size 0 bytes, capacity 0 bytes, 0 hits, 0 requests, NaN recent hit rate, 0 save period in seconds
Counter Cache               : entries 0, size 0 bytes, capacity 50 MB, 0 hits, 0 requests, NaN recent hit rate, 7200 save period in seconds
Token                       : (invoke with -T/--tokens to see all 256 tokens)
```

  By default, the key cache is set to store all the partition keys, and the row cache is disabled if you don't specify caching options while creating a table.

- **Partition summary**: If a partition key is not present within the key cache, the read process hits the partition summary next. The partition summary is an off-heap memory component that stores a sampling of the partition index. A partition index stores the location of all the partition keys within an SSTable. A partition summary stores a sample of these values. Suppose you set the index sampling interval to 128, the partition summary will contain every $128^{th}$ element of the partition index. Based on the partition summary, Cassandra figures out a range of possible partition key values.

- **Partition index**: The partition index resides on disk and stores an index of all partition keys mapped to their offset. After checking the partition summary for a range of partition keys, the partition index is searched to figure out the location of the partition key on disk. Searching a partition index involves a disk seek and sequential read. Next, the read process hits the compression offset map to find the data on disk.
- **Compresssion offset map**: The compression offset map stores pointers to the location on disk, where the partition exists. It is stored in off-heap memory and is accessed by either the partition key cache or the partition index. The desired compressed partition data is fetched from the correct SSTable(s) once the compression offset map identifies the disk location.

The entire read path has been summarized in the figure as follows:

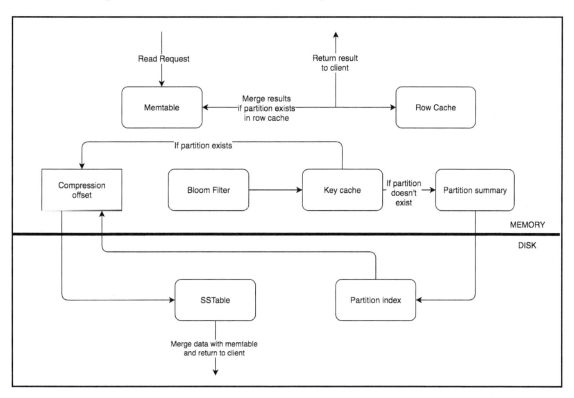

# Cassandra repair mechanisms

Since data is partitioned and replicated onto multiple nodes, there is a possibility that replicas might be out of sync. This is usually due to slow responsiveness of certain nodes or nodes being down. If multiple nodes are out of sync, there is a possibility of reading stale data. There is also a certain case when deleted data reappears. To fix these issues, Cassandra provides three main repair mechanisms. These mechanisms ensure that the data is in sync most of the time. The repair mechanisms are as follows:

- Hinted handoff
- Read repair
- Anti-entropy repair

## Hinted handoff

Whenever a node becomes unresponsive or down for a certain period of time, all the write requests to that node will fail. Cassandra keeps a copy of the partitions that were supposed to be written to the unresponsive node within a local hints table. The hints are stored for a certain configurable period of time. When the downed node comes up and starts gossiping with the rest of the nodes in the cluster, the hints are replayed to the downed node, and data is back in sync between all the replica nodes.

The coordinator node will eventually evict hints if the downed node doesn't come back up within the eviction period. The coordinator also stops storing hints related to a downed node if it is down for a configurable period of time.

## Read repair

Read repair is triggered during a read request. Consider a keyspace with replication factor 3. You send a write request to the cluster. The coordinator node will forward the write request to three relevant replica nodes. Suppose you read the same data with consistency QUORUM or TWO, and the coordinator node forwards the request to node 1 and 2. The coordinator node will then merge results from nodes 1 and 2 before returning them to the client. It will also trigger a background read repair on node 3, if enabled. This read repair ensures that the data on node 3 is in sync with nodes 1 and 2.

In read repair, Cassandra sends a digest request to each replica not directly involved in the read. Cassandra compares all replicas and writes of the most recent version to any replica node that does not have it. The ratio of times that read repair is triggered to the total read requests is configurable.

# Anti-entropy repair

**Anti-entropy repair** is triggered manually. Anti-entropy repair is very useful and is often recommended to be run periodically to keep data in sync. Often, hints and read-repair mechanisms are not sufficient to keep data in sync.

Cassandra accomplishes anti-entropy repair using Merkle trees, similar to Dynamo and Riak. Anti-entropy is a process of comparing the data of all replicas and updating each replica to the newest version. Cassandra has three phases to the process:

- Building a Merkle tree for each replica
- Comparing the Merkle trees to discover differences
- Streaming the relevant data

Why is running anti-entropy repair frequently so important? Consider a cluster with a replication factor of 3. Suppose a partition exists on nodes 1, 2, and 3. Suppose node 3 goes down and you issue a delete statement on this partition after the node goes down. Nodes 1 and 2 will have tombstones created. If node 3 doesn't come up within a certain period, the hint related to this deletion will be evicted. After the tombstones expire, the data is deleted from nodes 1 and 2, but it still continues to exist on node 3. When you trigger a repair, this data will be streamed to nodes 1 and 2 again. Thus, the deleted data will reappear. To prevent this, it is recommended to run a manual repair frequently or to be more specific, within a interval, which is lower than the tombstone eviction period.

 You can read up more on the repair process here: http://docs.datastax .com/en/archived/cassandra/3.x/cassandra/operations/opsRepairN odesTOC.html.

# Summary

In this chapter, you learned how to set up a multinode cluster by changing various configuration options. We also took a practical look at how consistency levels work and how Cassandra provides a balance between consistency and availability. We tried out various consistency levels including QUORUM and ANY for writes. We then took a quick look at the architectural aspects of Cassandra.

We looked at the write path, and how data was written to both memory and disk. Data was persisted to commitlog on disk to avoid data loss in case of restarts. Data is flushed to immutable SSTables when the memtables are filled up. The read path utilizes several data structures, both in memory and on disk, to optimize reads. We could enable row and key caching to avoid disk seeks. In case a partition was not found in cache, we would have to hit bloom filters and partition indexes to figure out the location of a partition within an SSTable. We also looked at the data repair mechanism provided by Cassandra to keep data in sync between replica nodes.

In the next chapter, we will build Java applications using DataStax Java driver to write data to Cassandra and read data from Cassandra. This will include creating a cluster object, fetching cluster metadata, and using prepared statements and batches. We will also look at some client optimizations, such as load balancing and retry policies.

# 12
# Application Development Using the Java Driver

Since the beginning of `Chapter 1`, *Getting Up and Running with Cassandra*, we have been using `cqlsh` to execute all queries. Whether it is reading or writing data, changing consistency level, or enabling tracing, `cqlsh` facilitates performing all these tasks with ease. When developing applications that work with Cassandra, we use various drivers, supported either by DataStax or by the open source community. During the course of this chapter, we will be focusing on the Java driver in particular, which is used widely, and most new changes go into this first. Cqlsh uses the Python driver underneath.

The Java driver is based on CQL3 and Cassandra binary protocol. It uses Netty-based transport, which provides high performance and is optimized for Cassandra. Prior to the Java driver, which is based on native protocol, thrift protocol was more popular. As newer versions of Cassandra rolled out, thrift became a limitation; communication was limited to request response paradigm, there were no notifications, no streaming, and so on. The solution to this was the native protocol, which was designed for CQL3. Thrift is going to be defunct soon.

The Java driver provides many capabilities, which further enhance the performance of querying over Cassandra. Some of these are as follows:

- **Node discovery**: Java driver automatically discovers new nodes that join the cluster and redirects queries to them based on the load-balancing policy you choose
- **Load balancing**: Java driver provides a bunch of load balancing policies to evenly spread out queries
- **Async execution**: Java driver allows asynchronous execution of queries allowing multiple simultaneous requests

- **Retry policy**: Java driver also provides several retry policies to retry failed queries
- **Prepared statements**: This feature reduces the data sent over network, which we will discuss later
- **Other features**: Java driver also provides other features, such as paging support, `QueryBuilder` API, speculative query execution, tracing, and so on

Two main features of Cassandra that Java driver provides is request pipelining and server-to-client notifications. Request pipelining allows us to stream multiple requests/responses over a single connection. Since each connection can handle more than one active request at a time, client libraries will need to maintain only a small amount of open connections. A low number of per-node connections helps scaling to large Cassandra clusters.

Also, servers can send events to clients, which eliminates the need for the client-polling servers for any cluster changes. The driver allows clients to register for certain types of event notifications. The currently supported events are cluster topology changes, such as node joining, node decommissioning, or node removal. When one of these events occurs, the server will push notifications to registered clients. This allows those clients to maintain a state of the Cassandra cluster up to date.

In this chapter, you will learn the following:

- Creating a cluster object
- Creating a session for querying
- Sending read/write queries
- Using prepared statements
- Using `QueryBuilder` API
- Asynchronous querying
- Paging support
- Driver policies

# A simple query

To begin with, we will create a cluster object, connect to Cassandra and execute a simple query. We will also fetch cluster metadata. I would recommend using the single-node cluster we launched in `Chapter 1`, *Getting Up and Running with Cassandra*, rather than the *3-node cluster* from the previous chapter. This is because the single-node cluster has all the tables and data required for this chapter. Before we begin, you should familiarize yourselves with any of the free IDEs available to edit, compile, and run Java code.

To compile and run Java programs from the command line, you can look at this article: `http://introcs.cs.princeton.edu/java/15inout/linux-cmd.html`.

There are multiple IDEs available, which make it easier to compile and run programs. Some of them are as follows:

- **Netbeans**: `https://netbeans.org/`
- **Eclipse**: `https://eclipse.org/`
- **IntelliJ IDEA**: `https://www.jetbrains.com/idea/features/`

I will be using Eclipse IDE for all my programs. While you get acquainted with Java, make sure you also look up how to add dependencies so you don't get any compile-time or run time errors. The dependency required for our project can be found here: `https://mvnrepository.com/artifact/com.datastax.cassandra/cassandra-driver-core/3.1.0.`

# Cluster API

The first thing required when creating a connection to Cassandra is creating a Cluster object. These are some of the classes related to a Cluster:

- `Cluster`: This represents a Cassandra cluster. This is the main entry point when connecting to a cluster.
- `Cluster.Builder`: This can be used to build a `Cluster` object.
- `Configuration`: This holds cluster configuration.
- `Host`: This represents a Cassandra node.
- `KeyspaceMetaData`: This holds keyspace metadata.
- `MetaData`: This holds metadata about the cluster.

`Cluster.Builder` is a helper class used to create instances of Cluster. This has several methods that help you set the configuration of Cluster, such as which nodes to connect to, enabling SSL encryption, enabling authentication, and other options.

To ensure that the Java driver can connect to the Cassandra nodes in your cluster, you must configure the following in the `cassandra.yaml` configuration file:

- `start_native_transport`: true
- `rpc_address`: IP address or hostname reachable by clients
- `native_transport_port`: 9042

# Getting metadata

Let's dive into some action by writing our first program, which will create a `Cluster` object and fetch some metadata from the cluster. Let's name the program `GetMetadata.java`:

```java
import com.datastax.driver.core.*;
public class GetMetadata {
  public static void main(String[] args) {
    Cluster cluster =
      Cluster.builder().addContactPoints("127.0.0.1").build();
    Metadata metadata = cluster.getMetadata();
    System.out.printf("Cluster name: %sn", metadata.getClusterName());
    for (Host host : metadata.getAllHosts()) {
      System.out.println("Host: " + host.getAddress() + "n");
    }
    cluster.close();
  }
}
```

Program 1: `GetMetadata.java`

Upon executing the previous program, you should see the result like this:

```
Cluster name: Test Cluster
Host: /127.0.0.1
```

You might get a different cluster name based on your configuration and a different number of hosts if you're running a multinode cluster.

Let's analyze the program, line by line:

```java
import com.datastax.driver.core.*;
```

To begin with, you import all the classes present within the `com.datastax.driver.core` package to use them. Here, you can find the full list of classes present within the package: `http://docs.datastax.com/en/drivers/java/3.1/`

```java
Cluster cluster = Cluster.builder().addContactPoints("127.0.0.1").build();
```

Next, we create a `Cluster` object using the `Cluster.Builder` API. The `build()` method creates the final `Cluster` object. All the other methods are used to configure the `Cluster` object.

The `addContactPoints()` function is used to add initial nodes to bootstrap the client. One of the contact points must be reachable by the client. Since we have a single node cluster, we pass the RPC address of the node (`127.0.0.1`) as an argument to the method. After making the initial connection, the Cluster instance knows about the complete cluster topology and not just the contact points provided. Changes in the cluster topology are pushed to the Cluster instance via notifications. Once the initial connection is made, the Cluster instance remains connected as long as any node within the connection pool is reachable.

The `build()` function may throw two unchecked exceptions: `NoHostAvailableException` and `AuthenticationException`. Since these are unchecked, you are not required to enclose them in try/catch blocks.

A more comprehensive `Cluster` object would include more methods to set the configuration:

```
Cluster cluster = Cluster.builder()
.addContactPoints("127.0.0.1").withRetryPolicy(...)
.withPort(9042).withSSL().withLoadBalancingPolicy(...)
.withoutMetrics().withoutJMXReporting()
.build();
```

Here, you have more methods that are used to set retry and load balancing policy, set the native transport port, enable SSL, and disable metrics and JMX reporting. You can also define the preceding `Cluster` instance as follows:

```
Cluster.Builder builder = Cluster.builder();
builder.addContactPoints("127.0.0.1");
builder.withRetryPolicy(...);
builder.withPort(9042);
builder.withSSL();
builder.withLoadBalancingPolicy(...);
builder.withoutMetrics();
builder.withoutJMXReporting();
Cluster cluster = builder.build();
Metadata metadata = cluster.getMetadata();
System.out.printf("Cluster name: %sn", metadata.getClusterName());
```

We can fetch the cluster metadata by calling the `getMetadata()` function. Metadata instance provides several functions, such as `getClusterName()`, which is used to get the cluster name of the Cassandra cluster and the `getAllHosts()` function, which is used to fetch all the hosts' information within the cluster:

```
cluster.close();
```

This method closes connections of all sessions of the `Cluster` instance and shuts down the `Cluster` instance.

# Querying

Here are some of the common types used for querying:

- `PreparedStatement`: This represents a prepared statement
- `Query`: This represents a query
- `BoundStatement`: This is created from a prepared statement with the values bound
- `Sessions`: This creates a connection to a Cassandra cluster and is used to execute queries
- `ResultSet`: This denotes the result of a query
- `Row`: This is a single CQL row

Let's execute a simple query to insert data into the `users` table of `my_status` keyspace and fetch some data. Let's the name the program `SimpleQuery.java`:

```java
import com.datastax.driver.core.Cluster;
import com.datastax.driver.core.ResultSet;
import com.datastax.driver.core.Row;
import com.datastax.driver.core.Session;

public class SimpleQuery {

  public static void main(String[] args) {
  Cluster cluster =
Cluster.builder().addContactPoints("127.0.0.1").build();
  Session session = cluster.connect();

session.execute("INSERT INTO my_status.users (username , email) VALUES
('greg', 'greg@gmail.com')");
  ResultSet rs = session.execute("SELECT * FROM my_status.users");
  for (Row row : rs.all()) {
System.out.printf("Username: %s, Email: %s, Location: %sn",
row.getString("username"), row.getString("email"),
row.getString("location"));
  }
  cluster.close();
  }
}
```

Program 2: SimpleQuery.java

Upon executing the query, you should get all the rows in the users table with columns username, email, and location printed per line. The result should look like this:

```
Username: greg, Email: greg@gmail.com, Location: null
Username: bob, Email: null, Location: Austin, TX
Username: happycorp, Email: media@happycorp.com, Location: New York, NY
Username: dave, Email: dave@me.com, Location: San Francisco, CA
Username: gina, Email: null, Location: Houston, TX
Username: eve, Email: eve123@hotmail.com, Location: Washington, D.C.
Username: carol, Email: carol@hotmail.com, Location: null
Username: frank, Email: frank@gmail.com, Location: Los Angeles, CA
Username: ivan, Email: ivan@gmail.com, Location: null
Username: alice, Email: alice@gmail.com, Location: null
```

Let's analyze the program, line by line:

```
import com.datastax.driver.core.Cluster;
import com.datastax.driver.core.ResultSet;
import com.datastax.driver.core.Row;
import com.datastax.driver.core.Session;
```

We changed the import statement to multiple import statements in order to import the relevant classes rather than the entire package:

```
Cluster cluster = Cluster.builder().addContactPoints("127.0.0.1").build();
Session session = cluster.connect();
```

After creating an Cluster instance, we create an instance of the Session object to execute queries by calling the connect() method of the Cluster instance.

A session holds connections of a Cassandra cluster. A session can hold multiple connections to each node and choose the node to be used for a query based on the policy set. A session also handles retries for failed queries based on the cluster policy.

A session has a couple of important methods:

- shutdown(): This shuts down the session instance and closes its connections
- execute(...): This executes the provided query string and returns the result set

The following code executes the query string, which is provided as an argument to the `execute()` method:

```
session.execute("INSERT INTO my_status.users (username , email) VALUES
('greg', 'greg@gmail.com')");
```

The query string is a simple query, which you have been running using `cqlsh` so far. This inserts a record with username `greg` and e-mail `greg@gmail.com` into the `users` table. You can use `cqlsh` to check whether the record was actually inserted:

```
ResultSet rs = session.execute("SELECT * FROM my_status.users");
```

This executes the query string, which reads the entire `users` table and assigns the result to the `ResultSet` instance `rs`. A `ResultSet` instance implements `Iterable <Row>`, over which we can iterate to fetch individual rows:

```
for (Row row : rs.all()) {
        System.out.printf("Username: %s, Email: %s, Location: %sn",
row.getString("username"), row.getString("email"),
row.getString("location"));
}
```

Here, we iterate over `ResultSet`. The `all()` method of the instance of `ResultSet` `rs` returns a list of rows. An instance of row has several methods, which can be used to fetch individual columns. `Row.getString("username")` is used to fetch the value of the `username` column for that particular instance of row.

# Prepared statements

CQL statements that are executed multiple times can be prepared and stored in a `PreparedStatement` object. The prepared statement is parameterized with ? placeholders for the literal values in CQL. The Cassandra server caches the prepared statement and returns an ID to the client. The client sends the ID when it needs to execute the prepared statement along with the parameter bindings. The server reuses the server-side prepared statement it has cached to execute the query. This is all done transparent to the application.

Let's run the earlier query using prepared statements and name the program `SimplePreparedQuery.java`:

```
import com.datastax.driver.core.BoundStatement;
import com.datastax.driver.core.Cluster;
import com.datastax.driver.core.ConsistencyLevel;
```

```
import com.datastax.driver.core.PreparedStatement;
import com.datastax.driver.core.ResultSet;
import com.datastax.driver.core.Row;
import com.datastax.driver.core.Session;

public class SimplePreparedQuery {

 public static void main(String[] args) {
 Cluster cluster =
Cluster.builder().addContactPoints("127.0.0.1").build();
 Session session = cluster.connect();

PreparedStatement ps1 = session.prepare("INSERT INTO my_status.users
(username , email) VALUES (?, ?)");
PreparedStatement ps2 = session.prepare("SELECT * FROM my_status.users
WHERE username = ?");
 BoundStatement bs1 = ps1.bind();
 bs1.setString("username", "alice");
 bs1.setString("email", "alice@yahoo.com");

 BoundStatement bs2 = ps2.bind();
 bs2.setString("username", "alice");
bs1.setConsistencyLevel(ConsistencyLevel.ONE);
 bs2.setConsistencyLevel(ConsistencyLevel.QUORUM);

 session.execute(bs1);
 ResultSet rs = session.execute(bs2);
 for (Row row : rs.all()) {
System.out.printf("Username: %s, Email: %s, Location: %sn",
row.getString("username"), row.getString("email"),
row.getString("location"));
 }
 cluster.close();
 }
}
```

Program 3: `SimplePreparedQuery.java`

Let's analyze the previous program again:

```
PreparedStatement ps1 = session.prepare("INSERT INTO my_status.users
(username , email) VALUES (?, ?)");
PreparedStatement ps2 = session.prepare("SELECT * FROM my_status.users
WHERE username = ?");
```

After importing the relevant classes and creating a `Cluster` and `Session` object, we declare two prepared statements. The first one is an `INSERT` query and has placeholders for `username` and `email`. The second one is a `SELECT` query and has a placeholder for `username`:

```
BoundStatement bs1 = ps1.bind();
bs1.setString("username", "alice");
bs1.setString("email", "alice@yahoo.com");
BoundStatement bs2 = ps2.bind();
bs2.setString("username", "alice");
```

Next, we have to bind values to placeholders in the prepared statement. To do this, we use `BoundStatement`. We create two bound statements each for both of the prepared statements. We use the `setString()` function to bind the relevant values:

```
bs1.setConsistencyLevel(ConsistencyLevel.ONE);
bs2.setConsistencyLevel(ConsistencyLevel.QUORUM);
```

We can also the set the consistency level for each query using the `setConsistencyLevel()` method. Here, we set the consistency levels to `ONE` and `QUORUM` for the consecutive bound statements:

```
session.execute(bs1);
ResultSet rs = session.execute(bs2);
```

Next, we execute the bound statements using the `session.execute()` method. This will ensure that only the values are to the server rather than the entire statement. The server uses the cached prepared statement along with the values it receives to execute the query. This reduces the data sent over the network, especially when you run the same query multiple times.

When we execute the previous program, we will notice that the `email` column value has been updated for the user `alice`:

```
Username: alice, Email: alice@yahoo.com, Location: null
```

# QueryBuilder API

`QueryBuilder` API provides another way to execute queries without using prepared statements. `QueryBuilder` has many methods to help generate dynamic queries. Some of these methods are as follows:

- Methods to select/insert/update/delete: `select()` and `update(String table)`
- Methods representing a `WHERE` clause: `eq(String name, Object value)`
- Methods representing an assignment: `set(String name, Object value)`

We will look at the `QueryBuilder` API to build the `INSERT`, `UPDATE`, and `SELECT` statements.

# Building an INSERT statement

First, let's write a program, which uses the `QueryBuilder` API to build an `INSERT` statement and execute it. Then, we will walk through each method used in the program. To demonstrate this, we will update the `email` of user `alice` and set the location as well. Let's the name the program `QueryBuilderInsert.java`:

```
import com.datastax.driver.core.Cluster;
import com.datastax.driver.core.Session;
import com.datastax.driver.core.Statement;
import com.datastax.driver.core.querybuilder.QueryBuilder;

public class QueryBuilderInsert {
 public static void main(String[] args) {
 Cluster cluster =
Cluster.builder().addContactPoints("127.0.0.1").build();
 Session session = cluster.connect();

 Statement statement = QueryBuilder.insertInto("my_status", "users")
.value("username", "alice").value("email", "alice@aol.com")
.value("location", "Los Angeles, CA");
 session.execute(statement);

 cluster.close();
 }
}
```

Program 4: `QueryBuilderInsert.java`

`QueryBuilder` provides the `insertInto()` method to create an `INSERT` statement. The `INSERT` statement is a subclass of the `Statement` class. There are two versions of the `insertInto` method:

- `insertInto(String keyspace, String table)`: Creates an Insert statement with the given keyspace and table names

- `insertInto(String table)`: Creates an Insert statement with the given table name

Both the earlier methods return an instance of the `Insert` class. The `Insert` class consists of methods to add `column` name and `value` pairs to the `INSERT` statement:

- `Insert value(String name, Object value)`: Add a column with the given name and value. You can chain this method multiple times to add multiple column name/value pairs.
- `Insert value(String[] names, Object[] values)`: Add multiple column name/value pairs to the `INSERT` statement.

Run the previous Java program. Upon checking the `users` table for the record with username `alice`, you will find that the e-mail has been updated and the location has been set:

```
username | email          | location
---------+----------------+-------------------
   alice | alice@aol.com  | Los Angeles, CA
```

# Building an UPDATE statement

Run the following program with the name `QueryBuilderUpdate.java` to create an `UPDATE` statement and execute it:

```java
import com.datastax.driver.core.Cluster;
import com.datastax.driver.core.Session;
import com.datastax.driver.core.Statement;
import com.datastax.driver.core.querybuilder.QueryBuilder;

public class QueryBuilderUpdate {

 public static void main(String[] args) {
  Cluster cluster =
Cluster.builder().addContactPoints("127.0.0.1").build();
  Session session = cluster.connect();

  Statement statement = QueryBuilder.update("my_status", "users")
  .with(QueryBuilder.set("location", "San Francisco, CA"))
  .and(QueryBuilder.set("email", "alice@hotmail.com"))
  .where(QueryBuilder.eq("username", "alice"));
```

```
session.execute(statement);
cluster.close();
 }
}
```

Program 5: `QueryBuilderUpdate.java`

The previous program is similar to the INSERT statement model. `QueryBuilder` provides the `update()` method to create an UPDATE statement. The UPDATE statement is also a subclass of the `Statement` class. There are two versions of the `update` method similar to `insertInto` method:

- `update(String keyspace, String table)`: Creates an Update statement with the given keyspace and table names
- `update(String table)`: Creates an Update statement with the given table name

Both the earlier methods return an instance of the `Update` class. The `Update` class has methods to add a WHERE clause:

- `Update.Where where()`
- `Update.Where where(Clause clause)`: Here, we are adding the WHERE clause using the `QueryBuilder.eq(name, value)` function, which sets the equality constraint where the `username` is `alice`

You can add assignments to the UPDATE statement using the `with()` method.

- `Update.Assignments with(Assignment assignment)`: We generate an assignment by calling the `set()` method for `QueryBuilder` API, which sets the column name/value pair
- `Assignment set(String name, Object value)`: This denotes the simple assignment of a value to a column
- `Update.Assignments and(Assignment assignment)`: `Update.Assignments` has methods to build the assignments. One such method we have used is the `and()` method

Both the `Update.Where` and `Update.Assignments` classes are subclasses of the `Statement` class and can be executed using the `execute()` method of a session.

After running the previous program and checking the users table via cqlsh, you will find out that the relevant columns have been updated:

```
username | email               | location
---------+---------------------+--------------------
   alice | alice@hotmail.com   | San Francisco, CA
```

# Building a SELECT statement

Run the following program with the name QueryBuilderSelect.java to create an SELECT statement and execute it:

```java
import com.datastax.driver.core.Cluster;
import com.datastax.driver.core.ResultSet;
import com.datastax.driver.core.Row;
import com.datastax.driver.core.Session;
import com.datastax.driver.core.Statement;
import com.datastax.driver.core.querybuilder.QueryBuilder;

public class QueryBuilderSelect {

 public static void main(String[] args) {
  Cluster cluster =
Cluster.builder().addContactPoints("127.0.0.1").build();
  Session session = cluster.connect();

Statement statement = QueryBuilder.select("username", "email",
"location").from("my_status", "users")
  .where(QueryBuilder.eq("username", "alice"));
  ResultSet rs = session.execute(statement);


  Row row = rs.one();
System.out.printf("Username: %s, Email: %s, Location: %sn",
row.getString("username"), row.getString("email"),
row.getString("location"));
  cluster.close();
  }
}
```

Program 6: `QueryBuilderSelect.java`

`QueryBuilder` API has two methods to return builder objects for creating the SELECT statements:

- `Select.Builder select(String... columns)`: This builds a SELECT query with the columns. We use this in our program specifying three columns
- `Select.Selection select()`: This builds a SELECT query without any columns specified

`Select.Selection` is a subclass of the `Select.Builder` class.

`Select.Builder` has methods to specify the table:

- `Select` from(String table)
- `Select` from(String keyspace, String table)

Both of the previous methods return a SELECT statement, which is a subclass of the `Statement` class.

`Select.Selection` adds methods specifying columns or data to select the following:

- `Select.Builder all()`: This selects all columns
- `Select.Selection column(String name)`: This selects the provided column
- `Select.Builder countAll()`: This selects the count of returned rows

Select class adds methods for creating a SELECT statement:

- `Select.Where where(Clause clause)`: This adds a WHERE clause to the SELECT statement. `Select.Where` is a subclass of `Statement` class
- `Select allowFiltering()`: This adds ALLOW FILTERING to the SELECT statement
- `Select limit(int limit)`: This adds the LIMIT clause
- `Select orderBy(Ordering... orderings)`: This adds the ORDER BY clause

`Select.where` class represents a WHERE clause in the SELECT statement. It can be generated by either calling `Select.where()`/`Select.where(Clause clause)` method or by the `Select.Where.and(Clause clause)` method.

Clause instances hold the details of the clause. Clause instances can be generated by several methods:

- `Clause eq(String name, Object value)`: Equality clause
- `Clause in(String name, Object... values)`: If the value of the `name` column is one of the provided values

Upon executing the preceding program, you will get the row with username `alice`:

```
Username: alice, Email: alice@hotmail.com, Location: San Francisco, CA
```

# Asynchronous querying

When executing a normal query, the call returns only after the query completes. When you call the `execute()` method of a session instance to execute a query, the call returns after doing I/O to the cluster, waiting for the cluster to execute query and getting a response from the cluster. Meanwhile, the querying thread is idle and blocked. It can't execute other queries.

Consider the following example where you're trying to load a lot of user data. We could execute the code in a loop thousands of times, but each iteration waits for `session.execute()` to finish:

```
public ResultSet insertUserData(/* Some user data) {
PreparedStatement insertUser = ...; // Prepare the statement
BoundStatement bs = ... ; // Bind the statement
return session.execute(bs); // Execute the query
}
```

A client executes `insertUserData()` in a loop. While waiting for the method to complete, the client won't execute other queries on the cluster. Only one node in the cluster will be servicing client requests at a time.

The main issues with this approach are as follows:

- The client runs often wait for a query result and stay idle
- Nodes in the cluster may not be fully utilized
- The performance is optimal

To avoid this issue of serially executing queries and making blocking calls, asynchronous querying was introduced. Asynchronous querying lets us execute queries without waiting for a response to the previous queries. Asynchronous querying is done via the `executeAsync()` method of a session instance. There are two forms of the method, one which takes a string as an input and another which takes a query object as an input:

- `ResultSetFuture executeAsync(String query)`
- `ResultSetFuture executeAsync(Query query)`

# Execute asynchronously

The `executeAsync()` method of a session instance executes a query asynchronously. The method is non-blocking. It passes a query to the underlying network stack and returns immediately. One thing to consider is it doesn't guarantee that the query was passed to a node or that it was valid. Query failures/exceptions are detected when you access the `ResultSetFuture`.

`ResultSetFuture` is a future on `ResultSet`. It includes all the methods of `Future<ResultSet>`. It adds the following methods for processing the results:

- `ResultSet getUninterruptibly()`: This method waits for the query to return and return its result
- `ResultSet getUninterruptibly(long timeout, TimeUnit unit)`: This is the same as the previous method and includes waiting for the timeout duration before throwing an exception

Both of these methods can throw the following exceptions:

- `NoHostAvailableException`, if a host cannot be contacted
- `QueryExecutionException`, if the query triggered an execution exception, which is usually thrown by Cassandra because it can't execute the query
- `QueryValidationException`, if the query is invalid
- `TimeoutException`, if the query didn't return before the timeout

To query asynchronously, you would just change the previous `insertUserData()` method to this:

```
public ResultSet insertUserData(/* Some user data) {
PreparedStatement insertUser = ...; // Prepare the statement
BoundStatement bs = ... ; // Bind the statement
return session.executeAsync(bs); // Execute the query - returns
```

```
immediately
}
```

# Processing future results

After executing query results, we may want to process the results of those queries. This can be done by creating an array of ResultSetFuture and looping through the array and calling future methods to get ResultSet. For the earlier query, you could do something like this:

```
ArrayList<ResultSetFuture> futures = new ArrayList<ResultSetFuture>();
for (int i=0; i< 500; i++) { // 500 inserts at a time
  futures.add( insertUserData(/*.. User data */ ) );
}

for (ResultSetFuture future : futures) { // Process future results
future.getUninterruptibly();
}
```

First, we instantiate an empty array called futures to store the ResultSetFuture objects.

In the first loop, we execute the insertUserData() method 500 times and add the result to the futures array.

In the second loop, we loop through the futures array and execute the getUninterruptibly() method to wait for a response for each query. We don't assign the result to a ResultSet object because we are doing INSERT queries and don't care about the results.

# Driver policies

The Java driver provides several policies to configure behavior. Some of the policies are as follows:

- **Load-balancing policy**: This determines which Cassandra host to contact for each query. The policy is made aware of any changes in the cluster topology. They ensure that downed nodes are excluded and decommissioned, or removed nodes are removed from the connection pool.

- **Retry policy**: This determines the course of action whenever failures occur. It's usually triggered when a timeout or host unavailable exception happens. This minimizes exception handling from our side by automating query retry of failures.
- **Reconnection policy**: This policy decides how often reconnection to a dead node is attempted.

# Load-balancing policy

As the name implies, the driver forwards queries to hosts based on the load-balancing policy chosen. Usually, this distributes the queries evenly amongst the nodes in the cluster. Java driver provides several load-balancing policies. You can create your own load-balancing policies as well.

To set a load-balancing policy, you will have to use the `withLoadBalancingPolicy()` method of the `Cluster.Builder` object:

```
Cluster cluster = Cluster.builder().addContactPoints("127.0.0.1")
.withLoadBalancingPolicy(LoadBalancingPolicy policy).build();
```

# RoundRobinPolicy

This is the default load-balancing policy. This is a straightforward implementation and chooses hosts in a round robin fashion to execute queries. This implementation is not datacenter aware. If a host fails in a query, the next one in the round robin is used.

Suppose you have three hosts in a cluster. Your query execution sequence could look like this:

- Query1: host1, host2, host3
- Query2: host2, host3, host1
- Query3: host3, host1, host2

To use this policy, create a `Cluster` object as follows:

```
Cluster cluster = Cluster.builder().addContactPoints("127.0.0.1")
.withLoadBalancingPolicy(new RoundRobinPolicy()).build();
```

# DCAwareRoundRobinPolicy

This policy is datacenter aware and routes queries to the local nodes first. There are two constructors for instantiating this class:

- `DCAwareRoundRobinPolicy(String localDc)`: This specifies the name of the local data center
- `DCAwareRoundRobinPolicy(String localDc, int usedHostsPerRemoteDc)`: This can configure the number of nodes to try in a remote data center

To use this policy, use the `withLoadBalancingPolicy()` method to set the LB policy, as follows:

```
Cluster cluster = Cluster.builder().addContactPoint("127.0.0.1")
 .withLoadBalancingPolicy(
 DCAwareRoundRobinPolicy.builder()
 .withLocalDc("localDc")
 .withUsedHostsPerRemoteDc(2)
 .allowRemoteDCsForLocalConsistencyLevel()
 .build()).build();
```

# TokenAwarePolicy

This policy adds token awareness on top of another policy. The requests will be routed to the nodes, which contain the token (or the partition). This policy is used when you query over multiple partitions. To use it in conjunction with `RoundRobinPolicy`.

To use this policy, create a `Cluster` object, as follows:

```
Cluster cluster = Cluster.builder().addContactPoints("127.0.0.1")
 .withLoadBalancingPolicy(new TokenAwarePolicy
 (new RoundRobinPolicy())).build();
```

# Retry Policy

Often, queries might fail due to temporary network outages or increased load on a node. It doesn't make sense to fail such queries immediately. Java driver provides a set of policies to ensure queries are retried a certain number of times before throwing exceptions. This accounts for temporary failures. You can create your own retry policy as well.

To set `retrypolicy`, you will have to use the `withRetryPolicy()` method of the `Cluster.Builder` object:

```
Cluster cluster = Cluster.builder().addContactPoints("127.0.0.1")
.withRetryPolicy(RetryPolicy policy).build();
```

Here are some of the retry policies available in Java driver:

- `DefaultRetryPolicy`: This policy retries a failed query a certain number of times. It retries queries on a read timeout where replica nodes were contacted but the read failed. It also retries queries on a write timeout when writing distributed log for batches.
- `DowngradingConsistencyRetryPolicy`: This ensures that a failed query may be retried with a consistency level lower than the initial query. This may break consistency guarantee of the query and could return stale data.
- `FallthroughRetryPolicy`: This never retries any query, and you implement retry logic in your application code.

# Summary

In this chapter, we learned how to develop applications using the Java driver to communicate with Cassandra. Throughout the chapter, we studied the various classes that are used to create a connection with a Cassandra cluster and execute queries. We looked at a lot of helper methods that can be used to configure a Cassandra connection and query execution.

To begin with, we started by using the `Cluster` API to create a `Cluster` object, which is the entry point to the Cassandra cluster. We used methods to set the initial contact points to create a Cassandra cluster connection and return an instance of the Cluster object. We then proceeded with creating an instance of Session, which is used to execute queries. Executed queries return the results as a `ResultSet` object. A `ResultSet` object implements `Iterable <Row>`, which can be looped over to fetch individual rows. Then, we wrote a couple of programs to perform the INSERT and SELECT queries using this knowledge.

After this, we created a prepared statement with parameterized portions, which is cached locally on Cassandra nodes. We took this prepared statement and created a bound statement by binding values. We then executed these bound statements to ensure that only the parameterized values are sent. The Cassandra node combines the cached statement along with the values it receives and executes the query. This could potentially save a lot of network I/O when a query is run multiple times.

We then proceeded with using the QueryBuilder API to create different types of statements. We created the INSERT, UPDATE, and SELECT statements and used various helper methods to pass column name/value pairs and set equality constraints. These statements were then executed to run the respective queries.

Finally, we looked at various optimizations, such as asynchronous querying and different policies, to make queries more efficient.

To further read up on the Java driver, please visit this page, which has a comprehensive list of all the features, including paging support, speculative query execution, logging, metrics, and other details (http://docs.datastax.com/en/developer/java-driver/3.1/manual/).

To finalize, the Java driver architecture can be visualized as follows:

# Peeking under the Hood

Over the previous 12 chapters, we've thoroughly explored Cassandra's capabilities from the perspective of application developers. All of our interaction with Cassandra has been through CQL, and we've explored a robust set of features available to us via the CQL interface. We've found that one of the big appeals of Cassandra is the rich set of data structures available to us for domain modeling; structures such as compound primary keys, collection columns, and secondary indexes are part of what sets Cassandra apart from other distributed databases.

As it turns out, CQL is an abstraction on top of a much less sophisticated data structure that underlies all the data stored in Cassandra. Commonly referred to as the **Thrift interface**, named after the protocol used to interact with Cassandra at this level, this layer represents all data using an ad hoc key-value structure called a **column family**. As developers, we will never need to interact with Cassandra at this level of abstraction, but it's illuminating to explore how the familiar CQL data structures are represented at the column family level.

In some contexts, you might hear the terms table and column family used interchangeably. In fact, CQL provides CREATE COLUMNFAMILY as an alias for the familiar CREATE TABLE command. This is a legacy of the gradual divergence of the CQL table structure from the underlying column family structure. In earlier versions of CQL, tables were mapped more or less transparently onto the underlying column family structure.
We will use the terminology preferred by the Cassandra developers, using table to talk about the CQL data structure and column family for the lower level structure available via the Thrift interface.

When we have completed exploring the Thrift interface, you'll have discovered:

- How to directly access Cassandra's low-level column family structures
- Column family representation of simple and compound primary keys
- The structure of collection columns at the column family level

# Using cassandra-cli

To explore the Thrift API, we'll use a new tool called **cassandra-cli**. Like cqlsh, cassandra-cli is a command-line interface to Cassandra, but it does not provide a CQL interface. Instead, cassandra-cli uses a small, purpose-built query language that allows us to interact directly with column families. Some cassandra-cli commands resemble their CQL equivalents, but it's merely a resemblance, not a relationship.

In recent versions of Cassandra, cassandra-cli is deprecated and will be removed from Cassandra 3.0. This should serve to underscore the fact that CQL is considered the way to interact with Cassandra: the Thrift interface is merely a curiosity, not a viable tool to interact with Cassandra in our applications.

Your installation of Cassandra should have the cassandra-cli executable in the same directory as cqlsh. Once we start it up, we should see something like this:

```
$ cassandra-cli
Connected to: "Test Cluster" on 127.0.0.1/9160
Welcome to Cassandra CLI version 2.0.7

The CLI is deprecated and will be removed in Cassandra 3.0.  Consider migrating to cqlsh.
CQL is fully backwards compatible with Thrift data; see http://www.datastax.com/dev/blog/thrift-to-cql3

Type 'help;' or '?' for help.
Type 'quit;' or 'exit;' to quit.

[default@unknown] █
```

Just as in cqlsh, we'll need to start by specifying the keyspace we want to interact with:

```
USE my_status;
```

Now that we've got cassandra-cli up and running, we can start exploring how our CQL3 tables are modeled at the column family level.

# The structure of a simple primary key table

To start with, let's have a look at the `users` table. To do this, we'll start with the `LIST` command that prints all the data in a given column family:

    LIST users;

This will print out a long list of information, grouped by `RowKey`. For brevity, the first couple of `RowKey` groups appear as follows:

```
RowKey: bob
=> (name=, value=, timestamp=1401412616531000)
=> (name=encrypted_password, value=10920941a69549d33aaee6116ed1f47e19b8e713, timestamp=1401412616531000)
=> (name=version, value=ec0c1fb1321f11e48eeb5f98e903bf02, timestamp=1409607341355000)
-------------------
RowKey: happycorp
=> (name=, value=, timestamp=1409607324125000)
=> (name=email, value=6d65646961406861707079636f72702e636f6d, timestamp=1409607324125000)
=> (name=encrypted_password, value=368200fa910c16cc644f3512e63b541c85fa2a3c, timestamp=1409607324125000)
=> (name=location, value=4e657720596f726b2c204e59, timestamp=1409607607205000)
=> (name=version, value=8a810110322011e48eeb5f98e903bf02, timestamp=1409607607205000)
```

Although we've never seen it structured like this before, the data here should look pretty familiar. The `RowKey` headers correspond to the username column in our CQL3 table structure. Within each `RowKey` is a collection of tuples, each tuple containing a name, a value, and a timestamp. We will call these tuple cells, in keeping with the terminology used in the cassandra-cli interface itself.

 You might encounter the word `column` being used for the name-value-timestamp tuples we are exploring here. Not only does that terminology invite confusion with the concept of a column in CQL3, but it's also a singularly misleading way to describe the data structure in question. We'll stick with *cell*, which is both unambiguous and more descriptive. Please excuse us for referring to collections of cells as column families-there is no better alternative.

# Exploring cells

Looking at the `name` attribute, we see things like `email`, `encrypted_password`, `version`, and `location`. Clearly, the `name` attribute of the cells corresponds to the names of columns in our CQL schema-although the relationship is more complex than it might appear, as we'll explore in the next section.

The `value` field in the cells is a bit of a mystery; given that the name contains column names, we might expect that the value would contain column values. However, what we see in cassandra-cli are just some inscrutable hexadecimal blobs.

As it turns out, under the hood Cassandra represents all data as hexadecimal byte arrays; the type system is part of CQL's abstraction layer. The cassandra-cli utility does give us a way to retrieve human-readable values of individual columns, using the `AS` keyword to explicitly specify the type. Let's try to read the value of the cell with the `name` value as `email`, from HappyCorp's user record:

```
GET users['happycorp']['email'] AS ascii;
```

The `GET` command allows us to access a single cell by first specifying the `RowKey` value, then the cell name. We can also omit the cell name to return all the cells at a given `RowKey`.

In this case, thanks to our use of `AS`, we can see a human-readable value for HappyCorp's email address:

```
=> (name=email, value=media@happycorp.com, timestamp=1409607324125000)
Elapsed time: 3.34 msec(s).
```

Thankfully, the CLI will remember our preference for reading emails in ASCII, and will accordingly print out all cells named `email` from the `users` column family for the remainder of the session.

# A model of column families: RowKey and cells

At this point, we've satisfied ourselves that each cell in a column family corresponds to a column name and value at the CQL level. The mapping between CQL3 tables and lower-level column families, so far, seems pretty straightforward. A table row's primary key value is stored in the `RowKey` field, and each cell contains a name-value pair that represents the value of the named column in the row.

We can make the relationship between the table representation and the column family representation more accessible with a visualization of each:

| The **users** table | | | |
|---|---|---|---|
| username | email | encrypted_password | location |
| **bob** | | 0x10920941… | |
| **happycorp** | media@happycorp.com | 0x368200fa… | New York, NY |

The **users** column family

bob — [ encrypted_password / 0x10920941… ]

happycorp — [ email / media@happycorp.com ] [ encrypted_password / 0x368200fa… ] [ location / New York, NY ]

We thus visualize the column family as a collection of RowKey values, with each RowKey linked to a collection of cells containing a name and a value. Note that not every CQL3 column is represented by a cell in every RowKey field; only when a given column has a value does it have a corresponding cell in the column family. This is consistent with our mental model of CQL3 tables, developed in the *Developing a mental model for Cassandra* section of Chapter 2, *The First Table*.

As it turns out, the similarities between column families and CQL3 tables take us this far and no further.

# Compound primary keys in column families

Now that we've established the relatively familiar-looking column family structure of users-a table with a simple primary key-let's move on to a table with a compound primary key. To start, let's take a look at home_status_updates, a fairly straightforward table. Recall that this table has a partition key timeline_username; a clustering column status_update_id; and two data columns, body and status_update_username column.

We'll use the `LIST` command to take a look at the contents of the column family and, beforehand, we'll use the `ASSUME` command to set the value output format to `utf8`. This has a similar effect as the `AS` modifier we used earlier, but it applies to all cells in a column family, rather than only cells with a specific name:

```
ASSUME home_status_updates VALIDATOR AS utf8;
LIST home_status_updates;
```

The output of the `LIST` command takes the same general shape as that for the `users` column family, but the way the information is arranged might come as a surprise:

```
RowKey: alice
=> (name=16e2f240-2afa-11e4-8069-5f98e903bf02:, value=, timestamp=1408823428694000)
=> (name=16e2f240-2afa-11e4-8069-5f98e903bf02:body, value=dave update 4, timestamp=1408823428694000)
=> (name=16e2f240-2afa-11e4-8069-5f98e903bf02:status_update_username, value=dave, timestamp=1408823428694000)
=> (name=cacc7de0-2af9-11e4-8069-5f98e903bf02:, value=, timestamp=1408821757668000)
=> (name=cacc7de0-2af9-11e4-8069-5f98e903bf02:body, value=carol update 4, timestamp=1408821757668000)
=> (name=cacc7de0-2af9-11e4-8069-5f98e903bf02:status_update_username, value=carol, timestamp=1408821757668000)
```

The output contains only a single `RowKey`, that is `alice`; it contains six cells with rather inscrutable names. Recall that in the *Fully denormalizing the home timeline* section of `Chapter 6`, *Denormalizing Data for Maximum Performance*, we populated the `home_status_updates` table with two status updates, both in `alice`'s partition of the table. So how does the information in the column family line up with the information in the CQL table we're used to?

To answer this question, look closely at the names of the cells. Take the second cell, which has the name `16e2f240-2afa-11e4-8069-5f98e903bf02:body`. This cell name appears to contain two pieces of information: a clustering column value and the name of a data column. The value of the cell is, straightforwardly, the value of the body column in the row with the `status_update_id` value `16e2f240-2afa-11e4-8069-5f98e903bf02`.

The reason we only see one `RowKey` value is because all the rows in the `home_status_updates` table have the partition key `alice`. What cassandra-cli calls a `RowKey` is, in fact, exactly what we have been calling a partition key the entire time.

# A complete mapping

With this insight, we can now generate a complete mapping between the components of a column family and the CQL-level table structure components they represent:

| Column Family Component | CQL3 Table Component |
|---|---|
| RowKey | Partition Key |
| Cell name | The values of clustering column(s), if any, followed by the name of the data column |
| Cell value | The value in the row/column identified by the partition key, clustering column(s), and the column name |

To reinforce this idea, let's apply our visualization from the previous section to the more complex structure of home_status_updates:

The main insight here is that every value in every row in alice's partition is stored in a one-dimensional data structure in the column family. At the column family level, nothing in the storage structure distinguishes the values in carol's status update row from the values in dave's status update row. The cells containing those values simply have different prefixes in their cell names; only at the CQL level are these represented as distinct rows.

# The wide row data structure

Another important observation is that, at the column family level, there is no preset list of allowed cell names. The cell names we observe in `alice`'s partition of the `home_status_updates` column family are derived partially from data calculated at runtime-namely, the UUID values of various status update ID columns. At the CQL level, tables must have predefined column names but no equivalent restriction exists at the column family level.

Looking closely at the cells in `alice`'s RowKey, we observe that they are in order: first, descending by the timestamp encoded in the UUID component of the cell name, and second, alphabetically ascending by the column name component. You learned in `Chapter 3`, *Organizing Related Data* that clustering columns give CQL rows a natural ordering, and now we know how the cells grouped under a given RowKey at the column family level are always ordered by the cell name.

The data structure that we observe at `alice`'s RowKey in `home_status_updates` is commonly called a **wide row**. Not to be confused with the rows we commonly interact with in CQL tables, wide rows are simply ordered collections of cells; each wide row is associated with a RowKey, which at the CQL level we call a partition key.

# The empty cell

We've so far ignored one curious entity in the column family data structure-each RowKey seems to have a cell whose value is empty, and whose name consists purely of a clustering column value and a delimiter.

Recall that, in a CQL row, there is no requirement that any data column contain data. A row consisting purely of values for the primary key columns is entirely valid. CQL makes this possible by storing an extra cell any time a row is created or updated that acts as a placeholder indicating that there is a row in the clustering column encoded in the cell's name. Thus, the existence of the row is guaranteed even if there is no data column to be stored as a cell in that row.

# Collection columns in column families

We've seen the surprising way in which the key structure of a CQL table maps to the underlying column family representation, but so far the values stored in CQL have mapped completely transparently into cell values at the column family level. While this is true for scalar data types, something much more interesting happens where collections are concerned.

# Set columns in column families

We'll start by looking at sets, which are the simplest of the three collection column types. Let's take a look at alice's row in the user_status_updates column family:

```
GET user_status_updates['alice'];
```

Recall that, by only using the bracket operator once in the GET statement, we'll retrieve all cells in the alice RowKey.

There are quite a few cells in alice's wide row, but we're particularly interested in those having to do with the starred_by_users column, which is a set:

```
=> (name=76e7a4d0-e796-11e3-90ce-5f98e903bf02:starred_by_users:626f62, value=, timestamp=1411314062536000)
=> (name=76e7a4d0-e796-11e3-90ce-5f98e903bf02:starred_by_users:6361726f6c, value=, timestamp=1411314212388000)
```

Note that the cell names here look like the cell names in home_status_updates, but with yet another component: a short hexadecimal string appended to the end. Unfortunately, there's no straightforward way to get cassandra-cli to print those hexadecimal strings in a human-readable form, so you'll have to take my word for it that 0x626f62 is the blob encoding of the string bob, and 0x6361726f6c encodes the string carol.

With this cleared up, we can observe that the underlying representation of a CQL set is a collection of cells, with each cell encoding one of the items in the set. The item is actually encoded in the cell's *name* by appending it to the usual combination of clustering column value and row name that comprises the name of a scalar cell.

Let's have a look at a set using the visual comparison we have been developing in the course of this chapter. For clarity, I've omitted everything unrelated to the set:

## The **user_status_updates** table

| username | status_update_id | starred_by_users |
|----------|------------------|-------------------|
| alice | 76e7a4d0... | {dave,carol} |

## The **user_status_updates** column family

| alice | 76e7a4d0...:starred_by_users:dave | 76e7a4d0...:starred_by_users:carol |
|-------|-----------------------------------|-------------------------------------|

This turns out to be a very effective way to represent a set at the column family level. When a new item is added to a set, the CQL abstraction simply adds a cell containing the item appended to the appropriate clustering column/column name combination. Removing items from the set is as simple as deleting the cell that encodes that item. In both cases, Cassandra can do the right thing without having to read the existing contents of the set.

# Map columns in column families

Although maps might seem like the most complex of the three collection column types, their column family level representation is actually simpler than that of lists, so we'll save lists for last. To get a sense of what map columns look like at the column family level, let's take a look at the **social_identities** map in alice's user record:

```
GET users['alice'];
```

Again, we'll focus solely on the interesting cells in the result:

```
=> (name=encrypted_password, value=8914977ed729792e403da53024c6069a9158b8c4, timestamp=1409605884231000)
=> (name=social_identities:74776974746572, value=2725634, timestamp=1411314494120000)
```

The structure of the cell names looks identical to the cell names used by set columns. However, unlike set columns, the cells encoding map columns have values in them. In a map, the map keys are stored in cell names, and the map values are stored in cell values. We can thus visualize a map like this:

The relationship between the underlying representations of map columns and set columns should come as no great surprise; many programming languages implement their set data type using an underlying map whose values are not meaningful.

Our reasoning about the process of insertion and deletion in sets also carries over to maps. Since, for any given map key that needs to be inserted or deleted, the CQL abstraction can calculate the corresponding cell name, map key-value pairs can be directly inserted and deleted without Cassandra needing to read the full contents of the column.

# List columns in column families

The last collection type we'll explore at the column family level is lists. Lists are the most complex collection types in a couple of ways. As you learned in Chapter 8, *Collections, Tuples, and User-defined Types*, lists have more available mutation operations than maps or sets. It also turns out that lists have the most complex underlying representation.

Let's take a look at the shared_by list in the user_status_updates table. Before we dive into the underlying structure, let's quickly open a cqlsh console and add a new value to the shared_by list of alice. When we last left this list, it only had a single username in it, which isn't really useful for the purposes of our exploration:

```
UPDATE "user_status_updates"
SET "shared_by" = "shared_by" + ['bob'],
  "shared_by" = ['dave'] + "shared_by"
WHERE "username" = 'alice'
AND "id" = 76e7a4d0-e796-11e3-90ce-5f98e903bf02;
```

Note that, by setting the `shared_by` column twice in our UPDATE statement, we can both prepend and append values to the list in a single query. Having done this, let's take a look at `alice`'s partition in the `user_status_updates` column family, focusing on the cells related to the `shared_by` collection:

```
=> (name=76e7a4d0-e796-11e3-90ce-5f98e903bf02:shared_by:4116d73041a611e4b4ad5f98e903bf02,
value=726f62657274, timestamp=1411314365135000)
=> (name=76e7a4d0-e796-11e3-90ce-5f98e903bf02:shared_by:e358efe0678711e4ac53f51fa8d64e2e,
value=626f62, timestamp=1415479406045000)
```

At first glance, the structure looks quite similar to that of set and map columns: the cell name consists of a clustering column value, a data column name, and finally some other list-related component. However, what is the list-related component?

It turns out that this value is a UUID; the hex string printed in cassandra-cli is in fact the usual UUID representation, just without the dashes. If we decode the UUID `e358efe0678711e4ac53f51fa8d64e2e`, the last one in the list, we'll find that it encodes the timestamp at which we appended `bob` to the list column.

# Appending and prepending values to lists

Our observation allows us to deduce that Cassandra appends items to list columns by creating a new cell whose name includes the current timestamp UUID. Since the value of timestamp UUIDs is monotonically increasing, this will ensure that the appended value is the last in the list, since it has the highest (newest) UUID. This way, Cassandra can construct the cell name for a newly appended list item without consulting the current contents of the list.

Now, let's take a look at the first cell in the list, the one whose value contains `dave`. Recall that we prepended `dave` onto the list, so we know that the cell name doesn't contain the current timestamp because that would put Dave at the end of the list, not the beginning.

Decoding the UUID in Dave's cell's name, `77d9443f854711d9ac53f51fa8d64e2e`, yields a timestamp several years old-February 23, 2005. Where does this timestamp come from? As it turns out, the following calculation yields it:

- Calculate how much time has elapsed since midnight UTC on January 1, 2010
- Calculate the timestamp corresponding to that duration before January 1, 2010

So while the UUIDs used to append to lists are monotonically increasing, the UUIDs used to prepend are monotonically decreasing, since we'll be subtracting an ever-greater duration from the *epoch* time of January 1, 2010. Since the first version of Cassandra to support lists was released in early 2013, we can assume that that particular epoch marker was chosen to ensure that all generated prepend timestamps would be smaller than all generated append timestamps.

## Other list operations

We've seen that the structure of maps and sets allows Cassandra to perform all supported mutation operations on those collection types without having to read the currently stored values. Unfortunately, the same is not true for lists. While appending and prepending to lists can be done discretely, other operations require scanning the existing contents of the list first.

If we take a moment to ponder the underlying representation of list columns, the reason is clear. If, for instance, we ask to remove the value `dave` from the list, there's no way for Cassandra to know which cell(s) contain that value without reading it. Even in the simpler case of deleting an element at a given position, Cassandra must look at the cell names to know which cell is at the position requested. So, it's worth keeping in mind that list mutations-except for appending and prepending-are naturally less performant than mutations on other collection types.

# Summary

Having spent the bulk of this book exploring Cassandra using CQL, we've now peeked under the hood to see how the robust data structures offered by CQL are in fact abstractions upon a much more rudimentary column family data structure. If nothing else, this is an opportunity to appreciate modern technology; as recently as Cassandra 1.1, the CQL data structures we take for granted were unheard of. Before Cassandra 0.7, CQL did not exist at all; the Thrift interface we explored in this chapter was state-of-the-art.

Our deep dive into Cassandra's internal data structures also helps us understand the underlying reasons behind facts that in previous chapters we'd taken as first principles. You learned in Chapter 3, *Organizing Related Data* that partition keys group related data, but now we know that in fact all the data under a partition key, or RowKey, coexists in a single wide row. Similarly, we already knew that clustering columns determine row ordering, but now we know that the sorting is actually happening to cells in a wide row, and the use of the clustering column as a prefix for wide row cell names generates the familiar behavior at the CQL level.

In the final appendix, we will do a brief survey of Cassandra's authentication and authorization functionality, and discuss the various tools Cassandra gives you for protecting your deployments against security vulnerabilities.

# B
# Authentication and Authorization

In our interactions with Cassandra in this book, we haven't concerned ourselves with authentication or authorization; whenever we connect to our local Cassandra instance, we're not required to provide any credentials, and there have been no restrictions on what kind of operations we've been able to perform. This is the default configuration for a Cassandra cluster and works well in many scenarios, in particular where network access to the machines running Cassandra is tightly controlled.

In some scenarios, however, it's useful to be able to control access to Cassandra at the database level itself-for instance, when a cluster is shared between multiple tenants or where a large organization needs to restrict access to sensitive data to certain departments or individuals.

For these scenarios, Cassandra does offer a full suite of authentication and authorization functionality; accounts and permissions are configured using CQL.
In order to enable authentication and authorization in our development cluster, we will need to make a couple of small changes to the cluster's configuration file, but we'll otherwise be operating in the familiar territory of cqlsh.

By the end of this appendix, you'll be familiar with:

- How to configure your cluster to restrict access to authorized users
- How to create a user
- How to change a user's password
- How to grant privileges to a user
- How to see the privileges granted to a user
- How to revoke privileges from a user
- Other steps you may want to take to secure your Cassandra cluster

# Enabling authentication and authorization

By default, Cassandra does not require user authentication when clients connect to the cluster, and it also does not place any restriction on the ability of clients to perform operations on the database. To change this, we will need to make a couple of minor modifications to our Cassandra instance's configuration file. Since modifications to the configuration file are typically a concern of deployment engineers, we haven't interacted with it in this book, so you may be wondering where to find it. Where it's located depends on your platform; the table below assumes you installed Cassandra using the instructions for your platform in the *Installing Cassandra* section of Chapter 1, *Getting Up and Running with Cassandra*. The following table gives you the location of the cassandra.yaml file on the respective platforms.

| Platform | Configuration file location |
|----------|------------------------------|
| Mac OS X | `/usr/local/etc/cassandra/cassandra.yaml` |
| Ubuntu | `/etc/cassandra/cassandra.yaml` |
| Windows | `C:\Program Files\DataStax Community\apache-cassandra\conf\cassandra.yaml` |

You will need to make two changes to the cassandra.yaml file. First, find the line that begins with authenticator: and change it to:

```
authenticator: PasswordAuthenticator
```

This change tells Cassandra to require a username and password when clients connect to the cluster. It does not, however, restrict access based on which user is logged in; to do that, we'll need to enable authorization. Find the line beginning with authorizer: and change it to:

```
authorizer: CassandraAuthorizer
```

Now our cluster will restrict the access of the logged in user based on the permissions that user has been granted. You will need to restart your Cassandra instance for the settings to take effect.

# Authentication, authorization, and fault-tolerance

Using the `PasswordAuthenticator` and `CassandraAuthorizer` strategies for authentication and authorization respectively, user credentials and granted permissions are stored in Cassandra itself. This means that, if the authentication data becomes unavailable, no clients will be able to access the cluster. For that reason, you will always want to set the replication factor for your `system_auth` keyspace to the total number of nodes in your cluster. Since our development cluster consists of only a single node, we don't need to make any changes; in production, however, you will almost certainly have many nodes in your cluster, and you'll want to make sure credentials and permissions are stored locally on every one of them.

For further information on configuring Cassandra authentication, including best practices when configuring authentication in a production cluster, see the DataStax Cassandra documentation at: `http://www.datas tax.com/documentation/cassandra/2.1/cassandra/security/securit y_config_native_authenticate_t.html`.

For more information on configuring authorization, see `http://www.data stax.com/documentation/cassandra/2.1/cassandra/security/secure _config_native_authorize_t.html`.

# Authentication with cqlsh

Now that we've enabled authentication on our development cluster, we will need to reconnect our cqlsh session with a username and password. By default, Cassandra has a superuser account whose username and password are both `cassandra`, so we can use that:

```
$ cqlsh -u cassandra -p cassandra
```

In a production cluster, of course, we would not want to have a superuser account with such an easily guessable password; however, for our purposes, this will work fine.

# Authentication in your application

The details differ from language to language, but the CQL driver for your platform should provide a mechanism for authenticated connections. Consult your driver's documentation for more information.

# Setting up a user

By default, Cassandra has one user account configured; its username is cassandra and it is a superuser, meaning there are no restrictions on what it can do to the database. When you connect as a superuser, it's essentially the same as if Cassandra did not have authorization enabled at all.

In order to do something useful with our access restrictions, we'll want to set up another user account that is not a superuser. Let's say one of the departments in the burgeoning MyStatus corporation is a data analytics team. This team needs access to read data from our Cassandra cluster, but has no need to add, change, or remove data. We'll set up a user account for this team that gives them only the access they need.

First, we'll use the CREATE USER command to add a user account for the analytics team:

```
CREATE USER 'data_analytics'
WITH PASSWORD 'strongpassword'
NOSUPERUSER;
```

Note, of course, that in a real deployment we would want to choose an actual strong password, for which the string strongpassword does not suffice.

The NOSUPERUSER option tells Cassandra that the new account is not a superuser, meaning it can't do anything it hasn't explicitly been granted permission to do. This is the default for new users, but we make it explicit here for clarity; replacing it with SUPERUSER would make the new user a superuser.

> For more information on the CREATE USER command, see the DataStax CQL documentation: http://www.datastax.com/documentation/cql/3. 1/cql/cql_reference/create_user_r.html.

# Changing a user's password

If we wish to change the password of an existing account, we can use the `ALTER USER` command:

```
ALTER USER 'data_analytics'
WITH PASSWORD 'verystrongpassword';
```

We can also append a `SUPERUSER` or `NOSUPERUSER` option to the end of this query to grant or revoke superuser access.

# Viewing user accounts

We can see existing user accounts, along with their superuser status, by accessing the users table in the `system_auth` keyspace:

```
SELECT * FROM "system_auth"."users";
```

Note that the use of the period between the keyspace name and the table name simply instructs CQL that we'd like to look into the `system_auth` keyspace, regardless of which keyspace, if any, has been activated by an `USE` statement.

As we can see, user accounts are stored quite transparently in the `system_auth.users` table:

```
 name            | super
-----------------+-------
       cassandra |  True
  data_analytics | False

(2 rows)
```

You may be wondering where and how passwords are stored. These live in a separate table, `system_auth.credentials`; passwords are not stored in plain text, but rather as bcrypt hashes.

# Controlling access

We've now created a user account for our data analytics team, but so far that user can't actually do anything in our database. We'd like to give the data analytics team read access to all the data in our application's keyspace, but no ability to modify data or schema structures. To do this, we'll use the GRANT command:

```
GRANT SELECT PERMISSION
ON KEYSPACE "my_status"
TO 'data_analytics';
```

Now the data_analytics user can read the data from any table in the my_status keyspace; however, it can't make any modifications to anything. The SELECT permission we used above is one of six that Cassandra makes available:

| Permission | Description | CQL commands allowed |
|---|---|---|
| **SELECT** | Read data | SELECT |
| **MODIFY** | Add, update, and remove data in existing tables | INSERT<br>UPDATE<br>DELETE<br>TRUNCATE |
| **CREATE** | Create keyspaces and tables | CREATE TABLE<br>CREATE KEYSPACE |
| **ALTER** | Modify the structure of existing keyspaces and tables | ALTER TABLE<br>CREATE INDEX<br>DROP INDEX<br>ALTER KEYSPACE |
| **DROP** | Drop existing keyspaces and tables | DROP TABLE<br>DROP KEYSPACE |
| **AUTHORIZE** | Grant or revoke permissions to other users | GRANT<br>REVOKE |

There is also an ALL permission that is simply shorthand for granting all six of the permissions listed above.

As well as granting a permission across an entire keyspace, we can also grant permissions to operate on a specific table. For instance, we might want to give the data analytics team full read/write access to the `status_update_views` table that we created in `Chapter 9`, *Aggregating Time-Series Data*, since the data in that table is primarily an analytics concern. To do that, we'll use `GRANT` to issue a permission on a specific table:

```
GRANT MODIFY PERMISSION
ON TABLE "my_status"."status_update_views"
TO 'data_analytics';
```

Note that we use `ON TABLE` instead of `ON KEYSPACE` here, and that we provide the fully-qualified name of the table we want the permission to apply to. Of course, if we've previously issued a `USE "my_status";` command in this session, we can refer to the table name without providing the keyspace name explicitly.

 The `GRANT` statement can be used to provide all manner of access, from a very broad mandate to a very narrow set of permissions.
For full details of the `GRANT` syntax, see the DataStax CQL reference:
`http://www.datastax.com/documentation/cql/3.1/cql/cql_reference/grant_r.html`.

# Viewing permissions

Much like user accounts, permissions are stored in a human-readable way in a Cassandra table, in this case the permissions table. We can see the effects of the permissions that we granted by reading from this table:

```
SELECT * FROM "system_auth"."permissions";
```

We'll see a row for each of the permissions we've granted:

```
 username        | resource                               | permissions
-----------------+----------------------------------------+-------------
 data_analytics  |                         data/my_status | {'SELECT'}
 data_analytics  | data/my_status/status_update_views      | {'MODIFY'}

(2 rows)
```

Note that the `resource` column contains a path to the keyspace or column family that the user has permissions on, and that the permissions column is in fact a set column. Note also that the `cassandra` user does not appear in this list; as a superuser, the `cassandra` user automatically has permission to do anything it wants, and does not need explicit authorization of the kind stored in the permissions table.

# Revoking access

Let us say that, having slept on it, we've reconsidered the decision to give the data analytics team read/write access to the `status_update_views` table. After all, the data in that table is generated automatically by the application, and there's no need for the analytics team to be able to modify it. Happily, we can revoke that permission just as easily as we granted it, using the `REVOKE` command:

```
REVOKE MODIFY PERMISSION
ON "my_status"."status_update_views"
FROM 'data_analytics';
```

The syntax of the `REVOKE` command is identical to that of the `GRANT` command, except that the `TO` keyword is replaced by `FROM`. We can check the `system_auth.permissions` table to satisfy ourselves that the permissions are how we'd like:

```
 username        | resource        | permissions
-----------------+-----------------+-------------
 data_analytics  | data/my_status  |  {'SELECT'}

(1 rows)
```

We can rest easy knowing that the only remaining access granted to the analytics team is keyspace-wide read-only permissions.

> For more on `REVOKE`, see the DataStax CQL documentation: `http://www.d atastax.com/documentation/cql/3.1/cql/cql_reference/revoke_r.h tml`.

# Authorization in action

Now that we know how to create user accounts and grant and revoke permissions to them, let's see how a non-superuser account behaves in practice. To do this, let's open up a new cqlsh session logged in with our data analytics team's account:

```
$ cqlsh -u data_analytics -p verystrongpassword -k my_status
```

The `-k my_status` option simply tells cqlsh that we want to interact with the `my_status` keyspace, saving us the effort of issuing a `USE` statement.

Now let's see what we can do. First, we expect to be able to read data with no problem; let's have a look at the `user_status_updates` table:

```
SELECT * FROM user_status_updates;
```

As expected, we have permission to read the contents of that table:

```
 username | id                                   | body
----------+--------------------------------------+------------------------
      bob | 97719c50-e797-11e3-90ce-5f98e903bf02 | Eating a tasty sandwich.
      bob | e93a7410-7344-11e4-a0e6-5f98e903bf02 |          Bob Update 1
      bob | e93bac90-7344-11e4-a0e6-5f98e903bf02 |          Bob Update 2
      bob | e9454980-7344-11e4-a0e6-5f98e903bf02 |          Bob Update 3
    alice | 76e7a4d0-e796-11e3-90ce-5f98e903bf02 |    Learning Cassandra!
    alice | e9367c70-7344-11e4-a0e6-5f98e903bf02 |        Alice Update 1
    alice | e93b3760-7344-11e4-a0e6-5f98e903bf02 |        Alice Update 2
    alice | e9443810-7344-11e4-a0e6-5f98e903bf02 |        Alice Update 3

(8 rows)
```

Now let's try making a change to some data. Though our analytics team certainly would have no malicious intent, perhaps at some point the analytics cat may sit on a keyboard, producing the following statement:

```
DELETE FROM "users"
WHERE "username" = 'alice';
```

That's quite an alarming query, but happily our authorization setup has saved us:

```
code=2100 [Unauthorized] message="User data_analytics has no MODIFY
permission on <table my_status.users> or any of its parents"
```

Recall that the MODIFY permission is needed to make any changes to existing data, including insertion and deletion. Since the data_analytics account only has the SELECT permission, our accidental attempt to delete alice's account is rejected. alice's data is safe.

# Authorization as a hedge against mistakes

We generally think of authentication and authorization as a mechanism to prevent intentional access to our data by nefarious actors. However, authorization can also be a powerful insurance policy against unintentional mistakes by well-intentioned people. In the preceding example, the data analytics team did not intend to do any harm, but without authorization in place, that pesky cat would have unwittingly caused data loss.

While the odds of a feline posterior producing a perfectly-formed CQL query are quite long, mistakes do happen. Using authorization to give each user the minimum level of access they strictly need, we can reduce the chance of a mistake turning into an emergency.

Of course, authentication and authorization are also an important tool to secure your data from those seeking unauthorized access. As it turns out, these are only part of the entire security picture; we also need to make sure our data is secure on disk and in transit.

# Security beyond authentication and authorization

The security afforded by Cassandra-level authentication and authorization only applies to clients connecting directly to your Cassandra cluster. Anyone who has physical access to the machines running Cassandra can access the data stored on disk; the same goes for anyone with SSH access to machines in the Cassandra cluster. Cassandra itself does not offer encryption for on-disk data, but DataStax Enterprise, a commercial distribution of Cassandra, does offer encryption of at-risk data. For more information, consult
http://www.datastax.com/documentation/datastax_enterprise/4.5/datastax_enterpri
se/sec/secTDE.html.

Data security can also be compromised in transit; anyone who can intercept traffic between your application and your Cassandra cluster can potentially gain unauthorized access to your data. Cassandra offers client-to-node SSL encryption that protects your data in transit between your application and your cluster. For information on setting up client-to-node encryption, see
`http://www.datastax.com/documentation/cassandra/2.1/cassandra/security/secureSS LClientToNode_t.html`.

Finally, normal operation of Cassandra involves passing data between different nodes in the cluster; if attackers can intercept inter-node communication, they can gain access to your data. Cassandra has the ability to encrypt all node-to-node traffic; for information on configuring node-to-node encryption, see
`http://www.datastax.com/documentation/cassandra/2.1/cassandra/security/secureSS LNodeToNode_t.html`.

# Security protects against vulnerabilities

We've covered authentication and authorization in depth and also mentioned a few other security measures available in Cassandra or DataStax Enterprise. However, not every deployment will need every security measure in place. What security measures you need depends on the sensitivity of your data and the security characteristics of your deployment. As an application engineer, you likely leave the details of deployment security to your sysadmins, but this table can provide a quick reference to what sort of security measures you should think about:

| Security measure | Vulnerability protected against | Alternative protections |
| --- | --- | --- |
| Internal authentication & authorization | Direct access to Cassandra cluster via CQL binary protocol | Restrict access to the Cassandra cluster to secure the private network |
| On-disk data encryption | Shell access to machines hosting the Cassandra cluster | Restrict shell and physical access to Cassandra hosts |
| Client-to-node encryption | Network link between the application and the Cassandra cluster | Restrict access to private network traffic using encryption or physical isolation |
| Node-to-node encryption | Network link between Cassandra nodes | Restrict access to private network traffic using encryption or physical isolation |

It's quite plausible that, with both your application and Cassandra deployment protected by a well-secured VPN, you may not need to concern yourself with any database-level security measures.

# Summary

In this final appendix, we explored Cassandra's ability to restrict access to itself using internal authentication and authorization. We saw that Cassandra offers simple configuration of user accounts and permissions using a collection of CQL commands provided for that purpose, and also that this information is stored transparently in tables in the `system_auth` keyspace.

We noted that internal authorization can be useful for traditional security concerns, but also simply as a hedge against mistakes. By limiting access to that which is strictly needed, we can reduce our vulnerability to user errors that can unintentionally cause major data loss.

We also noted that internal authentication and authorization are not the full security picture for a Cassandra deployment. While the details are beyond the scope of a book whose audience is primarily application engineers, we did a brief survey of other security measures a Cassandra deployment might undertake, and we briefly discussed situations in which those measures might be called for.

# Wrapping up

The first nine chapters of this book were devoted to learning CQL's major features and how to effectively use them. `Chapter 10`, *How Cassandra Distributes Data*, explored the special issues that application developers must keep in mind when using a distributed database such as Cassandra. In `Appendix A`, *Peeking under the Hood*, we took a look at the low-level data structures that were once part of the daily lives of Cassandra developers but now serve as an internal data structure underlying the more powerful abstractions of CQL. And, in this Appendix, you learned about the tools Cassandra gives you to keep your deployment secure.

This brings us to the end of the topics we set out to cover in this book. You should now be fully prepared to take advantage of Cassandra's powerful feature set, high scalability, and resilience to failure in your own applications. You know that Cassandra is better suited to some use cases than others; when a distributed database is called for, you're prepared to use the most powerful distributed database on the planet, efficiently and productively.

# Index

many-to-many relationship 104
one-to-many relationship 104
one-to-one relationship 103
eventual consistency 16, 241

# F

fault tolerance 321
federation 223
follow relationships
  inbound follows 99
  modelling 98
  outbound follows 98
  storing 99
  viewing 108
functions, Universally Unique Identifiers (UUIDs)
  reference link 81

# G

G1 garbage collector 32
gossip protocol 236
GRANT syntax
  reference link 325

# H

high availability
  about 12
  reference link 12
hints
  working 280
home timeline
  denormalizing 131
  displaying 129, 133
Homebrew 26
horizontal scalability 11

# I

immediate consistency 16, 241
inbound follows 99
INSERT statement 91
  building 293
inserts
  about 152
  collection columns 179
  conditional inserts 155

existing data, overwriting 152
lightweight transactions 155
UUIDs, advantages 155
verifying 153
IntelliJ IDEA
  URL 285
issues, concurrent updates
  collection columns, serializing 167
  concurrency 168

# J

Java Development Kit (JDK)
  about 21
  installing 21
  URL, for downloading 21
Java driver policies
  about 300
  load-balancing policy 300, 301
  reconnection policy 301
  retry policy 301
Java Management Extensions (JMX) 264
Java Runtime Environment (JRE) 21
Java Virtual Machine (JVM)
  about 209
  URL, for settings 209
Java
  URL, for downloading 26
JavaScript Object Notation (JSON) 91
JSON support
  about 91
  INSERT statement 91
  SELECT statement 92

# K

key cache 278
key-value pairs
  storing, maps used 177
keyspace schema
  viewing 142
keyspace
  about 29, 33
  configuring 33
  deleting, with schema 151
  selecting 30